Good Cruising

GOOD CRUISING

The Illustrated Essentials

ZORA AND DAVID AIKEN

with illustrations by
David Aiken

International Marine
Camden, Maine

International Marine/
Ragged Mountain Press

A Division of The McGraw·Hill Companies

10 9 8 7 6 5 4 3 2

Library of Congress Cataloging-in-Publication Data

Aiken, Zora.
    Good cruising : the illustrated essentials / Zora and David Aiken ; with illustrations by David Aiken.
          p.   cm.
    Includes index.
    ISBN 0-07-000749-7 (alk. paper)
    1. Coastwise navigation. I. Aiken, David, 1940–   . II. Title.
VK559.A35   1997
623.89'29—dc20
                              96-43714
                              CIP

Questions regarding the content of this book should be addressed to:

International Marine
P.O. Box 220
Camden, ME 04843
207-236-4837

Questions regarding the ordering of this book should be addressed to:

The McGraw-Hill Companies
Customer Service Department
P.O. Box 547
Blacklick, OH 43004
Retail customers: 1-800-262-4729
Bookstores: 1-800-722-4726

Good Cruising is printed on 60-pound Renew Opaque Vellum, an acid-free paper that contains 50 percent recycled waste paper (preconsumer) and 10 percent postconsumer waste paper. ♻

This book was typeset in Adobe Sabon, Americana, and Fruitiger.

Printed by R.R. Donnelley, Crawfordsville, IN
Typography and page design by Patrice M. Calkin
   from original format by Zora and David Aiken
Production and page layout by Janet Robbins
Edited by John Kettlewell, Migael Scherer,
   Pamela Benner, Jane Crosen

To cruising friends

Contents

Acknowledgments

It's not possible to list all those who taught us about traveling by boat—in some cases, we don't know their names. But we do acknowledge their help. Not only did they provide information for this book, they also added a lot to our enjoyment of cruising.

We thank all the boating people who contributed to *Good Cruising:* armchair cruisers, story tellers, waterway wanderers; anchor setters, line handlers, engine fixers; tugboat operators, crabtrap pullers, shrimp-net draggers; drawbridge openers, lock controllers, channel dredgers; plus FCC communicators, NOAA chartmakers, NWS forecasters, Army engineerers, and, of course, U.S. coast guarders.

Special thanks to the publishing people at International Marine, who put the accumulated information into book form: editorial director Jonathan Eaton, acquisitions editor John Kettlewell, managing editors Pamela Benner and Tom McCarthy, technical editor Migael Scherer, copyeditor Jane Crosen, and assistant director of art and production Janet Robbins.

Introduction

Whether your boating style is an afternoon of beach combing or a weekend at the club, a week's cruise up the lake or a year's trip down the coast, you're traveling by boat. As you cruise into unfamiliar waters, you'll probably find unfamiliar situations, and how you deal with them can make or break your boating day.

As a means of travel—even the most ordinary, everyday kind of travel—cruising is better when the boater has the right combination of knowledge and skills. While it may be impossible to prepare for every eventuality, some basic awareness can't hurt. For example:

What do chart notes like "Danger Zone" or "restricted area" mean?

Could you identify and enter a strange harbor at night?

How can you avoid grounding (and how get the boat off when it happens anyway)?

Can you find a secure anchorage?

How should you approach a working dredge, or pass a river tug pushing barges?

Good Cruising is a collective response to a lot of such questions. It is a companion book to our previously published *Good Boatkeeping*. While the first book focused on crew comfort and boat care, this book shows you how to handle typical boat-travel situations. It doesn't matter what kind of boat you're on—the suggestions in *Good Cruising* have been provided by experienced cruisers to help *all* boat travelers get the most good from their boating days.

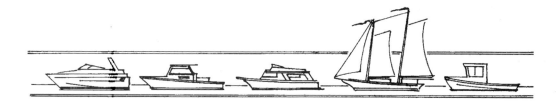

1 Charting Ways

When all your boating is done in familiar waters, you navigate by following familiar courses. Somebody shows you the local routes; you head for the gray house on the hill, or the small dock off the island, or the lone tree above the beach. Even a compass course is run more by habit than conscious aim. You go from place to place with the confidence that repetition—combined with local knowledge—brings.

When you want to expand your boating territory, you could look for other boaters to show you the new-to-you waterways, but the farther you travel, the more impractical that becomes. The easy alternative is to buy a chart of the area. Just as the road atlas guides drivers across country, so nautical charts guide boaters across the water. (If your destination is a river, inland lake, or canal system, your chart may be called a map, but both serve the same purpose.) In

a short time of "reading," you'll learn a lot about a place, and do it long before you ever leave your dock.

Charts and water maps differ from road maps in a number of ways, the critical one being that road maps give you a definite choice of specified routes to travel. Except for the single river or Intracoastal Waterway channel, most charts don't have established routes—no checkerboard of parallel paths with marked intersections, no familiar travel pattern of rights and lefts. On the plus side, there are few stoplights or no-passing zones. You travel as the seagull flies—or as the fish swims—*if* that path is a safe one, with "safe" defined by sufficient water depth and the absence of other hazards to boat navigation.

In home waters, you head for your harbor's entrance along a path formed by habit. In new-to-you waters, you may sight a big lighthouse across an expanse of seemingly open water; since there's no marked route, why not go there by the direct, shortest-distance rule? The problem, of course, is that the water may be hiding a lot of reasons for a detour. A direct course between you and the lighthouse might take you right across, or onto, a 3-foot shoal extending out from a point of land. There may be a spoil area (a "waterfill" site where dredged material was dumped) or a natural sandbar, a poorly marked wreck, or an unmarked rock. An accurate chart reading will show you these hidden dangers, and provide all the information you need to plan a safe route.

Charts show distance, water depth, and shoreline contours; you'll find marks to navigate by and marks to avoid. With a chart, you can establish a safe compass course to your destination and keep track of your progress and position. First, you need some familiarity with chart language.

COLOR CODES

Charts use different colors, or different tints of the same color, to separate landmasses from water. The water area is further separated into sections of "safe" depth or "shallow" depth.

On government charts published by NOAA (National Oceanic and Atmospheric Administration), solid land areas are a light brown; marshes or sandbars and other sometimes-submerged places are shown as green. Water is blue (where shallow) or white (where deep), though the dividing line is not the same on all charts.

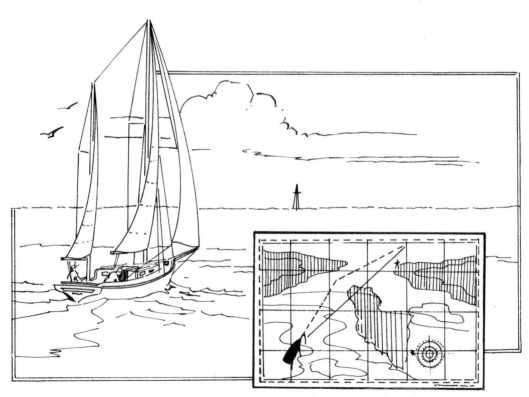

The most direct route might not be safe; a chart will show the hidden dangers.

• Government small-craft charts use 6 feet as the start of shoal water. On coastal charts, the line may be 12 or 18 feet or more.

• The division between deep and shallow water depends on the chart publisher's definition. Don't be surprised by a chart that sets the start of shallow water at 4 feet; always study the individual depth-sounding figures for the waters you plan to cruise.

• If you find yourself in a situation where you suddenly realize the water depths are 2 feet less than you thought, take the time to scribble some pencil shading over those places that are too close to your boat's draft, so you can see the good water more easily, and more quickly.

BOTTOM MARKS

Most U.S. charts indicate water depth in either feet or fathoms (1 fathom = 6 feet). Look for a statement near the title of each chart to verify the measurement system used.

• Sometimes, where it's critical, the charted depth figures will be printed with both fathoms and feet, with a large numeral used for the fathoms and a small numeral for the feet, as 2_3.

• The government has long planned a change to metric. It is a slow process, but necessary for the U.S. to conform to international charting practices. Because the metric system is a decimal (based on 10) system, it is far more logical than the arbitrary values of inches-feet-yards-fathoms-statute miles. All measurements relate to multiples or divisions of the basic meter unit.

• To help in the changeover process, remember that a meter is just slightly more than a yard (1 meter = 3.28 feet), so 2 meters is a bit more than a fathom.

• In coastal areas, actual water depth changes with the tide: two highs and two lows on most days in many places. Charted depths are established either by averaging all low tides in a given cycle (mean low water) or by using only the lower of the two daily low tides for the average (mean lower low water). The chart will specify MLW or MLLW. Most U.S. charts now use MLLW. Either way, since the figures on the chart are averages, at some times the water will not be as deep as charted. The literal up side is that the two high tides will bring deeper water, a most useful phenomenon for the captain who wishes to skim a sandbar or refloat a grounded keel. With all the variables inherent in a shifting bottom contour, the cautious captain doesn't cut depth allowances too close.

• Besides showing how deep the water is in a given area, charts often show what's on the bottom (sand, mud, grass, etc.). These indications are especially helpful when you're looking for an anchorage. If you know an area has a hard or rocky bottom, you may choose to look elsewhere.

TOP SIGNS

Just as the tide affects water depths (effectively "changing" charted depth figures), so does it affect overhead clearances, usually given above mean high water (MHW). If the boat height is too close to bridge clearance at high tide, a few hours' wait is all that's necessary to pass safely under a bridge.

BASIC MARKS

Charts show the boat traveler the location of an assortment of markers, or navigation aids. Most of these aids—whether in the form of a floating buoy or a dayboard on a fixed piling—are either red or green. In an

Port (left) side: odd number on green flat-top "can" buoy or square daybeacon. Starboard (right) side: even number on red pointed "nun" buoy or triangular daybeacon.

earlier marking system, the now-green marks were black, so if the odd black mark is sighted, just think green. (A few other odd marks will be described later.)

• On the paper chart, the navigation aids may be represented by little diamond shapes, some with a circle of color at one end. Other chart symbols look like exclamation points. Both the colored circles and the exclamation points indicate lighted aids. If the chart doesn't show actual colors, it will indicate the mark's number or have a chart note, either of which will identify it.

• Intracoastal Waterway charts will show parallel rows of triangles and squares, along with some exclamation points. All are navigation aids: either buoys or daybeacons (also called daymarks or dayboards) marking the sides of the navigation channel. The exclamation points are lighted; the triangles and squares are not.

BOATING'S THREE Rs

One of the first things new boaters hear about navigation is red-right-returning. It doesn't mean red always stays on your right, but it's a good start for learning some of the characteristics common to channel markers.

The three Rs refer to the safe passage when coming in from sea, and also apply to almost all harbor entrances inland. Red buoys or daymarks will mark the right (starboard) side of the channel. Once you determine where the reds should be (relative to which way you're traveling), you'll know where the green belong, too. While a straight lineup of reds opposite greens would show an obvious channel, a single outer mark or a dogleg channel is not so easy to read.

• In some rare instances, a harbor has two entrances, and one may not conform to the 3-R rule. For example, the harbor may be part of a U-shaped side channel, and both ends of the oxbow intersect the main channel. If the side channel is marked consistently along its entire semicircular shape, then the marks at one end will not comply with the red-right rule—one more reason to check charts carefully.

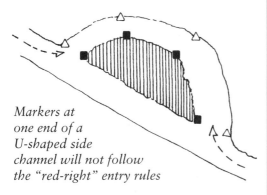

Markers at one end of a U-shaped side channel will not follow the "red-right" entry rules

• Large channel buoys may not show a shape difference between red and green, but daymarks do; triangular reds and square greens are easy to identify, even against the sun. In some areas, birds' nests can sometimes cause temporary confusion.

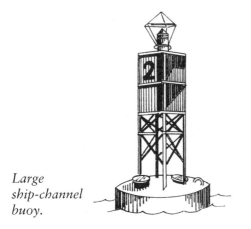

Large ship-channel buoy.

• Smaller buoys have distinctly different shapes: reds are cone-shaped "nuns," while greens are flat-topped "cans."

By the Number

All red marks, whether ship channel buoys or marina entry marks, will show even numbers, and all green marks, odd.

Once this becomes part of your boating subconscious, you *cannot* misread a 3 or a 5 as an 8, or an 8 as a 9, etc. The number—odd or even—must conform to the color of the mark.

The illustration on page 4 has all of red's characteristics: Red, even number, triangle (or pointy-top nun).

Another memory help for red mark numbers: think Evinrude (evenred).

NOISY MARKS

Some navigation aids make noise with bells, horns, gongs, or electronic whistles, a good solution to the problems caused by poor visibility in fog or rain (and as a backup identifier for a bad light). The chart provides this information, too; see Chapter 3 for details.

BIG MARKS

All major harbor entrances have some kind of major light. Visible from the farthest distance are the lighthouses, some planted on shore, others constructed in the water some distance from land. By daylight, their distinctive shapes stand out on the horizon, making an easy target to aim on. Charts show the specific characteristics of each lighthouse: height of the tower, pattern of light flash, range of visibility, fog signal. Chapters 2 and 3 explain lights and sounds in more detail.

ODD MARKS

Rows of triangles and squares are easy enough to follow, and just so you don't get too complacent, or worse, bored, you'll occasionally see different types of marks. Some mark the sides of the channel, some don't. Either way, you need to know what they mean.

Preferred Channel

Just when you get the red and green separated, along comes a mark that displays both. The colors will be in horizontal bands, and the mark is a junction, or "preferred channel" buoy, marking an intersection of two channels. Use the top band as your navigation aid for the main channel. (Some junction marks can be passed safely on both sides, but not all; check the chart.)

Isolated Danger

Another horizontally banded buoy marks an isolated danger. Colors are black over red, with two black spherical topmarks in a vertical row on top. Since the buoy is anchored above or near the danger, don't get too close.

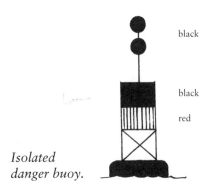

black

black

red

Isolated danger buoy.

Harbor ID

A few buoys or daymarks display letters instead of numbers. Often, their location explains the significance of the letters. (AH, Annapolis Harbor; BR, Back River.) These provide yet another way for you to verify your position, or find a harbor entrance mark.

Safe-Water Mark

If you see a red-and-white vertically striped mark, it's okay to pass on either side; this is a mid-channel, or fairway mark (also called "safe water" mark), often used as the outermost sea buoy, with a red spherical topmark to help identify it.

The same vertical red and white stripes may be seen on a beachball "spherical" buoy or on an octagonal dayboard, all serving the same purpose.

One exception to the safe-water rule might still be found on an inland lake or waterway (see pages 8 and 14).

Cardinal Buoys

The use of cardinal buoys is more common in Canada than in the U.S. These buoys are all yellow and black, but the pattern of the colors (and sometimes topmarks as well) indicate which is the safe passing side. For example, when you see a cardinal buoy with a color pattern indicating North, you know the safest water is to the north of the buoy. Specific patterns for each buoy are shown in various references, including Chart No. 1 (see page 8).

Special Marks

Occasionally, you'll see a yellow buoy. These don't mark the side of a channel; they're used to mark special features like a military target, fishnet area, or traffic separation pattern.

Again, consult the chart or other references, such as a Coast Pilot (see page 17).

Diamond-Shaped Daymark

Another odd mark is diamond shaped, and subdivided into four smaller diamond sections. Top and bottom segments are colored, the sides white. These, too, are special-purpose marks, often used to locate or call attention to a charted point of land or a pier or jetty—some feature outside the normal navigable channel.

Mooring Buoy

A white buoy with a horizontal blue band around its middle is a mooring buoy. (Larger buoys are for larger boats or barges, so don't anchor close by.)

Exposed Location Buoy

If a lightship is still in use today, its function is to house a museum. In its former life, however, it was a floating lighthouse, marking a location where a real lighthouse could not be built.

Lightships were first replaced by superbuoys, or Large Navigation Buoys (LNBs), that were 40 feet in diameter and nearly 40 feet high. Those monster markers are now being replaced by Exposed Location Buoys (ELBs), still large at about 9 feet in diameter.

Regulatory Marks

Another family of attention-getters are white buoys or dayboards with orange markings, which may be charted as simply "sign." A circle of orange on a white background will usually have a slow or no-wake caution; a diamond shape is a danger sign, and if the diamond shape has an X in the center, it tells boats to keep out.

Range Marks

In some areas, pairs of range marks (vertically striped dayboards) are used to indicate a safe, mid-channel course. The lower, front board is usually positioned in the water, near the side of the navigation channel. The upper board is usually on land some distance back. When a boater approaches on the correct, mid-channel course, the stripes of the two boards will appear to be in vertical alignment.

On the chart, the ranges may be identified by their light characteristics, or by their

Regulatory buoys or dayboards are white with orange markings.

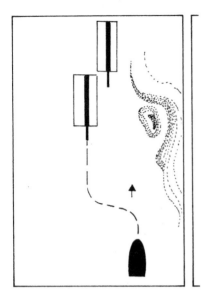

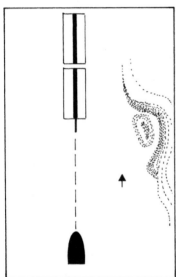

Boat is on a safe, mid-channel course when vertical stripes on range marks are visually aligned.

marked letters *and* by a line showing the course they indicate: a solid line shows the area of navigation; a dotted line continues the visual lineup of the two marks.

• The lower range mark may share a post or platform with a waterway channel marker, but the range board itself will not be a red or green numbered mark. Some ranges are lettered.

Dual-Purpose/ICW Marks

In some places, the Intracoastal Waterway (ICW) channel coincides with a return-from-sea river channel, and the same navigation aids serve both systems.

To confirm that a buoy or dayboard is an ICW aid, look for some yellow marking on it: a yellow triangle means ICW red side; a yellow square, ICW green side. A yellow horizontal band gives no lateral instruction; it just indicates that the mark does pertain to the waterway (for example, on a range mark).

River Marks

Marks for western rivers are now similar in structure and follow the same color separation as coastal waterway aids. (See Chapter 17 for information peculiar to river navigation.)

CHART DECODER

In addition to locating and identifying navigation aids, charts provide a lot of useful information about the areas they cover; you can find prominent landmarks, land and underwater contour lines, bridge and powerline clearances, and much more.

Most charted information is given in shorthand, but the charting folks thoughtfully printed a whole book to help you read the code. When you buy your first chart, also buy the book *Chart Number 1: Nautical Chart Symbols, Abbreviations, and Terms.* (See sample sections on pages 9 through 13.)

(text continued on page 14)

Chart Number 1:
Nautical Chart
Symbols, Abbreviations,
and Terms.

A *Chart Number, Title, Marginal Notes*

Schematic layout of a chart (reduced in size)

1. Chart number in national chart series.

2. Identification of a latticed chart (if any): D for Decca; Loran-C overprinted for Loran-C; Omega overprinted for Omega.

3. Chart number in international chart series (if any).

4. Publication note (imprint).

5. Stock number.

6. Edition note. In the example: Fifth edition published in May, 1989.

7. Source data diagram (if any). For attention to navigators: use caution where surveys are inadequate.

8. Dimensions of inner borders.

9. Corner coordinates.

10. Chart title: May be quoted when ordering a chart, in addition to chart number.

11. Explanatory notes on chart construction, etc. To be read before using chart.

12. Seals: In the example, the national, and International Hydrographic Organization seals show that this national chart is also an international one. Purely national charts have the national seal only. Reproductions of charts of other nations (facsimile) have the seals of the original

producer (left), publisher (center) and the IHO (right).

13. Projection and scale of chart at stated latitude. The scale is precisely as stated only at the latitude quoted.

14. Linear scale on large-scale charts.

15. Reference to a larger-scale chart.

16. Cautionary notes (if any). Information on particular features, to be read before using chart.

17. Reference to an adjoining chart of similar scale.

CHART DECODER (PAGES 10–13)

Positions, Distances, Directions, Compass

var	Variation
mag	Magnetic
brg	Bearing
T	True

Tides, Currents

MLW	Mean Low Water
MHW	Mean High Water
MLLW	Mean Lower Low Water
MHHW	Mean Higher High Water
2 kn ⇒	Current, general, with rate
vel	Velocity; rate
kn	Knots
ht	Height
fl	Flood

Depths

Rep	Reported, but not surveyed
3 Rep	Reported, but not confirmed sounding or danger
(symbol)	Limit of dredged area

Nature of the Seabed

S	Sand
M	Mud
Rk; rky	Rock; rocky
Wd	Weed
stk	Sticky
so; sft	Soft
h; hrd	Hard

Lights

Example of a full Light Description

 Fl (3) WRG 15s 21ft 11M

Fl (3)	Class of light: group flashing repeating a group of three flashes
WRG	Colors: white, red, green, exhibiting the different colors in defined sectors
15s	Period: the time taken to exhibit one full sequence of 3 flashes and eclipses: 15 seconds
21ft	Elevation of focal plane above datum: 21 feet
11M	Nominal range

Leading Lights

 Lts in line 270° Leading lights with leading line (firm line is fairway)

Supplementary Symbol

Riprap surrounding light

Buoys, Beacons

	G	Green
	Y	Yellow
	RG	Multiple colors in horizontal bands, the color sequence is from top to bottom
		Lighted mark
		Buoy with topmark
RW	ODAS	ODAS buoy (Ocean Data Acquisition System). Data-collecting buoy of superbuoy size
□ ▲ ▨		Beacon with color; no distinctive topmark

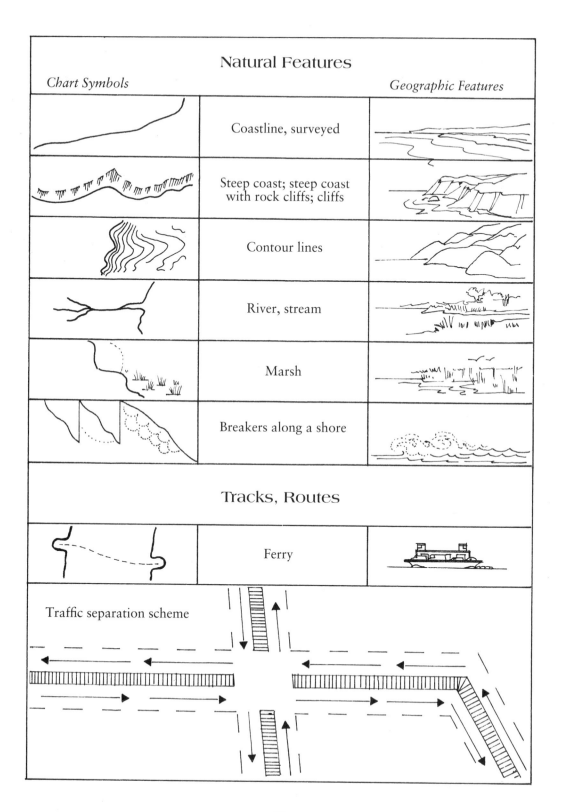

Natural Features

Chart Symbols		*Geographic Features*
	Coastline, surveyed	
	Steep coast; steep coast with rock cliffs; cliffs	
	Contour lines	
	River, stream	
	Marsh	
	Breakers along a shore	

Tracks, Routes

	Ferry	

Traffic separation scheme

Cultural Features

Symbol	Description	Illustration
■ ▨ ▢	Buildings in general	
	Motorway; road (hard surfaced)	
	Railway, with station	
	Tunnel	
	Airport	
	Fixed bridge	
	Opening bridge (in general)	
	Lifting bridge	
	Bascule bridge	
Tower Overhead Power Cable Authorized CL. 140 FT Tower	Power transmission line with pylons and safe overhead clearance	
	Bridge under construction	

Landmarks

Chart Symbols	Landmarks	
Tank Tk	Tank	
Spire	Church spire	
Cupola (Cup)	Cupola	
Chimney (Chy)	Chimney	
R Mast TV Mast	Radio mast; television mast	
	Factory	
HS	High school	
HOSP	Hospital	
PO	Post office	
CG CG CG	Coast Guard station	

(text continued from page 8)

The navigation aids in U.S. and Canadian waters are positioned according to a marking system established by IALA (International Association of Lighthouse Authorities). Though international is part of the name, there is not a single, universal buoyage system followed worldwide. Some countries follow the IALA-A system, which follows red-to-port. The red-to-starboard in North American waters is part of IALA-B.

Along U.S. coasts, the red-right rule for IALA-B applies when a boat is headed in a southerly direction along the Atlantic Coast, westerly along the Gulf Coast, and northerly along the Pacific Coast.

State Waterway System

The markers for the Uniform State Waterway Marking System use smaller buoys, and they may all be can-shaped. Reds are still right, but the port-side cans are either black or green. In this system, a red-and-white vertically striped mark tells you not to pass between the mark and the nearest shore (check your map or chart). Fortunately, this system is in the process of changing, so markers will be consistent with coastal navigation aids.

CHART USE

While it may be gratifying to be able to read a chart, its primary function is to help you travel safely on the water. The connecting links between the chart and your boat are the direction indicators (chart orientation and compass rose) and the distance measurements.

Direction

Charts are drawn to a grid system based on imaginary lines that circle the Earth horizontally and vertically. Horizontal divisions (parallels of latitude) start at the horizontal middle of Earth (the equator, or 0

degrees) and increase north or south to 90 degrees at each pole. Vertical lines (meridians of longitude) start at Greenwich, England (0 degrees, or prime meridian), and increase to 180 degrees east or west.

Large coastal charts are printed so that north is at the top of the chart, but even if a chart grid is angled on the paper, direction is easy to determine. Look for the circle of numbers called the *compass rose*. Most compass roses will show an outer ring indicating true north, and an inner ring for magnetic north. (The two are not in the same place, a bit of trivia that you could successfully ignore until now.) The difference between true and magnetic north is termed *variation*; Chapter 4 will explain more about it, showing how you can transfer chart knowledge to actual boat travel.

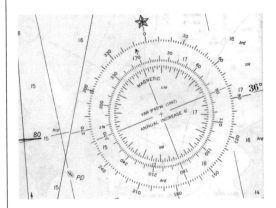

Distance

You can measure distance on a nautical chart by referring to the chart's scale legend, or you can take it directly from the latitude divisions printed at the side of the chart. One full degree of latitude divides into 60 minutes, and each minute of latitude is a nautical mile.

The subdivision of minutes, however, is commonly done in tenths of minutes (rather than a division of 60 seconds). A quick study of the numbers marking the subdivisions of latitude should clarify the basis of measurement used.

• Offshore charts are measured in nautical miles; inland charts, including Intracoastal Waterway strip charts, give distance in statute miles, though the scale also includes a measurement for nautical miles.

• When charts are changed to the metric system, the figures that will be changed include water depths, overhead clearances, and heights of towers, and other landmarks. While distances formerly measured in statute miles will be given in kilometers, the nautical mile measurements are unaffected.

Metric Equivalents

1,000 millimeters		
100 centimeters =	}	1 meter
10 decimeters		
1 dekameter =		10 meters
1 hectometer =		100 meters
1 kilometer =		1,000 meters

Comparisons

• A statute mile is 5,280 feet.

• A nautical mile is 6,076 feet, or 1,852 meters.

• A nautical mile is 1.15 statute miles (roughly 7 nautical miles = 8 statute miles).

• 1 kilometer = 0.62 statute mile or 0.54 nautical mile.

CHART TYPES

Charts are available in different scales, for different purposes. Charts covering large areas are useful for general course planning, while detailed harbor charts add a big safety factor when heading inland.

Charts are published by government agencies and by a number of private businesses, all using the same information (there is no copyright on government publications; soundings come from the same surveys).

• You'll find color differences and size differences. Some are individual charts, some are grouped into regional books of charts. Look at all the charts available; think about how (and where) you'll use them.

• For example, if you have a big nav station and a convenient flat surface in the wheelhouse, a big chart may be fine. If you have *no* nav station and a tiny cockpit, you may do better with one of the book charts.

• Even the book charts give you a choice of sizes, from 8½ by 11 inches to 17 by 22 inches.

• The government's original small-craft chart series, called "strip charts," fold into their own neat file folders—once you figure out the folding system.

• NOAA has chart catalogs for five areas. Each is a fold-out brochure showing what charts are available in each region. You can list the numbers of all the charts you need to cruise a particular area.

• A combination of coastal charts (in the 1:80,000 scale) and small-craft charts (1:40,000 with harbor inserts) is usually adequate for all but out-of-the-way gunkholing, when you want the most detailed charts you can find.

• For chart information (coastal and Great Lakes), check a local marine store, or write to Distribution Branch, N/CG33, National Ocean Service, NOAA, Riverdale, MD 20737. Or call 1-800-638-8972.

• For river maps and inland waterway information, contact the U.S. Army Corps of Engineers. Addresses are provided in the NOAA chart catalog.

• For charts of Canadian waters, write Hydrographic Chart Distribution Office,

Department of Fisheries and Oceans, P.O. Box 8080, Ottawa, Ontario K1G 3H6, Canada. Or call 613-998-4931.

• Several companies print nautical charts on waterproof paper, an obvious advantage for longevity. They are available at many marine stores.

• If you want to take the time, you can try waterproofing your own charts, with Map Seal. If you don't find it at the marine supply store, call Campmor and ask for a catalog: 1-800-226-7667.

• One more option: you can purchase photocopies of government charts from Bluewater Books & Charts in Fort Lauderdale, Florida. The charge is about half the price of a new chart. Call 1-800-942-2583.

CHART UPDATE

When buying a chart, check with NOAA for the date of the most recent edition. All charts are not reprinted on the same schedule; busy harbors are done more often than remote areas.

Charts show their age by the dating information given in the lower left border area of flat charts, near the chart number. On small-craft charts, look near the bottom of the cover of the folder the chart came in. While it is expensive to buy new charts with each new issue, you *can* keep your old charts updated, so you'll know if markers have been moved or renumbered, or if an old bascule bridge has been replaced by a new fixed span.

Notice to Mariners

The Coast Guard publishes regional issues of the Local Notice to Mariners, to keep boaters informed of changes to charts and other publications (like Coast Pilots and Light Lists, described later in this chapter). The notices are based on government-collected data, and refer to depth soundings, navigation aids, new obstruc-

tions or dangers, plus scheduled regattas or military operations—anything that affects navigation. Make notations of all permanent changes directly on the chart.

To receive the Local Notice to Mariners, call the Coast Guard District serving your area (listed in the Yellow Pages under United States Government, Transportation Department, Coast Guard). Request that your name be added to the mailing list (the service is free). If you don't know what district you're in, call the Coast Guard Boating Safety Hotline: 1-800-368-5647.

• Also available from the Defense Mapping Agency is the Notice to Mariners (not local), but since this contains information for worldwide navigation, it is prepared mainly for commercial and military interests and not usually needed by the ordinary coastal recreational boater.

• Computer enthusiasts can get the information, if they really need it, through the Defense Mapping Agency computer. For information about computer access, write: Navigation Department/NAVINFONET Staff, Mail Stop D-44, Defense Mapping Agency, 4600 Sangamore Road, Bethesda, MD 20816-5003. Or call 301-227-3732. The E-mail address is: NAVINFONET@dma.gov.

BOATING LIBRARY

To supplement chart information, navigators should add a few reference volumes to the bookshelf.

Light List

An excellent source of updated information, Light Lists are published annually by the U.S. Coast Guard, by region. These books give detailed descriptions of lighted navigation aids all along the area covered. You can find out what a lighthouse looks like, so you'll know what to look for. You can check that lighted aids have not changed their lighting sequence since your chart was issued. You'll find geographic coordinates for entry marks. (Chapter 2 covers actual light identification in detail.) *The International Marine Light List & Waypoint Guide* covers the waters from Maine to Texas, including the Bahamas, in one volume.

Coast Pilot

Other helpful onboard references are the Coast Pilots from NOAA. These are published for nine specific regions, and provide general descriptions of the areas, plus details on harbors, navigation cautions, anchoring, or small-craft facilities. Most important, they explain the otherwise maddening "refer-to" notes on charts (as in, "Danger Area: see note A," which then refers you to the Pilot).

Tide Tables

The information contained in tide tables makes navigation so much easier—and safer. It is helpful to know the times of high and low tide at a given location, and it can be critical to know the expected height of a tide (even on a daily basis, the two highs may not be the same). The tables show times and heights for major locations, then give time and height differences for a lot of secondary locations. These books are now published by International Marine.

Tidal Current Tables

Current tables go a step beyond tide tables to give you an estimate of the times of slack water, and the times of maximum current flow (both ebb and flood), plus the expected velocity of current at maximum flow. These can influence a decision on whether or when to cross a bay or move upcurrent. The tables are now published by International Marine.

Tidal Current Charts

Current charts are sets of almost duplicate charts (11 of them) of a particular area,

Savannah, Ga., 1997
Times and Heights of High and Low Waters

From Tide Tables 1997: East Coast of North and South America, Including Greenland, *International Marine, 1997.*

the difference being that each chart shows the expected direction and velocity of tidal currents for a specific "tidal" hour. By using them in conjunction with tide tables, the navigator can plan good times to cross the bay or enter the harbor, and avoid the bad. He can also adjust course to compensate for current set. Unfortunately, NOAA has discontinued publishing many of these.

Cruising Guides

One more category of books can make any cruising easier, even if they don't add more technical detail. These are the cruising guides, the boater's equivalent of a tourist guide. They supplement navigation information, and most add the tourist dimension by listing marinas, boatyards, and all the support businesses a traveling boater might need. Most include sidebars on places to go and things to see, so the boat traveler does not stay confined to harbor, but sees all the special sights.

been possible, with depths of 6½ feet, to lay along-side the nearly perpendicular bank. However, this is limestone and requires considerable bumpering, as the banks do slope slightly outward. There is no sturdy growth along the bank to which you can tie up; you would probably need to carry out anchors to use as substitute bow-and-stern bollards.

The bottom appears to have only a coating of mud over rock; holding is only fair.

The cut is surrounded on all sides by high banks, so it requires considerable agility to get out of a skiff. Since there is nothing to which you can tie up, you'll need to take along a dinghy anchor.

This is not an attractive anchorage; the view closely resembles barren desert hillocks. There are dirt roads on both sides of the basin, and cars often are parked beside the water while local families spend the day fishing. If you are able to get ashore, you can stretch your legs on the access roads. In an emergency, you could walk to the town of Epes, about 1.25 miles to the northwest.

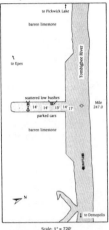

Epes Industrial Cut, *Mile 247.0*

to Pickwick Lake

barren limestone

to Epes

scattered low bushes

Tombigbee River

14' 14' 15' 14' 17'

Mile 247.0

parked cars

barren limestone

N

to Demopolis

Scale: 1" = 720'

GAINESVILLE CUTOFF

⭐ 🔵 🔵🔵 🔲

No facilities

Chart: TTWW76; see sketch map page 108

Mile: 265.9   **Pool:** 73.0 feet

This offchannel anchorage is just below Gainesville Lock on the western bank, up the old river section that leads northwest to Gainesville Dam. So far we have never seen barges stored here, and this is a good stop if you are overtaken by darkness when heading upriver and do not want to attempt lockage in the dark. The anchorage is not recommended if the river is rising. There can be strong currents and considerable drift, since the dam is just upstream.

Depart from the main channel when the old river to the west opens clearly. Slightly favor the southern bank when entering; depths generally will hold from 20 feet to more than 30 feet.

A short distance up the old river is an overhead power line whose clearance is unknown; it could be a hazard. Proceed up the old river only until well off the channel, and anchor east of the cable. The bottom is mud over a scoured surface, and it may be difficult to set the anchor.

You can take a dinghy up the old river to the bridge, where you can land the skiff and scramble up the bank. From there it is a short walk to Gaines-ville. Main Street is only about a block from the river.

Mile 217.0 - Mile 266.0   107

From Cruising Guide to the Tennessee River, Tenn-Tom Waterway, and Lower Tombigbee River, *by Thomas, Marian, and William Rumsey, International Marine, 1991, 1995.*

Personal narratives can add even more to the enjoyment of a new place. While some people prefer to make their own discoveries, others like to gain from the experience of those who've gone before.

With any of the travel-related books, look through them before your cruise. Besides gaining some familiarity with the territory, you'll have a basis for choosing where to go, and perhaps, where not.

Local Knowledge

While it is impractical to try to navigate solely on the basis of verbal directives, it doesn't hurt to supplement written and charted information with some practical experience. As you expand cruising waters, your circle of boating friends will also grow. Find the willing—and reliable—sources, and note their local knowledge directly on your charts.

CYBERCHARTS

On the simple premise of first-things-first, this chapter has ignored the newest solution to the chart-folding puzzle: the electronic chart plotter. It is covered in Chapter 4.

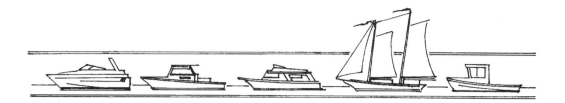

Reading Lights

Boaters describe night travel as either fun or frightening; there are few in-betweens. You may choose to be a daytime boater for many reasons, but it is still important to know how to find your way after daylight fades. The best-laid plots of captains are often waylaid by temperamental engines, broken bridges, even the U.S. military. With a little practice, some preparation, and often a bit of patience, you can read and follow night lights. You'll stop worrying about getting in before dark as you start to enjoy the peripheral benefits of night travel: bright cityscape, glowing moonrise, sparkling stars.

The night navigator watches all lights—the stationary lights along a shoreline, on buoys or anchored boats, or the moving lights that indicate moving boats.

SHORE LIGHTS

Sometimes, night travel entails an overnight run along a coastline, where navigation is mostly a simple matter of counting sea buoys or lighthouses (or towns and water tanks) until you get to the one you want. Other times, the shortest distance between two ports cuts an angle course that first leads you away from shore, then brings you back in near your destination.

City Loom

From offshore, your first indication of landfall may be a large, if vague, dome-shaped area of light along the horizon—the *loom* of a city.

One of the most interesting looms lights the night sky along the New Jersey coast. It's red, and it shows brighter and brighter with each closing mile. The rosy glow doesn't come from any navigation aid, though it accomplishes that purpose better than any ordinary mark. The red rooftop signs of the Trump and Harrah Casinos are the unmistakable trademark of Atlantic City.

Major Lights

On other nights, at other cities, your first sign of harbor lights will be a faint hint of a light flash. You may dismiss it as distant fireworks (or farther-distant lightning), but the closer you get, the brighter the light and the more obviously regular the flashes. Finally, you'll see it clearly enough to time the flash and confirm that it's "your" light.

HARBOR LIGHTS

The lighthouse or major shore light at a harbor entrance will have a specific light characteristic (perhaps "flashing white at 15-second intervals" or "two flashing white at 20-second intervals"). Charts indicate the flash pattern, the height of the light, and its range of visibility under ordinary conditions. As you approach, you can confirm the charted information and usually add to it, by looking up the light in your Light List.

Once you're sure of the general location, look for other identifiable shore lights or buildings: antennas, stacks, a church or other large building that may be noted and

located on the chart. Even at night, silhouettes of such structures can help you find entry marks: Where is the charted channel in relation to the landmarks?

Lighthouse Red Sector

Not all lighthouses are built on land; some are a good distance out in the water and must be passed on the "safe" side. Study the chart indication for one of these, and you may see a noted "red sector" where dotted lines radiate outward from the light in a circle-dissecting pattern. The red sector is that section of the circle where it is unsafe for boats to approach.

If boaters start to approach the light on a heading that would lead into the danger area, they will see a red light from the lighthouse instead of white. (The revolving light is shielded by panes of glass all around. It shines through clear glass to indicate the safe sector, and through red panes to signal danger.)

If you see red when the light flashes, you're approaching from a dangerous direction. Alter course until you see the light flashing white.

ENTRANCE CHANNEL

When you're approaching a harbor entrance from offshore, check the chart to see what markers will lead you in.

Outer Sea Buoys

Coming in from offshore, the single fairway marker farthest out to sea should be your first mark encounter. All of these have the same red-and-white-striped coloring, and the same light pattern: the Morse code A (dot-dash) flashed by a very bright white light. Usually, sea buoys are far enough from shore lights so they stand out clearly, once you're close enough to the mark to identify the light pattern.

Channel Markers

Once you find the sea buoy, a rough compass course will help you locate the first set of channel markers. (Use the Light List to double-check the light patterns shown on the chart.) You'll be looking for red and green lights, the same colors as the buoys.

Practice counting seconds so you can time the light flashes of any navigation light. The long-used method of inserting "1,000" before the number still works, at least closely enough to distinguish between 2½-, 4-, or 6-second intervals. As soon as you see a flash, start counting "one thousand and one, one thousand and two, one thousand and three. . . ."

Use a stopwatch, if you like being right-on, but practice counting along with the watch, for those days when the watch has been misplaced.

Following a straight channel is easy, but when a channel turns, you must follow the correct sequence of lights (for example: a 4-second light, then a quick flash, another 4, then a 2½). Aiming for the wrong light would put you right out of the channel.

The end of a jetty may be marked by a post or tower directly on the structure, or by a buoy in front of it. Again, check the chart so you know what to look for.

Range Lights

The striped-board range marks that keep boats in center channel by day do the same job at night, using lights instead of stripes. If the chart does not specify the light characteristic of a set of ranges, check the Light List (range lights can be any color). Often, they're obvious even without a written description; once you know where to expect them, you'll be attuned to recognizing them quickly.

LIGHT LIST

A current Light List is a necessary reference when you're cruising to new waters. Even if your charts are all brand new, they don't have space to include all the information you'll get from the book.

Characteristics of Lights

1. **F—Fixed:** A light showing continuously and steadily.

2. **Occulting:** A light in which the total duration of light in a period is longer than the total duration of darkness, and the intervals of darkness (eclipses) are usually of equal duration.
   2.1 Oc—Single-occulting: An occulting light in which an eclipse is regularly repeated.
   2.2 Oc (2)—Group-occulting: An occulting light in which a specific number of eclipses is regularly repeated as a group.
   2.3 Oc (2+1)—Composite group-occulting: A light similar to a group-occulting light, except that successive groups in a period have different numbers of eclipses.

3. **Iso—Isophase:** A light in which all durations of light and darkness are equal. (Formerly called *equal interval light.*)

4. **Flashing:** A light in which the total duration of light in a period is shorter than the total duration of darkness, and the appearances of light (flashes) are usually of equal duration.
   4.1 Fl—Single-flashing: A light in which a flash is regularly repeated up to 30 times per minute.
   4.2 Fl (2)—Group-flashing: A light in which a specific number of flashes is regularly repeated as a group.
   4.3 Fl (2+1)—Composite group-flashing: A light similar to a group flashing light except that the groups have varying numbers of flashes.

Characteristics of lights, from International Marine Light List and Waypoint Guide, Maine to Texas, *1996.*

Every light has an identifying number, so you'll know exactly what the Coast Guard is talking about when their broadcast Notice to Mariners mentions an off-station buoy or an extinguished light. Major lights are also named, and their location is given in latitude/longitude coordinates; there's no mislocating marks.

You'll find physical descriptions of unusual structures (example: "red conical tower on gray cylindrical pier") so you know what to look for by day. Height and range details suggest at what distance you start to look, day or night. You'll know if you can expect a fog signal, radio beacon, or RACON (radar beacon).

Naturally, for night navigation, the flash pattern of each light is shown, and the Light List shows a graphic representation of what each light code means. While most of the abbreviations are obvious, a few benefit from the visual picture.

OTHER LIGHTS

• Most lighthouses show white lights (a few mix a color with the pattern) or add a colored sector. White lights also flash the Morse code A of fairway buoys, and the double flash of isolated danger marks.

• Buoys show red and green lights to match their color.

• When a light marks a place where special caution is needed (at a sharp turn in a channel, or on a wreck), the light will be quick-flashing.

• Away from channels, you may see the yellow light of a yellow buoy.

• Bridges are lighted: reds on the piers (both sides) and greens marking the centerline above the navigation channel.

• Oil well structures are not listed in the Light List, but they're charted, and it's

doubtful you could mistake such a huge platform for anything else.

• On the Intracoastal Waterway, you should be able to travel from lighted mark to lighted mark in safe water. By traveling light to light, interim daymarks will be passed with a wide margin. (Note: This is not the case on other waterways—for example, on the Inside Passage to Alaska.)

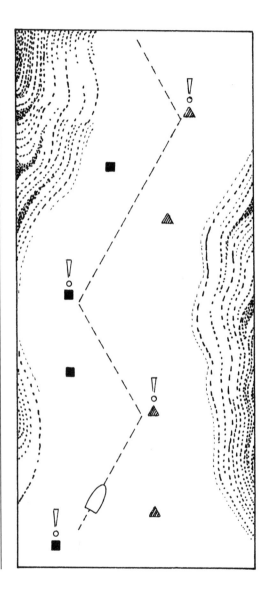

• If the sea is rough when you first spot a light, don't even try to figure its flash characteristics. More often than not, it's not flashing at all; you're just getting an interrupted view because you and the light are on top of a wave at the same time. However, lights can, and do, fail from time to time—never rely on one aid to navigation to fix your position.

• Lighted buoys are powered by batteries charged by little solar panels. The on-and-off mechanism is automatic, responding to outside light or darkness, much like city street lights, leaving them relatively maintenance-free for prolonged periods of time.

• Commercial boats frequently run at night, and may scan a channel with a bright spotlight sweeping from shore to shore. These captains travel the same waterway often; they're familiar with the route and the potential trouble spots. Except for delivery captains in a hurry, most recreational boaters prefer to travel only by day.

BOAT LIGHTS

After setting a compass course for a destination, boat captains navigate at night according to information they read in the light patterns displayed by other boats. Lights not only can tell you what type of boat you see, but also whether it is anchored or underway, and if moving, what general course it's on. Recognizing these light patterns is the first step in determining whether you maintain or alter course according to the rules that govern boat traffic: the U.S. Coast Guard's *Navigation Rules: International— Inland* (see Chapter 5).

Though most recreational boats follow the Inland rules, you should be aware of the division between *inland* and *international* waters. This is known as the *demarcation line*. Sometimes it's clearly charted, usually close to harbor exits. (Inland does *not* extend to what are normally considered offshore boundaries.) Lighting requirements described here are for inland rules, unless otherwise noted.

Definitions

Recreational boats are either powerboats or sailboats. A sailboat that is motoring is considered a powerboat. Sportfishing boats are also included with powerboats; for rule purposes, "fishing vessel" applies to commercial boats only.

A vessel is "underway" when it is not anchored, tied to shore, or aground.

A vessel is "not under command" if some exceptional circumstances exist, and it cannot maneuver.

A vessel is "restricted in its ability to maneuver" when its work restricts motion (as with a dredge or a vessel working on a pipeline or cable).

Lights should be shown from dusk to dawn or whenever visibility is restricted, by rain or fog or whatever. When visibility is severely limited, sound signals can supplement light signals (see Chapter 3).

First Sight

A faint white light is usually the first indication you'll have of boat traffic (though a sailing boat moving toward you would be the exception). The white light could be a masthead, stern, or anchor light; even a giant cruise ship first appears as a tiny glow. You won't be able to identify the vessel until you're close enough to see more lights.

• Once you can separate, visually, a colored side light, or two masthead lights, you can picture the boat they're connected to. When you know how the boat is faced, you can judge if and when you need to alter course to avoid a close encounter of the marine kind. If you do decide to change course, do it in an obvious way, so the captain of the other boat understands your intention.

Common Lights

Light requirements for recreational boats are usually shown in the state's boating regulations pamphlet (which most boaters get when first registering the boat). They're also found in the federal government's booklet *Federal Requirements for Recreational Boats*, which you can usually find at a marina or boating supply store; or call the Coast Guard Boating Safety Hotline, 1-800-368-5647.

• "Captain's" courses use flash cards to help students memorize light combinations. Make up your own cards; they'll have colored dots positioned as you would see lights of a boat coming toward you, moving away, or at a side angle.

Sailboat Lights. When sailing, the typical under-20-meter sailboat will show red and green side lights and a white stern light. (The side lights are often combined in one unit at the bow.) In addition, the captain can choose to add two lights at the top of the mast: red over green.

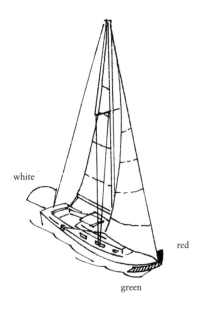

An alternative arrangement for the under-20-meter boat is to carry a tri-color light at the top of the mast: red and green side lights and a white light showing aft.

Either of these combinations is acceptable under inland or international rules.

Powerboat Lights. Powerboat lights have variations, too. The under-20-meter boat shows a single white masthead light, red and green side lights, and a white stern light.

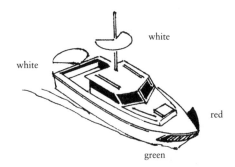

A larger-than-50-meter boat *must* show two masthead lights (one forward, one aft), and a smaller powerboat *may* show two.

A motoring sailboat is considered a powerboat. Here, the "masthead" light will not be literally at the top of the mast, but is usually carried about spreader height on the front of the mast.

Check often to be sure your lights are working.

Other Boat Lights

If your boating takes you places where you'll see more than small pleasure boats, you'll need a more complete light reference—one that includes commercial fishing boats, or tugs, barges, and freighters. Look for regional publications that are most pertinent, or go to the source: *Navigation Rules: International—Inland*, required to be on board recreational boats longer than 12 meters. Find the rule book at larger marine stores (usually those that sell charts)

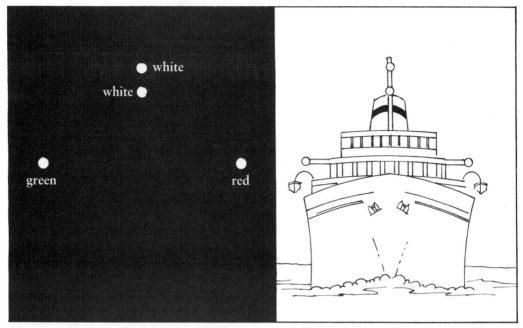

Powerboat, head-on view. (Alter course to avoid collision.)

Powerboat showing port side profile.

or write for a copy to: Superintendent of Documents, U.S. Government Printing Office, Washington, DC 20402 (cost is $8).

Big Powerboats. Megayachts, freighters, and cruise ships all show the same lights: side lights, stern light, a masthead light forward, and a second masthead light aft, positioned higher than the forward light. (And by the time the boat gets close enough for a silhouette, you'll see a bunch of deck lights and cabin lights—and Christmas lights, if it's the right season.)

Towing Astern. The recreational boater is well advised to stay a good distance away from any commercial traffic, but one particular combination is a special danger. The tug towing a barge can be a real problem. Often, the barge is towed so far behind the tug (up to a half mile) that boaters don't realize they're connected. The required

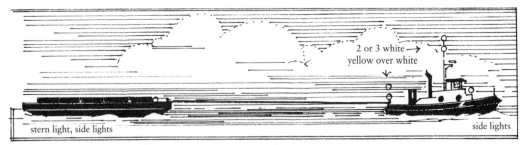

2 or 3 white →
yellow over white

stern light, side lights

side lights

A tug towing a barge might be difficult to identify because of the distance between the two.

lighting arrangement is apparently not a sufficient warning, as many accidents have occurred even though these vessels are properly lighted.

The lights to watch for are: on the towing boat, two or three white lights in a vertical lineup (the number of lights depends on the length of the tow); side lights; white stern light *and* a yellow light shown above the stern light. The barge being towed shows only ordinary side lights and stern light.

The same caution applies to tugs towing rafts of logs, which are low and very hard to see at night.

Fishing and Trawling. Commercial fishing boats also show two lights in a vertical line, but their colors are red over white. Trawlers—those vessels dragging some kind of fishing apparatus—show green over white. (All show side lights and stern light.)

Restricted in Ability to Maneuver. This one's important to remember: these boats cannot get out of your way. A vertical lineup of red, white, red is your signal to keep clear.

Pilot Boat. One more vertical combination: Pilot boats show two all-around lights, white over red—in addition to side and stern lights.

Submarine. If you ever see double white masthead lights *and* a flashing amber (three flashes in as many seconds, then off for 3 seconds), you are looking at a submarine. Do not pass close.

Police Boat. If a flashing blue light comes your way, expect the local law-enforcement boat.

Little Boats. Small sailboats (less than 7 meters) and rowboats can show red and green side lights if they want to, but the only required light is a flashlight to shine in time to prevent a collision. ("Portable" running lights are available, too: a flashlight with red and green sectors.)

Anchored Boats. Under-50-meter boats show one all-round white light, "exhibited where it can best be seen." If the boat is less than 20 meters, and you're anchored in one of the officially recognized anchorages, you're not required to show an anchor light, though it can't hurt to call attention to your location if there's much traffic in the area. (In the unfortunate situation of your boat being hit while anchored, the insurance company will probably ask about an anchor light.)

Vessels Aground. A grounded boat would show an ordinary anchor light and, if practical (for boats over 12 meters), two all-round reds aligned vertically.

DAY SHAPES

Just as different lights give us information about other boats at night, so different shapes tell us something about boats by day. The same rules that define light patterns for different types of boats also require day shapes to indicate different types of boating activity. These are not flags or sign-boards, but three-dimensional objects, of a black material and of a size appropriate to your boat.

Sailboat Under Power

If a sailboat has sails up but is also under mechanical power, it should show a cone shape forward, with point down. (If the boat is under 12 meters, it does not need the cone in inland waters.)

Anchored Boats

Whether power or sail, all anchored boats should show a single ball shape in the forward part of the boat. (This is one rule where the dividing line is not 12 meters; even a 20-foot boat should comply.)

Fishing Boats and Trawlers

The day shape is the same for fishing boats and trawlers: an hourglass of two cones in a vertical line, with points together. (Boats under 20 meters long can substitute a basket.)

If fishing gear is extended farther than 150 meters from the boat, another cone (apex up) should be shown in the direction of the gear.

Restricted Maneuverability

Those vessels that can't move must show a vertical lineup of ball, diamond, ball.

Dive Boats

A code flag "Alpha" can also be used to show inability to maneuver. Not an official day shape according to federal navigation rules, but worth mentioning, is the divers' flag: the familiar red with white diagonal stripe that indicates diving activity.

Dredge

One of the recreational boater's least favorite sights along a route is a dredge. We should be glad to know the channel is being maintained at proper depth, but we wish the maintaining were out of sight. "Dredge" means the channel has shoaled, so where is the shoal, and, equally worrisome, how do you get past all this stuff?

The typical dredge is a mass of equipment: pipeline, anchor buoys, cables, often two or three small workboats. The channel

A dredge is restricted in ability to maneuver; shows day shapes of ball-diamond-ball. Also, on the safe passing side, two diamonds; side with obstruction, two balls.

is dotted with survey flags, and until you're practically on top of it all, you can't see any clear channel.

As you might have guessed, a dredge is one of those vessels "restricted in ability to maneuver." At night, it shows three vertical lights: red, white, red; by day: ball, diamond, ball. In addition, if an obstruction exists, you'll see two vertical red lights or two ball shapes on the side of the obstruction. On the safe passing side, you'll see two vertical green lights, or two diamond shapes.

Despite all this information, you should *still* call the dredge operator on VHF radio. You may think you see a clear path, but underwater cables will not be visible; you must be sure the operator knows you want to pass so he can lower the cables. According to one operator, the biggest problem they see is the boater who either has no radio, or chooses not to use it. He takes a chance, guesses wrong, goes aground, and then blames the dredge. As noted earlier, dredges are our friends!

One suggested solution to the clear-channel problem was to use red- and green-flagged posts on the appropriate sides of the temporary channel. Recreational boaters are so conditioned to red and green, it would be easy to follow. However, such colored flags would constitute placement of navigation aids by persons other than the proper agency, so it was not allowed.

If at first that seems foolish, think about how Americans love to sue anybody for anything that goes wrong, and you can understand why an apparently simple solution was neither simple nor a doable solution.

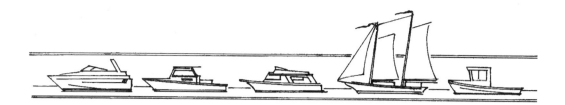

3

Hearing Aids

With the increased popularity of marine electronics in recent years, it's been suggested that unless you have such navigation help on board, you'd better stay in port whenever visibility is less than great. But few boaters start out in a proverbial pea-soup fog, so that's hardly helpful advice to anyone caught by a suddenly descending and totally enveloping cloud.

Even when the boat *has* a magic position finder, the captain should have backup strategies for dealing with fog or downpours. There are times when you can't count on the most basic of navigation help—your own eyesight—until it may be too late to act.

The purpose of all sightings, of course, whether by eye or by electronics, is to avoid hitting anything: another boat, a buoy, a shoal, even the shore. There will be times when you won't be able to see

these things, but with the help of some well-placed hearing aids, you will be able to avoid them.

As with lighted aids, you'll hear sounds from stationary sites (buoys, shore stations, the shore itself) and sounds from movable objects (other boats).

SHORE SOUNDS

Sound signals are given to provide information to boaters when visibility is restricted. Though often called fog signals, they are just as welcome and useful in a driving rainstorm.

Lighthouse Horns

Thanks to innumerable mystery movies, the most familiar sound signal is the basic foghorn. Though the plot might thicken

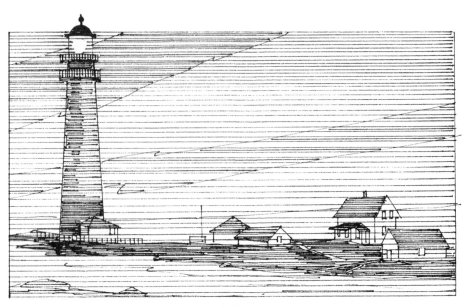

Each lighthouse has a particular sound characteristic.

with the two-tone horn, most actual fog-horns are not that interesting.

Each lighthouse is identified by its phase characteristic—the sound pattern of how many blasts it sounds at what time intervals—which will be noted on the chart and in the Light List (i.e., one blast every 15 seconds, or two blasts every 30 seconds).

Usually, lighthouse foghorns sound only during actual fog or other times of reduced visibility; those few that operate continuously are so noted in the Light List.

If someday you are trying to stare through a fog bank and are expecting to hear a nearby foghorn, keep in mind that the fog you're in may not even reach all the way to the shore lighthouse, so the horn will not be sounding. Also, if the signal is turned on and off by an electronic activator, there is no guarantee that it will be working. This is one of those times when prudent mariners don't rely on only one source of information.

Background Noise

When you're traveling close to a shore-line, you may hear noises other than the warning horn. These include car horns, and maybe a siren or two, mixed with ordinary traffic sounds. (These should set off a red light in your brain, as should the sound of breaking waves—even gently breaking waves spell shore or shoal, neither of which should be on your course.)

Occasionally, a third sense gets into the act: the pungent odor of a paper mill or fish-processing plant will alert you to a presence you'd like to avoid for more than the obvious reason.

SOUND BUOYS

When the air is so thick you can't see a horizon, you'll never see a buoy, either, unless you have the misfortune of finding it by running into it. To aid the finding and avoid the colliding, certain buoys will announce their location with a sound signal.

Unlike lighthouse signals, most of these sounds have no fixed phase characteristics because they're activated by wave action, which could only be described as variable. You'll hear either an occasional muffled

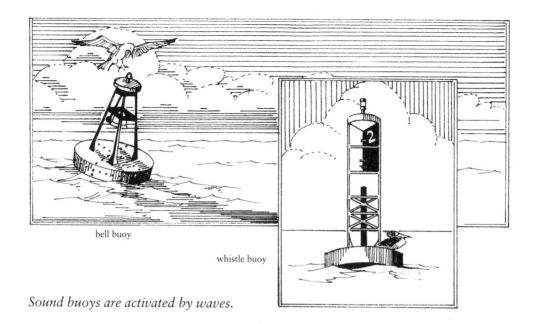

bell buoy

whistle buoy

Sound buoys are activated by waves.

sound, or a continuous clatter or hoot, depending on the state of the water and the type of sound-producing device on the buoy. Seldom is the water so calm that you would hear nothing at all, though that is a possibility that must always be considered.

Bell Buoy

A bell buoy works well with the bouncy-platform principle: a very slight wave action rocks the buoy enough so the bell will be struck by one of four hammers, all hanging outside the bell, waiting for an appropriate angle for contact.

Gong Buoy

Equally basic is the gong buoy, but instead of using a single noise-maker, it has four, each producing a different tone. While bells can play only a monotone rhythm, gong buoys could conceivably play a rhythmic tune.

Whistle Buoy

Wave motion also prompts the almost eerie sound made by a whistle buoy. Ac-

cording to the Light List's glossary of terms, the buoy produces the sound "by emitting compressed air through a circumferential slot into a cylindrical bell chamber." Whatever—it works, and it's not likely to be confused with any ordinary sea sounds.

Combination Buoy

A mark described as a combination buoy is one that has both a light and a sound signal, though calling them "lighted bell buoy" or "lighted gong buoy" seems clearer—and shorter.

BOAT SOUNDS

Since weather may render the boat's navigation lights as useless as the shore lights, boats should also send sound signals, not because the rules say so (though they do) but in plain old self-defense. If everyone made noise continuously, there would be no time for listening, so boats follow specified patterns of nautically correct noise.

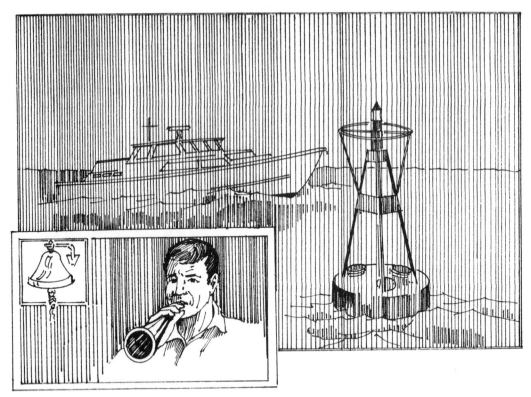

Navigation rules require boats to have some sound-making device on board.

To send signals, you must have a sound-making device on board. Over-12-meter boats should have a whistle and bell; under-12-meter boats don't need both, but must have something to use to make noise. A whistle is really a horn.

The type of signal each boat sends is dictated by the type of boat as well as by what it is doing, whether moving through the water, towing another boat, purposely anchored, or aground. When regulations call for a short blast, that means 1 second; a long blast is 4 to 6 seconds.

Powerboat

If you hear one long blast every couple of minutes, expect to also hear the engine(s) of a powerboat moving through the water. If the same boat stops "making way" (engine still on), it signals with two long blasts at the same 2-minute intervals.

Sailboat (and more)

If the 2-minute intervals are interrupted by one long, then two short sounds, you can't be sure what to expect. It could be a sailboat, a fishing boat (that is fishing), a towing boat, or any boat "restricted in ability to maneuver." At least you can assume it won't be traveling fast. (Regardless of boat type, "fast" should not be a consideration in restricted visibility, but not all boaters understand "should not.")

Towed Boat

One long and three short indicates a vessel being towed. The signal should be sounded shortly after the towboat's one long, two short.

Pilot Vessel

If you hear the unusual combination of four short blasts given along with a set of ordinary fog signals, you're hearing a pilot vessel.

Anchored Boats

Though few recreational boats actually do so, anchored boats *should* sound the truly distinctive signal of a bell ringing rapidly for 5 seconds. Do this at the prescribed 1-minute intervals, and everyone on board will be wishing fervently for an immediate lifting of the fog.

If you're lucky and are anchored in a designated anchorage (those so noted on the charts), and presuming the boat length is under 20 meters, you can officially ignore the 5-second jingle bells.

Aground Boat

A foggy day could qualify as one of the worst times for a grounding, and for obvious reasons you'll want to send as many messages as you can, warning others to stay away. Do the ordinary anchored-boat signals, and add three separate bell strokes before and after the 5-second rapid ringing session. Repeat the whole sequence every minute—and hope the tide will soon rise.

FOG STRATEGIES

Even without loran, GPS, or radar, there are things you can do when caught by a fog bank.

Locate Yourself

When you see the ground-level cloud of a fog bank rolling toward you, make a note of your position (as close as you know it) and the time, then look at the chart and write down the sequence of navigation aids you should be passing soon. Especially note those that are sound buoys or shore foghorns; estimate the time required to get close enough to hear them, and start listening, intently.

Lights On

Even though visibility seems like zero, navigation lights should be turned on. A red or green glow might cut through fog earlier than the outline of a boat and thus give another boat another few seconds' warning.

On Watch

You probably won't have to assign crew to specific lookout posts; everyone on board will be looking as hard as they can. It is amazing how thick air can become, and frightening to see how abruptly a boat can drift out of the haze and drift back in, with only a few seconds of visual contact.

The person who watches from the bow should be the crew who has the most astute hearing; sound will be the more likely aid, giving you a longer time for evasive action. By the time you *see* another boat, it may be too late to maneuver out of the way.

Go Slow, Go Quiet

You shouldn't need navigation rules to tell you to go slow when you can't see. The rules' definition of slow—speed appropriate to prevailing circumstances and conditions—leaves way too much room for interpretation and, unfortunately, those who need to be told don't listen anyway.

Occasionally, you should slow all the way to a stop; though looking is not an option, you'll be able to listen better for other boats, buoy signals, or shore sounds. Often, this quiet time will yield a distant bell, or a not-distant-enough sound of a boat moving through the water, either of which might be a course-altering signal.

Not Quite Stop

If you hear another boat's fog signal, go as slowly as you can, while still maintaining steering ability.

Sound Direction

At times, the apparent direction of a sound is unreliable in fog; you can easily

Stop and listen.

misjudge the location of its source, especially in an area where steep cliffs or bluffs along the shoreline deflect the sound. Distance, of course, is a guess even in clear weather, and fog does muffle sound.

Timing Is Everything

Because required signaling is timed, many people give signals "on the minute." So, assuming all watches are close, if you give your signals on the half-minute, you'll have the theoretical advantage of a better chance to be heard.

Seek and Ye May Find

Make note of the progress along your course more often than usual; try to confirm position with each buoy you're supposed to pass. If you seem to be missing a sound buoy, take some short sidetracks and go looking for it. If your general course is westerly, aim north for a short distance, then come back to course; then south a short distance, and again return to course line. Proceed west about a half mile, then do the north-south routes again.

Reflect Yourself

Everybody should hoist a radar reflector, to make the job of boat location easier for those boats that have radar.

Wait It Out

If you were boating in an out-of-the-main-way place when the fog rolled in, you may want to poke your way as close to shore as possible, and drop a hook till the fog rolls out again.

Move well away from shipping lanes; try not to cross them in a fog.

Shore Leave

If you take the dinghy ashore when it's foggy, think about how to return to the anchored boat. Someone on board the big boat could make anchored-boat sounds, but if a number of boats are all obeying the anchor rules, you may row from wrong boat to wrong boat for awhile. Another option is to send some other noise, like Beethoven's Third or Buffett's newest comeback.

Clear Sky

Check shore stations both ahead and behind. If it's clear one way, you may choose to go for it, hoping, of course, that the fog does not choose to follow your lead.

Think Before You Call

Do not call the Coast Guard to ask when the fog will clear at a given location.

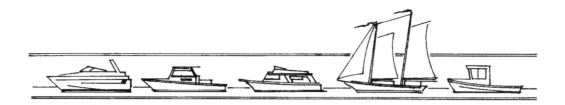

Tracking Courses

It's no surprise that electronic navigation aids are popular; they're fast, accurate, reliable, and generally amazing. Nobody questions their place as navigation tools, except, perhaps, to suggest they be placed on board only *after* boatowners have mastered the more traditional arts of navigation.

The problem with putting all your faith in one black box is twofold. The obvious someday-it-will-break warning is usually ignored by the faithful; either they choose not to believe it, or they're prepared with their definition of backup—a battery-operated version of their favorite position finder. The second problem is harder to define; it's about missing out on the satisfaction that comes with learning.

In today's hurry-up world of push-buttons, appealing to a sense of pride in knowledge and/or seamanship might border

on the naive, but it works for some people. Based on the assumption that (1) nobody likes to be ignorant and (2) nobody likes to be lost, this chapter can give you a start on developing basic piloting skills.

PILOTING AND "DEAD" RECKONING DEFINED

All boaters should know how to navigate by piloting and dead reckoning. You should learn these skills even if an electronic position finder is on board. The instant information provided by a Global Positioning System or loran unit is grand, but it's not much use to the boater who can neither plot the position on a chart, nor determine where to go next.

Piloting is what you do as you steer your boat from navigation mark to navigation mark. If each mark is within sight of the next, there's never any doubt as to your position. You're at number 12 or number 14 or somewhere between. To pilot your boat, you need only to look and steer.

When marks are too widely spaced to travel mark-to-mark visually, you steer the boat on a compass course that connects your present location A to your destination B. You can only estimate your position in the between-marks area, based on how long you've been traveling at what speed since you left A. You "deduce" approximate positions: *dead reckoning* (or "ded" reckoning) is a running estimate of your position, based on direction, distance, and speed.

You'll need a few basic tools to help you stay found, and you'll probably *want* a few more.

The necessaries: compass, charts, depthfinder (leadline), parallel rules, dividers, timepiece, pencils, erasers.

The desirables: binoculars, rangefinder, hand-bearing compass, electronic depthsounder, loran, or GPS.

The extras: night scope, radar, electronic chart plotter.

NEED TO KNOW: DIRECTION

To keep a record of your dead reckoning (DR) track, you must be able to connect the boat's position to charted positions. The compass helps you do that.

On your boat, you read direction by sighting over or across your compass. In most cases, the compass is mounted along the boat's centerline, and the front of the compass points in the direction you're traveling.

On charts, you read directions on a compass rose—usually twin circles of tiny hatch marks—imprinted in a few locations on each chart.

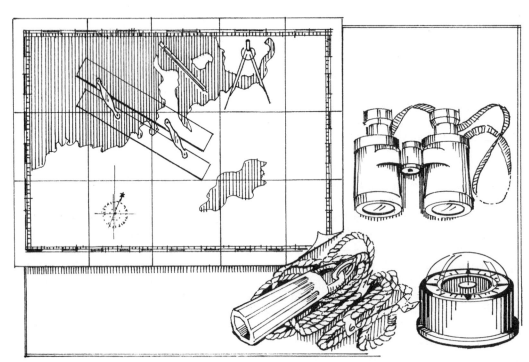

Tools for navigation.

The card inside your boat's compass, and the compass rose on the chart, are both divided and marked in increments of a 360-degree circle.

Variation

The outer ring of a compass rose shows an arrow at true north, and the inner ring, at magnetic north. A magnetic compass needle points to magnetic north, not to the true geographic north pole. It's not necessary to know *why* this is so, only that it *is* so.

The difference between these two norths is called *variation*, and it is not a constant difference; it "varies" with geographic location, and it changes with the passage of time—two more details it's necessary to file in memory.

If a particular chart does not have an inner rose to show you the variation, a chart note will tell you the variation for that area.

Reading the Rose

To determine what course to steer, get a pencil and your essential plotting tool—the parallel rules (rulers). (With this simple but clever device, two same-length rulers, usually clear plastic, are connected in such a way that a course line can be "moved" across a chart surface while retaining the same parallel directional line.) Draw a pen-

cil line on the chart from A (location) to B (destination). Take the parallel rules, and lay the edge of one rule along the pencil line. Find the nearest compass rose.

Hold one ruler in position flat on the chart, and slide the other ruler as far as the connecting bars will allow. Then hold the second ruler steady while you move the first rule up to the new position. Repeat the process as you "walk" your A–B line to a compass rose.

When you get there, place one edge of a ruler so it touches the marked center of the rose. Imagine the ruler as an arrow pointing in the direction you want to travel; sight along the ruler's edge from the center to the ring, and read the number of degrees at the place where ruler crosses circle. That's your course: true course if you read the outer ring, magnetic if you read the inner.

Deviation

Since your compass finds direction according to magnetic north, it would seem logical to use the inner (magnetic) circle of the compass rose to determine what course to steer. And it would be, except there's one more thing to consider.

Each boat has its own set of offsets caused by magnetic influences on board, and these must be factored into course-plotting. These offsets are called *deviation*—

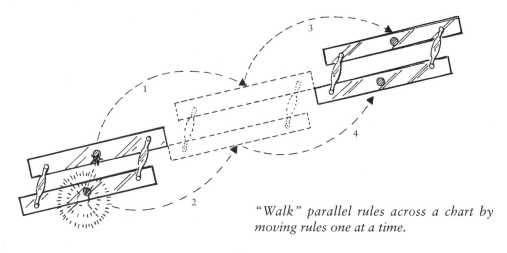

"Walk" parallel rules across a chart by moving rules one at a time.

the difference between the boat's compass readings and the chart's magnetic directions. To make it even more interesting (or frustrating), deviation is not a constant, either; it changes according to the boat's heading. For the most accurate course-plotting, each boat should have a record of this information in the form of a deviation table or deviation card specific to that boat.

Course Correctors

You must make adjustments to convert charted courses to compass courses, or to convert the boat's compass readings to the charted course.

Information on magnetic variation—the number of degrees and the direction—is found on the chart in the center of the compass rose. If it's a new chart, so variation figures are up-to-date, you can just read the magnetic ring on the compass rose, rather than convert true to magnetic.

Information on compass deviation—the number of degrees and the direction—should be found on each boat's deviation card.

Add or subtract the degrees, as required, according to the following memory device. This column of words has been used for years. You can "read" the words up or down, depending on which conversion you wish to make. Besides remembering the column, you must remember DAW: "down add west."

Once you remember "down add west," logic tells you to subtract east on the down side. And, having established that, do the opposite with both on the up side.

"COMPASS" in the column gives you the course to steer; it's the resulting number after adjustments for both variation and deviation have been made. The total of those two adjustments is called *compass error*. Examples:

If variation is 4 degrees east and deviation is 3 degrees east, compass error is 7 degrees east.

If variation is 4 degrees east and deviation is 2 degrees west, compass error is 2 degrees east.

If variation is 4 degrees east and deviation is 4 degrees west, *no* compass error.

Here's another memory device to use when correcting for variation and deviation. (1) When going from chart to boat: "east is least" (subtract easterly deviations and variations); "west is best" (add westerly deviations and variations). (2) When going from boat to chart, simply do the opposite (add if east, subtract if west).

More Compass Basics

• The compass dial is divided into 360 degrees numbered clockwise. North is 0 degrees, east is 90, south 180, and west 270. Memorize these cardinal numbers to avoid common "opposite" errors.

• To find reciprocal, or opposite, bearings: If the number is less than 180, add 180; if the number is more than 180, subtract 180. Examples:

Reciprocal of 40 degrees is 40 plus 180: 220.

Reciprocal of 240 degrees is 240 minus 180: 60.

• Because it's easier to add or subtract round numbers, here's a quick way to find

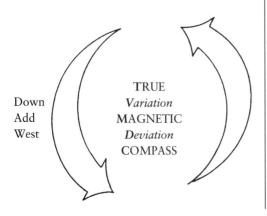

Down
Add
West

TRUE
Variation
MAGNETIC
Deviation
COMPASS

reciprocals without pencil and paper: First add or subtract 200 (an easy number), then subtract or add 20 (another easy number) to adjust for the difference between 200 and 180. It sounds more confusing than it is.

Example:

$$315 \\ -200 \\ \overline{115} \\ +20 \\ \overline{135}$$

$(315–180 = 135)$

Example:

$$45 \\ +200 \\ \overline{245} \\ -20 \\ \overline{225}$$

$(45 + 180 = 225)$

• Just remember that if you subtract the 200, you add the 20; if you add the 200, you subtract the 20.

On the East Coast, a magnetic compass points west of true; on the West Coast, it points east of true. In between (the line runs roughly through the Great Lakes and down to the Gulf of Mexico) there are places very close to true. We don't have to remember that; each chart reminds us of the variation for its area.

If your chart is not brand new, you may need to allow for a change in variation from that shown on the inner ring of the compass rose. A chart note will show the annual variation change; a few minutes won't make a noticeable difference in your computations, but if it's an old chart and the difference is a degree per year, you must consider it.

Compass Adjusters

Compasses can be adjusted to minimize deviation. See your neighborhood compass adjuster, or read a good book about it and try to do it yourself. Captain Bill Brogdon's *Boat Navigation for the Rest of Us* (International Marine, 1995) has a good section on adjustment.

If you hire someone to do it initially, watch and take notes. Some other time, on this boat or the next, you may want to do it again.

Deviation Table

After the adjusting has done all it can, you can make up your own deviation table. Find the deviation figures by running along the course lines of a number of different ranges, to see how your boat's compass reading compares to the charted course heading.

Charted range marks are best, but you'll need more than you're likely to find in one area, so use whatever charted objects can be conveniently aligned visually as a range. Note their direction according to the chart's magnetic rose; then steer on the range a few

Find pairs of charted objects to use as ranges.

times, and note the boat's average heading. Compare the compass course steered to the charted course; any difference is the deviation for that heading.

If you're steering 40 degrees and the chart shows 52 (magnetic) the error is 12, but which direction? Look at the "DAW" arrows in the figure on page 38. To get from your compass reading 40 to the magnetic 52, you must read up, and since compass is the smaller number, you must add 12 to get to 52. And by the arrows, up adds east, so your deviation is 12 degrees east.

If that doesn't compute, try "compass least, add east."

• If you hear someone talking about "having the compass swung" or "swinging the boat," it means they're checking the boat's deviation.

• A deviation table usually lists deviation figures for 15-degree intervals.

• An alternative to a numbered list for deviation is a more visual display using two compass roses, with both norths aligned. The outer circle shows compass; the inner magnetic. At the 10- or 15-degree intervals, draw a line from magnetic to the deviation correction for compass, so the space between the circles will seem to have sun rays tilting toward the direction of deviation. This makes it easier to see at a glance which way to steer to correct.

Backward Compass

Most compasses are read at the front of the dial or card. A mark (the lubber's line) helps you read the numbers more accurately. With some compasses, you read direction of travel from behind, much as you do with a car compass sitting on the dashboard. People claim they get accustomed to this, but it can be confusing, especially because bearings taken by sighting across the compass will also be "backward."

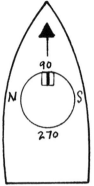
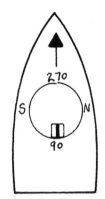

Lubber's line at front of compass dial   Backward-reading compass

NEED-TO-KNOW: DISTANCE

Charts have latitude scales (printed on side borders) and longitude scales (printed on top and bottom borders). You can use the latitude scales to measure distance, but always check the intervals on the particular chart you're using, to be sure what each division represents. One minute of latitude (1/60th of a degree) is 1 nautical mile. After minute number 59, a new degree number begins. Further subdivision of minutes is usually shown in fractions of minutes, *not* as 0 to 60 seconds.

To measure the nautical miles from where you are to where you want to go, use your dividers (second essential plotting tool). Set them at a convenient measure (2, 3, or 5 miles) along the latitude scale, then "walk" the dividers along your penciled course line, counting the miles as you go.

• Dividers—whether brass or stainless— should be easily separated with one hand, but stiff enough to hold the set measure as you walk the distance along the course line.

• When using the latitude scale to measure distance, use the section of the scale closest to the latitude you're traveling through (don't measure at the bottom of the chart if your travel area is at the top).

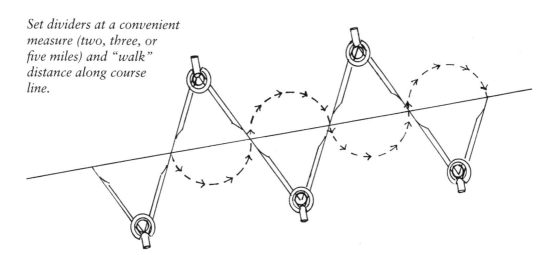

Set dividers at a convenient measure (two, three, or five miles) and "walk" distance along course line.

• River maps, Intracoastal Waterway charts, and maps of inland areas are measured in statute miles, the standard 5,280 feet. Ocean and coastal charts use nautical miles: 6,076.1 feet, or 1 minute of latitude.

• To convert nautical miles to statute, use a factor of 1.15. Seven nautical miles is roughly equivalent to 8 statute miles.

• A nautical mile is 1.852 kilometers.

• A knot is the time it takes to travel a nautical mile; you don't travel 6 knots in distance but in time. At a speed of 6 knots, you'll travel 12 nautical miles in two hours.

• Knot may be abbreviated as kn or kt.

• If you do use a chart's printed scale for a mileage measure, be sure to start measuring from the zero mark, not from the subdivided mile printed to the left of zero (see below).

NEED TO KNOW: SPEED

Speed can be measured directly through a speed log (your boat's speedometer) or it can be figured mathematically from how long it takes to travel a specified distance. (A third alternative is to cheat and read the GPS or loran.)

• If you choose the old way, run back and forth along a charted measured mile, assuming you have one close to home port. Besides elapsed time, keep track of engine RPM, and other factors like tide/wind situation, barnacle growth on the hull, how much excess weight you might be carrying. Run the course a number of times at different RPM until you have a good estimate of average speed at those RPM.

• If you have no measured mile nearby, you can still run the speed tests by establishing your own marked course. Start at the water tank and stop at the radio tower, for instance, or run from marker number 2 to marker number 34. Measure the distance between the two points on the

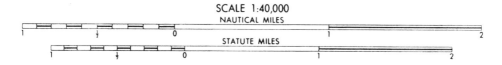

SCALE 1:40,000
NAUTICAL MILES

STATUTE MILES

chart, and use basic math to determine your speed.

Basic Math Formulas

Speed equals distance divided by time, or

$$S = \frac{D}{T}$$

For example, if distance is 6 miles, and time to run is one hour, then speed is 6 mph:

$$S = \frac{6}{1} \text{ or } 6$$

If you don't want to run one-hour segments, convert the formula to minutes: first, multiply distance by 60, then divide by the number of minutes:

$$S = \frac{D60}{T}$$

For example, if distance is 3 miles and time is 30 minutes, multiply 3 by 60 (180) and divide by time (30); speed is 6 mph:

$$S = \frac{3 \times 60}{30} \text{ or } \frac{180}{30} = 6$$

• If you need to determine distance, use these formulas:

$$D = ST, \text{ or } D = \frac{ST}{60}$$

• If the unknown factor is time, use these:

$$T = \frac{D}{S}, \text{ or } T = \frac{D60}{S}$$

IT HELPS TO KNOW: DEPTH

Electronic depthsounders have been around so long they can't qualify as new gadgets, though they do get more sophisticated with each new model. For basic navigation, all you need to know is: How deep is the water?

The original bottom finder still works: the *leadline*, a length of line with a chunk of lead attached to one end. The line is marked, usually in 1-foot increments starting at the chunk of lead. To use it, you toss the lead into the water ahead of the boat (of course, holding onto the other end of the line). As the boat moves forward, hold the line taut. When it's vertical, the mark on the line closest to the water's surface shows you how deep the water is—or is not. You must do this depth-checking at idle speed, to enable a hurried back-down, if the bottom contour is shoaling quickly.

• A leadline is simple, accurate, and doesn't break, unless the line portion is suffering from a severe case of mildew.

• A side benefit of the leadline is handy when you're checking out possible anchorages. The bottom of the lead is usually hollowed out to pick up a sample of what's on the bottom. If you see sand or mud, you'll know which anchor to choose. If you see clean lead, you can assume a hard or scoured bottom, and you may choose to look elsewhere.

• Put some water pump grease on the bottom of the lead to encourage its sample-gathering ability.

• Water depth is an important factor for piloting. In an area where depth contours are relatively even, you can tell how far from shore you are by the depth of the water. (Remember, high tide will cause a frequent, obvious increase in charted depths, and an extreme low tide, a marked decrease.)

MORE HELPERS

Here are some of the "desirable" navigating tools. While not absolutely essential to actual plotting, they add a big measure of accuracy to piloting.

Binoculars

Binoculars make the navigator's job so much easier. It's much better to identify a mark before the boat gets too close—especially if the positive ID tells you this mark is *not* the one you want.

Today's models are smooth, sleek, compact, and easy to hold.

Size. Most boat binoculars are 7 × 50. The 7 describes the magnification power: how many times larger you see the object. The 50 is the diameter of the forward (objective) lens in millimeters. This diameter is fairly large, for good light-gathering ability. While larger magnification might seem desirable from a viewing aspect, the binoculars would be difficult to hold steady on the unstable platform of a boat deck.

Coating. A rubberized coating—now almost standard on binoculars—is usually done for shock and water resistance, though on some models, the coating actually makes the binoculars water*proof.*

Focus. Focusing can be accomplished with a traditional center focus, or with individual eye adjustments. Now you can even choose "pre-focused": no adjusting necessary. Of course, these will not be as sharp as the others, but they're adequate for most usage, and when many people might be using the same binoculars, they save a lot of the frustration caused by constant readjustment.

Added Features. Some binoculars have a compass built in, some add a rangefinder; with one sighting you read the bearing of the object, its distance away, and maybe its number, too.

Night Scopes

The latest vision helpers on the market are night viewers. These handy "glasses" manage to gather the smallest amounts of available light, then send it back to the viewer in a way the human eye can see. What is blackness to the naked eye is suddenly identifiable, separated into water, sky, perhaps towers or marks, and other boats. The "picture" is always green, so color recognition is not possible. Some are in binocular form, some monocular—any one a welcome addition to the navigator's tool kit.

Hand-Bearing Compass

By sighting across your boat compass, you can take bearings on another boat or a landmark, but this is not the most accurate

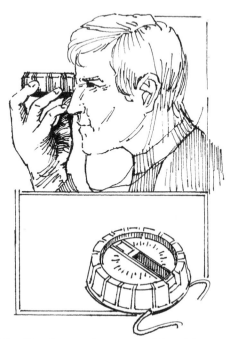

The "hockey puck"—a small hand-bearing compass—is easy to use.

way to get bearings. It's better to use a hand-bearing compass, one with sighting aids that allow you to look at the compass and the object together.

One model sets the compass atop a grip-type handle. A crewmember holds it at eye level, aims at the object, and reads the bearing when the sighting marks on the compass are in line.

The "handiest" hand-bearing compass is described as the "hockey puck," for obvious reasons. Tiny enough to hold with your fingertips, the compass is popular because it's easy to use and still provides a precise reading.

ELECTRONIC HELPERS

Electronics easily become essentials. How did we ever find our way without them?

Bottom Finders

An electronic depthsounder is one of those things best described by, "You don't know what you've got till it's gone." It's your version of X-ray vision, and you come to rely on it more than you realize.

With newer depthsounders (or echo locators) you can get a wonderful graphic color display of bottom contours and passing fish, or you can settle for a basic digital display.

Depending on who installed your depthsounder, you may need to adjust it so it reads from the water's surface rather than from the position of the transducer. (Or, just remember you'll go aground when it reads 3, even though your draft may be 5.)

Position Fixers

Despite relatively minor inaccuracies, both loran and GPS will keep you closer to "found" than traditional navigating methods, and on the basis of safety (and redundancy) many people now consider one or the other as necessary boat equipment.

Both provide almost-accurate fixes al-most all the time. Both compute courses, headings and bearings, speed, distance, and time to go—they'll even ring an alarm if you stray too far off course, or if your boat tries to drift out of an anchorage. Both store individual waypoints (destination coordinates) and entire routes made up of groups of waypoints.

• Coordinates are a statement of position, given in degrees of latitude and longitude, including the north and west identification to indicate the appropriate hemisphere.

• Loran and GPS units are usually preset to show magnetic headings and bearings. (Check the manual.)

LOng RANge Navigation (loran). With a loran navigation system, shore-based transmitters send signals, and the onboard loran computes position based on the time interval between sending and receiving. Originally, positions were stated in *time differences*—TDs—and navigators plotted these positions on Loran C charts (a loran grid overprinted a regular chart). Now, most lorans provide positions in both TDs and lat/long coordinates.

Loran is noted for its repeatability—enabling the captain to return to the exact same spot readings were taken. For this reason, loran users continue to hope the system will not be phased out, though the completion of GPS will most likely signal the end of the maintenance of the loran system.

Global Positioning System (GPS). GPS units get their information from a system of satellites. Developed for the military, GPS technology was then made available for general use, though the civilian version was not as accurate as the military. Boaters' GPS is said to be accurate within 100 meters 95 percent of the time—just wrong enough to cause trouble if navigators are not aware of the limitations.

GPS unit.

The government plans to make the more precise signals available for civilian use soon. Meanwhile, it's possible to correct the built-in "error" with a Differential GPS, which claims to bring accuracy to within 15 meters. Expect to pay more for a DGPS.

Like other electronic items, GPS units are more compact each model year; hand-held models are popular now.

Waypoint Pinpoint. With electronics, you can update or confirm your DR track. Read the present position coordinates from the GPS or loran; then use the dividers to pinpoint position on the chart. First, find the correct mark on the latitude scale. Place one point of the dividers on the scale mark; open the dividers till the other point touches the nearest grid line (these overprint across the whole chart). Hold the dividers in that open position and move across the chart till your hand is near the boat's approximate position, and pencil in a short line. In the same way, mark the longitude point. The pencil marks cross at your location.

• A book of waypoints, used with loran or GPS, might seem to be all the navigation equipment you need, but waypoint-to-waypoint navigation is only good if you know the direct course between the two is clear of dangers. Only course-plotting on charts (whether paper or electronic) can confirm that.

• Without traditional navigating skills, you might not recognize a problem. Example: With the electronics, it's easy to put in a wrong waypoint. If the box says to steer 270 degrees, and you had no background to help you realize that west would put you solidly aground, you'd *go* aground.

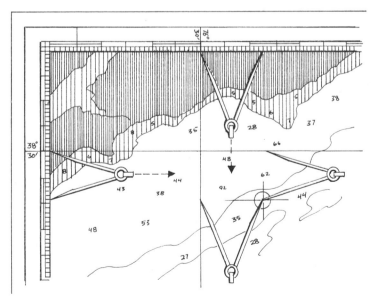

With dividers, transfer present-position coordinates from GPS or loran to chart.

• Boaters should remember that most navigation charts are based on surveys made long before any electronic aids existed, so it's unlikely even a precise electronic position fix would match the charted location. Use these fixes with care; don't run an inlet in fog based on only a GPS reading.

• Keep a book of the waypoints you store, by waypoint number and by place, as well as the coordinates, for checking or for backup.

• Too many people are content to navigate waypoint-to-waypoint, often according to coordinates provided by someone else (including chart publishers). It takes only a few seconds to double-check coordinates and courses, and you should do so.

• Electronics show you what *leeway* means. You will be amazed to see how fast a boat can go through water sideways when wind or current is persistent. The electronic navigator computes course corrections for you; no need for old-fashioned current vectors. (Can you plot a current vector? See the next section under "Piloting Practice.")

Electronic Charting

Chart plotters display charts on video, bringing them to the screen section by section so you can navigate mark-to-mark, or waypoint-to-waypoint. You still see everything that's on the paper charts: marks, colors, notes—and if the plotter is connected to a GPS, you'll see your boat too, as a "cursor."

You can buy a plotter as an independent unit; it may have a built-in GPS, or you can attach the one you already have on board. You'll buy charts by groups, on cartridges.

You can also buy a chart plotting program for a personal computer; the charts will be on disk, CD-ROM, or cartridge.

Some plotters have "windows" to display the same kind of information you'd see

on the GPS: speed, ETA, time to go, cross-track error. In fog, you can steer by its "vision," always remembering that it's only as accurate as the GPS allows.

While a chart plotter is an interesting add-on, don't get rid of your paper charts. The electronic version should not be the only source of chart information on board.

Radiobeacons

You can take bearings on radiobeacons, the first electronic system of navigation. Though the system is being phased out, the Coast Guard still maintains some beacons on the coasts and Great Lakes. A beacon may be on a lighthouse, a large buoy, or somewhere along a coastline; codes are charted so you'll know the location of the code you hear. To get a line of position from a radiobeacon, you need a *radio direction finder* (RDF), a radio receiver with a directional antenna that moves, pointing in the direction of the signal's station.

You can still use a basic RDF: a small, portable AM radio. If you're coming in to Florida from the Bahamas, and you wonder how far the Gulf Stream kicked you north, tune in to your favorite Fort Lauderdale station. Hold the radio up "broadside" to the shore, and turn it slightly side-to-side. When it's loudest, you're facing Lauderdale.

Radar

You can get good directional and distance information from radar, though it's hardly a necessity unless you do a good portion of your boating in fog. Naturally, once accustomed to using it, many boaters would not leave port without it.

• Larger navigation buoys are designed to be effective radar reflectors, but a radar beacon (RACON) is installed on some aids, so radar-users will get a much better reading. The Light List shows their ID codes.

• It is surprising how many radar owners are unfamiliar with its use. Since the information you get from radar depends on some interpretation, it's a good idea to test it when visibility can confirm what you think you "see" on radar.

• Videos have long been available to show basics of using electronics, and now software programs provide more hands-on instruction.

Helping Electronics

Turn on the electronics only after you've started the engine, or a power surge might damage them.

PILOTING PRACTICE

Perhaps if dead reckoning had a better name, it would be more desirable to learn. Think of the "deduced" explanation, and play Holmes and Watson.

Track Record

You know how to find direction, distance, and speed. Now put it all in writing in chart shorthand, to maintain the *DR track*—your best estimate of position based on speed and elapsed time run along a given course.

First, draw a pencil line on the chart along the route you intend to follow. Start from a known position (the lighthouse on the pier or the outer sea buoy), and take up the course you've drawn. Note the time at the mark, and write it on the chart. You're traveling at 7 mph, and you plan to stay on the same course for awhile. At each hour interval, make a note along the course line at the 7-mile mark where you should be, based on your speed.

When you change course for any reason, write down the time of change and the new direction.

Continue this record until you come to another known position—another buoy perhaps. Note the time you pass it, and start a new DR track from that mark.

If the second buoy was supposed to be along your course line, and you were actually a half mile to starboard, that's okay; DR is not perfect navigation. But it does give you an approximate position, and it starts a habit of staying aware of your location. It's a good habit—if fog rolls in or thunderstorms come down, you should be able to find your way by yourself. And even an approximate position is a much better answer to a "Where are you?" question than "I don't know."

Even if your DR track becomes more of an electronic track record (recording hourly lat/long positions from the GPS), it's still a good practice. If the electronic quits, you will have a recent position fix.

DR Notes

Establish some consistent way to mark your DR track on the chart, so everyone on board can read and use it. The course line is commonly labeled by course (C) and degrees, in true or magnetic, written above the line. Speed (S) and/or distance (D) is written below the line. To show an estimated position, draw a dot with a semicircle over it; for a fixed position, use a full circle around the dot, or use an X instead. A course is always written with three digits (even if the first two are zeros, as in 005 degrees). Each position mark should have time noted above it, and this is most clear when noted by 24-hour time, where 2 P.M. is 1400.

• When you use the 24-hour clock in speech, say "zero eight hundred" not "oh eight hundred." To say "hours" after the numbers is unnecessary and incorrect (but don't tell the movie people).

• Use a fairly soft pencil to record all this information, so you can erase it easily later. Plain school-pack No. 2 pencils are okay; some navigators prefer to use an H lead, a good compromise between erasability and sharper point-holding.

- Keep a tiny pencil sharpener or a sharp knife handy; a fat pencil line can make your course questionable by a few degrees.

- Eraser choice: Art gum is very effective; kneaded erasers are less messy (no gum crumbs); plastic works well, too, without damaging the chart surface. Look in art supply stores if you don't find what you need in office supply.

- Use a pen to enter courses you will run frequently from your home port. Why go through the same basic course plot every weekend?

- Some people never write anything permanent on charts; others note in large print things like light flash characteristics on a lighthouse or channel marks (for night entries). Rough compass courses are sometimes useful, especially if it's a visually confusing channel.

- If your compass is not adjusted, or you don't have a deviation card, make notes of the compass courses you run regularly; even if these do not match chart courses, they will show *you* what course to steer, if visibility gets iffy. Make notes for both directions—in and out—because a simple reciprocal would probably not work without compensation for deviation.

- Sticky Post-It notes are handy at a navigation station. Note the day's tides, or anchorage choices, or course changes (especially good at night, so the next person has a ready reference).

- Use a red light when doing chart work at night, and you won't destroy your night vision.

- For chart work, course plotters and protractors are alternatives to parallel rules. All are sold with instructions, but try to watch someone using the item to be sure you want it before you buy one.

Bearings

A *bearing* is the compass direction from your boat to an object you see. (A *reciprocal bearing* is the direction from the object back to you: find the reciprocal by adding or subtracting 180 degrees.) The line between you and the object is a *line of position* (LOP); you are positioned somewhere along that line.

Example: A lighthouse is visible off the starboard bow at a bearing of 20 degrees. To plot the line on a chart, set the parallel rules on a line from the center of the compass rose to 20 degrees, walk the line to your general location, and draw a pencil line from the lighthouse to you along the same parallel.

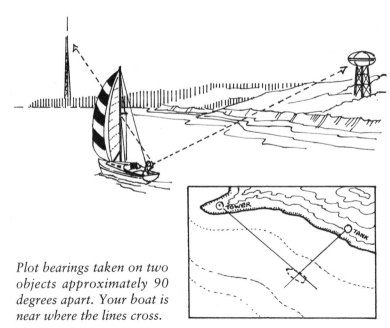

Plot bearings taken on two objects approximately 90 degrees apart. Your boat is near where the lines cross.

This is now the reciprocal bearing, because you started the line at the lighthouse and drew the line toward the boat.

One such bearing can't pinpoint your location, but two such bearings can come close. Find another object (best if it's about 90 degrees away from the first). Take another bearing, plot the reciprocal, and the two LOPs should cross somewhere near your estimated position. Now you've found yourself. Note the time, and proceed with a new beginning for a DR track.

This example conveniently ignored adjusting bearings for deviation. In practice, to be accurate, you would adjust your figures so all plotting was done using the same basis, whether true or magnetic or compass. Since course notes are labeled, everyone looking at the chart would know what the figures show, so all plotting would use the same basis.

• When you take a bearing with your boat compass, it will be magnetic, *and* it will reflect your compass's deviation. Correct the bearing for deviation and variation before plotting, if you want all to be expressed in true. (Remember the up-down DAW arrows.)

• Once more:

Variation is the difference between true and magnetic.

Deviation is the difference between magnetic and compass.

Combined adjustment for variation and deviation is *compass error*.

• Most people cannot judge the distance between boat and shore. A range finder would be one way to find out; a depth contour might also give you an approximate.

• Another way to "read" distance is by taking two bearings on a shore landmark: Mark the chart once when the mark is at 45 degrees off your bow, and again when

it's at 90 degrees. Measure the charted distance between the marks; the distance between you and shore will be the same.

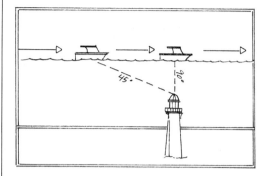

• Once you've confirmed that the light or tower is the right harbor, take a bearing on your approach and plot it, to be sure you're coming in at a "safe" angle.

Mark Checks

• When running a shoreline, just look around, and you can probably estimate your position relative to objects you can identify: buoys, water tanks, radio towers, stacks. Sometimes, a prominent landmark will be charted, like a church or a large hotel.

• If you're cruising in wild areas, look for some charted topographic features: an obvious hill or a stand of tall trees.

• Measure the distances between buoys so you can estimate your arrival time. If you don't see one when expected, *it* may be off station, or *you* may be off course or speed. Try to look for the buoy along a planned path, with short side trips perpendicular to the course line. Keep track of these maneuvers, so you can always return to your DR course.

Current Corrections

After correcting a few DR tracks, you realize how much current affects your intended course. It is possible to alter the course you steer, in an effort to compensate for the current—with mixed results.

First, estimate the current's speed and direction (or look up the information on a current chart). Then, make a current diagram to give you a corrected course. Pretend you want to cross a current that flows north at an average 3 knots. The direct compass course to your destination would be 90 degrees, and your boat travels 6 knots.

Use a plotting sheet or a convenient compass rose. Draw the 90-degree direct course line. Pick a unit of measurement (½ inch) and draw a line north 3 units long (1½ inches); that's how far the current would take a drifting box in an hour's time. Your speed is 6, so set the dividers at a six-unit measure (3 inches). Put one point of the dividers at the north end of the current line, and swing the dividers across the 90-degree course line. Mark the line where the dividers' second point touches. Now, draw a line from the north end of the three-unit current line to the six-unit mark on the direct course line; that's the course you should steer.

• Tidal current charts show approximate time, direction, and velocity of current flow. If you have a small boat or a weak engine, or are under sail, pay close attention to these, so you can time your entries or exits to coincide with flood and ebb of tide.

STAR WATCHERS

The *other* navigating method—the original one—uses the relative position of sun and stars (at given moments in time) to establish the mariner's position. Very few cruising people need to know celestial navigation, because only a small percentage of boaters cross oceans in small boats. But even coastal cruisers sometimes study celestial, because they *want* to.

Many books have been written on the subject (and tapes can also help tutor you), but try to borrow a how-to book before you buy it. Some excellent navigators unfortunately are not good teachers, and with this subject, the learner must stay motivated.

BE A PRUDE

There are thousands of navigation aids in U.S. waters. Not all will be perfectly operational at all times. Memorize the following, believe it, and act as though you believe it:

"The prudent mariner should not rely solely on any single aid to—or method of—navigation."

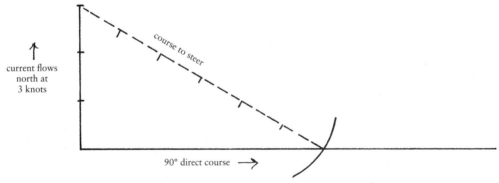

current flows north at 3 knots

course to steer

90° direct course →

Establish course-to-steer by plotting direction and velocity of current.

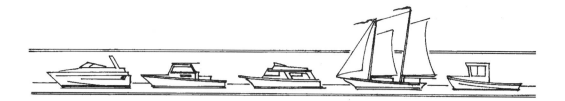

Minding Rules

Most boating areas don't have traffic lanes; there are no stop signs, and no "go" lights. Lacking such obvious aids to travel, boaters rely on a set of navigation rules, in which a right-of-way is dictated according to boat type (or means of propulsion) and the relative positions of the boats involved. When two boats get close enough to each other that a risk of collision exists, both captains should react and maneuver in whatever ways the rules direct, to assure safe passing. On a perfect waterway.

MOTORBOAT BASICS
Meeting Head-On
Even without a marked "road," when two boats are approaching almost head-on, road driving has given Americans a "right-reflex" that fortunately coincides with navigation rules: Keep to starboard so boats will pass safely port to port. In this situation, neither boat has any *privilege* or right-of-way; both must respond with a starboard move.

Crossing
Crossing situations are not as simple; without benefit of a marked intersection, confusion may come from not recognizing when a collision course exists. When you first sight a boat ahead and off to one side of your course, take a good look at its general bearing. Pick an identifiable spot on your boat (stanchion, windshield support) that visually aligns with the other boat from your vantage point. As the boats close, see if that bearing changes noticeably. If it *does* change, you should pass safely without altering course; but if you continue to see the boat in the same position above the stanchion, the two boats

may be on a collision course, or near enough that you should proceed with collision-avoidance tactics.

Power Meets Power. By the navigation rule book, when two powerboats are involved, the boat to starboard is the "stand-on" boat (or "privileged," according to former rule-wording) and the other must give way, early and obviously. Think of a four-way stop sign, where the car to the right goes first.

Power Meets Sail. When a powerboat and a sailing sailboat are involved, the powerboat gives way, regardless of the relative boat positions. However, sailors should remember that a motoring sailboat is a powerboat, for purposes of determining right-of-way.

SAILBOAT BASICS

When two sailing sailboats meet, right-of-way depends on each one's position relative to the wind. If the wind is on different sides, the boat with wind on the port side gives way. (This is why sailors scream "Starboard!" with such gleeful authority.)

If both boats have wind on the same side, the boat to windward gives way (but nobody screams "Leeward!").

• For the truly innocent non-racing sailors, it's not nice to pass another sailing sailboat on its windward side. This is regarded as "stealing" the wind, whether you give a friendly wave or not.

OVERTAKING

The boat that's passing another stays out of the other's way in the process; the boat being overtaken is the "stand-on" boat.

• The stand-on boat should maintain course and speed in all meeting or passing situations, but this is especially important in overtaking situations.

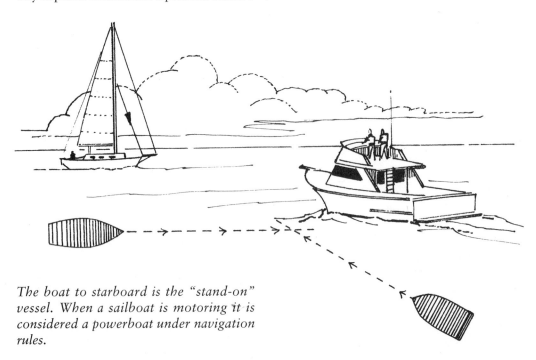

The boat to starboard is the "stand-on" vessel. When a sailboat is motoring it is considered a powerboat under navigation rules.

- If you wish to pass a sailing sailboat, sound the appropriate signal so the sailboat captain knows you're there. You don't want to be surprised at an inopportune moment by a tacking drill that turns the sailboat directly into your path.

MEETING THE BIG BOATS

Rules regarding recreational boats and big commercial boats are easy to understand: Let the big guys go first. The only rule you need to remember regarding ships, tugs, and barges is "Keep clear." No "I can beat that ship." No "I am a sailing boat and have the right-of-way." You probably can't. You may not. Keep clear.

In restricted areas, the rule is very clear: Sailing vessels shall not impede passage of a vessel that can navigate only within a narrow channel.

Even away from narrow channels, the message should be clear. Too often, boaters do cross in front of freighters, a foolish mistake, whether done out of ignorance or arrogance. If the motor were to quit, or a sailor misjudged the wind strength, there's no chance for a plan B.

The typical big ship is steered from a position toward the stern. Its structure creates a blind zone reaching as much as two ship-lengths ahead. The blind spot on a freighter might be a quarter mile long. Even if the captain *saw* your boat in front of the ship, he could not stop quickly enough to avoid hitting you.

Numbers to Remember

- A big ship might travel ½ mile or up to 3 miles before it could stop, depending on its speed and the state of a tidal current. Keep clear.

- At 8½ knots, a tug-and-barge combination will cover a nautical mile in about 7 minutes. Most ships travel faster; at

12 knots, a nautical mile takes 5 minutes. Typical stopping distance required for a ship doing 12 knots is about a mile. Keep clear.

- When necessary to cross ship channels, do it quickly (the fastest route is a perpendicular crossing) and very cautiously. In fog, don't. Keep clear.

- See Chapter 17 for more on commercial traffic and river travel.

Half-up Submarine

In certain places along the coast, the waterways connect with or cross big ship channels, and you may one day be surprised by a really odd-looking vessel coming your way. The rounded top of a submarine looks even stranger because of the unusual bow wave it is pushing—more of a bow bubble, as water lifts and flows over the mostly underwater hull. This is not just another powerboat; don't get too close for your picture-taking. Be especially cautious of the disturbed water behind the visible portion of the sub.

Seaplane Runway

Another wakeup call for the captain is the sight of a seaplane first descending, then landing somewhere ahead of your course, and continuing in a direct path toward you. Once the plane is on the water, the rule says it's just another powerboat, but initially it's an intimidating sight nonetheless.

PASSING SIGNALS

Whistle signals serve to notify another boat of a captain's intended action. In theory, the signals should be given—and answered—before the indicated action takes place (at least, in inland waters). In practice, if an overtaking boat signals its intent to pass, and the overtaken boat slows to idle and moves to starboard, it's obvious the signal was heard and acknowledged, but if you like to blow the whistle, do it anyway. Often, a wave—a friendly wave—will indicate the message was received and agreed to.

Under international rules, the signals are given as notification of action; no response is required, except in an overtaking situation.

• People have devised some elaborate ways to distinguish the one-whistle and the two-whistle side in passing situations. Here's one that's easy to recall. Think of the word association "two port—Newport." Two whistles (two toots) means the vessel is going to port. If a vessel behind you toots twice, look over your left shoulder; the boat will overtake and pass on your port side. Once you remember "two-port—Newport," a logical process of elimination says the other signal—one toot—means the opposite: the vessel intends to go to starboard. (So, look over your right shoulder.)

If you're moving along a narrow channel and hear a three-toot signal close by, look for a transom in motion: somebody's back-ing out of a slip or away from a dock. Watch carefully, no matter *what* signal you hear—they're all attention-getting devices.

If you hear five or more toots—someone is sounding a look-fast danger signal, and you may need to know why.

• Sometimes, you'll be given passing in-structions over the VHF radio; you'll be told to pass on the one-whistle or the two-whistle side. Keep a small drawing show-ing a graphic explanation of the one- and two-whistle passing sides; in a think-fast situation, you don't want to be hoping you guess right.

If you see two boats headed for trouble, sound the danger signal and hope the mes-sage gets to the right person.

• Summary of whistle signals for meeting/passing situations:

One toot: I'm altering course to star-board.

Two toots: I'm altering course to port.

Three toots: Engines are in reverse.

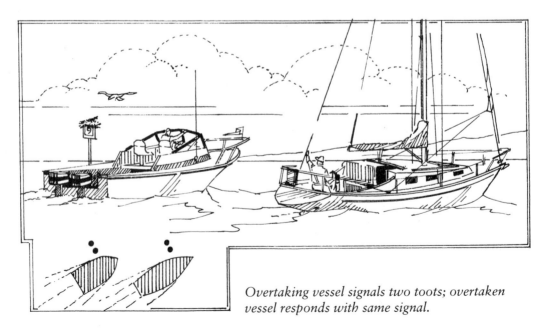

Overtaking vessel signals two toots; overtaken vessel responds with same signal.

Five or more: Danger!

• The same signals can be given with light flashes as well as sound; the number of flashes carries the same message as the corresponding number of whistle blasts.

PASSING TECHNIQUE

Along narrow channels, when you're moving at your top speed of 6 knots, and a fast boat comes up behind you at *its* top speed of 30-something, courtesy (and self-interest) dictate a slow-down—by you.

All slow-boaters should realize if they don't slow to idle, a passing powerboat will be forced to pass at an awkward speed. The mid-range speed, neither planing nor idle, creates the bad wake that sends the dish drainer flying.

Some boaters choose not to believe this, and maintain their 5- or 6-knot speed; the powerboat gets to 9 or 10, and there goes the wake. A simple slow-down and shift into neutral can prevent a wake roll. Most powerboat captains are aware of the problem and will pass at idle speed, if the passee will allow it.

Where space allows, powerboats often maintain their speed; the slow boat turns into the wake for a few up-and-down bounces rather than a lot of uncomfortable sideways rolls.

STAY-SAFE RULES

Some people are fond of observing that rules are made to be broken; here is a rule instructing you to break rules—for a reason: ". . . Special circumstances . . . may make a departure from rules necessary to avoid immediate danger."

If the rules say you're the stand-on boat, don't insist on retaining your "right" no matter what. The other guy may not know you're right, or he may not

care; all boaters are not equally smart, polite, or perhaps even sober. Whichever the reason, nobody wins a game of nautical chicken.

• You may read or hear different terms to explain who does what: a "burdened" vessel "gives way" because it does not have right-of-way. A "privileged" vessel "stands on" because it *has* right-of-way.

• In any close crossing situation, the "give-way" boat should alter course early and obviously. The "stand-on" boat should maintain course and speed.

• In general, unpowered vessels (rowboats and sailing sailboats) have right-of-way over powerboats, but in a narrow channel, the big commercial boats go first and everybody stays out of their way.

• The wording in some rules leaves a lot of room for interpretation: "safe speed"; "if risk of collision exists"; "act early and obviously"; "in ample time"; "change to be readily apparent." They all suffer from the same lack of real definition as "common sense," so guess on the side of safety. Stay clear.

• "Every vessel . . . at all times . . . shall maintain a proper lookout." (For sight and sound, even when the radar's on and especially when the autopilot's steering.)

• In a crossing situation, once you realize you are the give-way boat, turn (obviously) and aim off the stern of the other boat. Once you've made it clear that you *are* giving way, you can angle back and steer toward the other boat's transom, following a wide arc back to your original course (see illustration on page 56).

• Some nights, visibility is good; with bright moonlight and good binoculars, you can make out a boat shape as well as its lights. Other nights are so black, you must rely on lights only, and distance perception is difficult, a good example of why

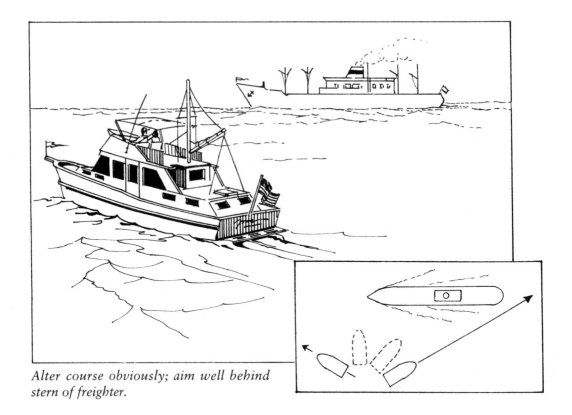

Alter course obviously; aim well behind stern of freighter.

"early and obvious" altering of course is important.

• In a busy, high-traffic area, before making an obvious alteration of your course, look around to be sure nobody's sneaking up behind you without a signal.

• Don't forget to use your radio as a collision-avoidance help. Listen to Channel 13 whenever you're in an area that's busy with commercial traffic, or on the appropriate channel in an area with a Vessel Traffic Service, where vessel movement is directed by one station.

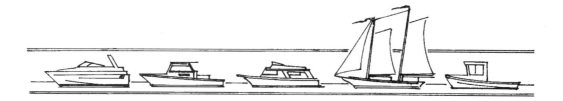

6 Sending Calls

At one time, one of boating's better benefits was the escapist part: hop on board, untie lines, and in half an hour you could be worlds away from any connection to land, literal and otherwise. No bumper-to-bumper traffic, no crowds of people, and—high on the list—no land noise. Your mind was clear to wander at will, without threat of any intrusive ringing in your ears. You knew in the back of your mind that you *could* be in touch through the trusty old ship-to-shore radio, but that was mostly a matter of *your* choice.

But that was then; and now, more often than not, escapism isn't part of the picture. The trusty VHF radio gets so much use, the Federal Communications Commission (FCC) recently approved another channel (09) for recreational boaters to use as a hailing channel. Many of today's boaters would rather go *with* than without, and with the

constantly changing technology, there's no need to be without communication. Computers go to sea along with modems and faxes; if the phone access must be there, why not the phone itself?

It's not only the "branch offices" that carry all this sophistication around. It's any techno-fan who also happens to own a boat. Isolation need not be the name of today's boating game.

BASIC VHF

VHF (very high frequency) radio has been the ship-to-shore and ship-to-ship standard for recreational boats for some time, having replaced earlier AM radios many years ago. Made in ever smaller packages, these radios are not required equipment, though a good argument is made that they should be. Even if you *do* want to be alone, a link to help is a good thing. Though VHF is not the only choice for a phone away from home, it is still the most popular form of communication on small boats.

Call Sign

You can buy a VHF radio from an electronics store or a catalog, and if you're staying in U.S. waters, you'll be able to install it and use it immediately: no license is required for most recreational boats. Use your boat's name as your call sign.

If you plan on voyaging outside the U.S. or your boat is longer than 20 meters, you'll need a station license to use the radio. This is a no-study, no-test license; all you need to do is fill out the appropriate form, pay the appropriate fee, and the FCC sends you a license with your very own call sign, a combination of letters and numbers that identifies your "station" (the boat).

If the radio dealer cannot provide the FCC form, call the FCC at 1-800-418-3676 and ask for form 506. Filing instructions will be part of the package. You get a temporary call sign upon filling out the form, so you can start to use your radio right away.

Boaters traveling outside the country also need a Restricted Radiotelephone Operator's Permit (a lifetime permit, no test; ask for FCC form 753).

CALL MONITORING

When the radio's installed, you can listen to Channel 16 for a half day; you'll learn how to make calls, and probably how *not* to as well.

Turn on the radio. If it's squawking a lot, fiddle with the squelch button (the one next to on-off) till the static stops. Now you're monitoring.

Channel 16 is the official hailing and distress channel, and if your radio is turned on, it should usually be tuned to 16. That way, emergency calls have the greatest chance of being heard and answered.

Call Making

Until recently, all calls were initiated on 16 (other options will be covered later). Once contact is made, boats switch to a "working channel" to have their conversation.

To make a call: Hold the microphone a few inches away, push in the key (button) on the microphone, and speak. Use low power unless you are calling someone more than a few miles away. When you're through talking, release the key and listen for a response. (You cannot speak and listen at the same time, as you can with a telephone.)

Try to make calls using the least amount of words. To call your friends on *Nova*, say, "*Nova, Nova, Nova*, this is *Munchkin*." Responder says, "*Munchkin*, this is *Nova*, switch 68." *Munchkin* says, "Switching 68" or "Roger, 68," and you both switch to Channel 68, where you have a brief conversation. When you're finished, say, "*Munchkin* out and back to 16."

When calling in another country, add your call sign after the boat's name.

• If you don't get an answer to your initial call, wait at least 2 minutes before trying again. Some people repeat a call so quickly, they don't give the callee a chance to answer.

• When it's time to choose a working channel, don't try to be polite by asking your friends what channel they might like. It really doesn't matter, and it requires added transmissions, thereby wasting time on the hailing channel.

Radio Talk

So far, marine VHF has not adopted much of the slang popularized by CB radio, but for clarity, some terms help make transmissions more specific.

A few examples:

Break = New subject to follow.

Wait = Stand by.

Over = It's your turn to talk.

Affirmative/Roger = Yes, understood.

Out = I'm through with the conversation.

You may someday find it useful to know the phonetic alphabet, to spell out the boat name, or to clarify a call sign. Memorizing it is a good way to pass the time during a quiet night watch. If you don't do night trips, tack a card next to the radio showing the alphabet.

Alpha	November
Bravo	Oscar
Charlie	Papa
Delta	Quebec
Echo	Romeo
Foxtrot	Sierra
Golf	Tango
Hotel	Uniform
India	Victor
Juliet	Whiskey
Kilo	X-ray
Lima	Yankee
Mike	Zulu

Dual-Channel Monitoring

Though you're required to monitor Channel 16, it's also smart to monitor Channel 13 when you're in an area with a lot of commercial traffic. This is the calling

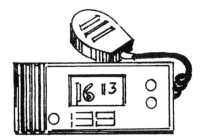

and working channel for commercial boats. Most newer VHF radios have the two-channel monitoring capability.

On Channel 13, you'll hear calls that may pertain to your immediate location; you'll know if a bridge will open soon for a tug (and you may be able to go through at the same time). You'll know if a ship is about to back into the channel or appear around the next bend. A tugboat captain may want to call you to establish passing procedure, or you may want to call the tug to be sure of the safe side.

In some areas, you will use 13 to call bridges and locks; look for a blue-and-white sign on the bridges, showing a phone and 16/13. (In Seattle, however, bridges prefer horn signals, and 13 use is discouraged for non-commercial boats.)

• When you must call a towboat and you can't see its name, give a mile mark or other clear geographic description: "Calling the southbound tow at mile number 234" or "Calling the northbound tow located just south of Hickman."

• Channel 13 is a preset low-power channel, so you won't be reaching a big number of boats.

• In a few high-traffic areas, commercial vessel movement is monitored and regulated by one station under a Vessel Traffic Service system. New York Harbor, the Chesapeake & Delaware Canal, and Puget Sound are three such places. In the Bahamas, Nassau Harbour Control keeps track of recreational boat traffic as well as commercial.

Three-Channel Scan

With radio traffic increasing right along with boat traffic, Channel 16 is suffering from overload, but Channel 09 can now be used as a hailing frequency by recreational boats.

When you're *not* in a busy commercial boat area, you may want to monitor Channels 16 and 09. Soon, you'll want a radio that can scan three channels, so you can monitor the required 16, talk to bridges on 13, and listen for your cruising friends on 09. Some models already have this capability; this will be the big reason for a radio trade-up.

VHF CHANNELS

How do you know what channels to use for conversations? The FCC tells you.

22 Alpha

The first one to remember is the Coast Guard's primary working channel: 22. Coast Guard broadcasts will always say "22 Alpha." This means the U.S. channel 22; as long as you don't accidentally push the international button on your radio, your 22 will be 22 Alpha.

The Coast Guard will announce safety broadcasts periodically on Channel 16; you'll be told to switch to 22, where you'll hear about navigation hazards (a light gone, something adrift) or a problem with a bridge, the approach of a significant weather system, or a boat that's late (missing) according to its float plan.

Chatting Channels

Recreational boats talk to each other or to marinas and boatyards on Channels 68, 69, 71, 72, and 78. In the Great Lakes, add 79 and 80.

You can connect to land phones through a marine operator on one of the following channels (check locally to learn which ones are used): 24, 25, 26, 27, 28; 84, 85, 86, 87, 88. Marine operators will call you on 16, but will not respond to your call on 16; you must call them on the marine operator channel for the area you're in. Call just as you would a boat: "Miami Marine Operator, this is *Munchkin*," etc. Give the operator the calling information, and you'll either be connected right away, or the operator will call you back later when contact is made.

If a shore person wants to find you, they call the Marine Operator in the area and give the boat name; the operator will put out a call on Channel 16, telling you which channel to switch to for your "traffic."

Channel 06 is used for inter-ship safety, not for casual conversations.

Channel 11, 12, 14, and 17 are for port operations or Vessel Traffic Service; 83 is for the Coast Guard Auxiliary. These are not for recreational boat use.

Other Channels

You'll listen to the weather stations: 1 through 9 are listed as weather channels, but the NOAA broadcasts are heard on Channel 1, 2, or 3. In Canada tune to Channel 21 or 83.

One channel (70) is set aside for the special use of "digital selective calling" (DSC) whereby boaters with the right kind of radio can have private conversations on the VHF.

VHF EMERGENCY CALLS

The VHF is used all the time to call for help with ordinary boating problems, from empty gas tanks to broken props or stubborn starters. More serious calls for help are divided into three categories, each identified by an attention-getting radio call.

Mayday: From the French *m'aidez* (help me), "Mayday" is the international signal for distress, to be used only in the event of serious, immediate danger to life or property.

Pan Pan: From the French *panne* (breakdown or hard times). If a situation does not constitute an immediate threat, but is still a bad situation, call "Pan Pan" (pronounced *pahn-pahn*).

Securité: Least urgent of the distress calls is "Securité" (say-*cu*-ri-tay). You'll hear big boats use it to announce they're about to round a bend, or back out into a channel, or come through a narrow cut. You may hear it to preface an urgent weather notice.

Receiving Distress Calls

When you hear a distress call, grab a pencil and jot down the position report, description of the boat—whatever you catch. Then check your chart to see if you are close enough to do anything.

The Coast Guard will sometimes switch distress calls to Channel 22, but often the emergency call stays on 16. If you think you are in a position to assist, contact the Coast Guard, and report your position and estimated time of arrival at the distressed boat. Then follow their directions.

• Even if you are in no position to help directly with the emergency, you may be in the geographic position that allows you to hear the distress caller and the responder, while they do not hear each other. You will then act as a go-between, or "Mayday relay."

• Respond directly to an emergency call only if the Coast Guard does not, or if the Coast Guard later asks you to communicate with the distressed boat.

MAYDAY MAYDAY MAYDAY		*First priority distress signal. "Mayday" is used to indicate grave and imminent danger to life or vessel.*
PAN PAN PAN PAN PAN PAN		*Second priority urgent communication. "Pan Pan" is used when the safety of the vessel or person is in jeopardy.*
SECURITÉ SECURITÉ SECURITÉ		*Third priority safety message. "Securité" is used for messages about the safety of navigation or important weather warnings.*

• Monitoring distress calls adds to your background experience, too; whether handled well or poorly, you will learn by listening. Someday, you may be grateful for the knowledge.

Sending Distress Calls

If you ever need to send a Mayday, here's the proper way:

On Channel 16, call, "Mayday, Mayday, Mayday, this is *My Boat, My Boat, My Boat.* Mayday *My Boat.*" Then give your location, state the problem and what kind of help you need, tell how many people are on board, describe the boat, and end with "This is *My Boat,* over."

Now stop and listen. If you hear no response, say it again. If there's no response after the second call, switch to another channel (Channel 22, the Coast Guard working frequency, is a good place to start) and try again.

USING THE VHF

FCC Rules

• The ship station license is good for 10 years; the FCC will notify you when it's time to renew the license.

• During the term of the station license, notify the FCC in writing if you change the boat name or number, or your name or address.

• If you sell the boat, mark the station license "cancel" and send it to: FCC, 1270 Fairfield Road, Gettysburg, PA 17325-7245.

• If you have a station license, display it near the radio. (Write the call sign in large characters and post it near the radio.)

• Recreational boaters are *not* required to have a copy of FCC rules on board, but they *are* required to comply with those rules.

• You do not have to keep a radio log.

• Keep pencil and paper handy to jot down information pertaining to emergency calls.

Portable Communication

In addition to the regular VHF, many boaters find a hand-held version most handy, in the cockpit or on the flybridge as well as in the dinghy when diving or fishing.

Calling Tips

• Radios have buttons to switch between high power and low power, or between U.S. and international frequencies. Sometimes you push the button by mistake; check both if you're having trouble transmitting.

• When giving a caller the working channel number, say the numbers in separate digits, as "six, eight" or "seven, two" rather than sixty-eight or seventy-two.

• "General" calls—those not directed to a specific station—are okay only in an emergency. Though it is common practice to make a general call for a radio check, FCC rules do not show this is acceptable.

• Do *not* call the Coast Guard on Channel 16 for a radio check.

• When you answer someone's call for a radio check, it is helpful to report your location as well as the quality of the transmission, as "loud and clear [or weak but readable] 2 miles south of Charleston."

• For years, the only way you could call home from the boat was through the local phone company's VHF marine operator. Now, even VHF has more choices. Many private companies provide access to marine calls; you can arrange a billing account with the company, or you can make collect calls.

• Don't give out your credit card or phone card numbers over the VHF; call collect if you have no other billing arrangement.

• When you're trying to call someone, wait 2 minutes between attempts, and if you get no response after three calls, wait 15 minutes before you start again.

VHF Etiquette

• If you get peeved with another boater, before you spout off over the VHF, think about all the people who must listen to you *other* than the source of the peeve. To someone with no knowledge of the situation, you will come across the airwaves sounding like a jerk, a pompous ass, a fuddy-duddy, an impolite person—choose one or more. (Better for your mental state if you can learn to laugh, or at least feel sorry for the other person's ignorance.)

• VHF is not a private telephone. Long conversations are never necessary and seldom desirable, but they *are* inconsiderate. Challenge yourself to keep calls as brief as possible.

• If someone leaves the mike "keyed," intentionally or not, nobody within a certain area can use the channel. (New radios have an automatic un-keyer, one reason to hope the right people buy a new radio.)

VHF Don'ts

• Don't try to call Fred in the middle of a Mayday. In an emergency situation, *clear* the radio. (One would like to assume these calls interrupt because the caller has not heard the Mayday, though that's hard to believe considering the Coast Guard's radio is audible for many more miles than an ordinary VHF transmitter.)

• Anyone sending a fake distress call must be seeking the prize for stupidity. To explain why would be wasted effort, but explaining the penalties might have some effect: prison and fines, including the not inconsiderable cost of a search-and-rescue effort.

• Don't use bad language.

• Don't ask the Coast Guard: "When will the fog lift?" or "Can I get into a harbor before the thunderstorm hits?"

• Don't use high power unless you need it. It interferes with other traffic.

CELLULAR PHONES

Cellular phone accessibility and range is expanding all the time; the question is not can you have a phone, but do you want one? The idea that only doctors need instant communication is an old idea indeed. Need or want, many people feel lost without the easy connection to—whomever.

Obviously, there are many reasons why quick communication is good. Illness: yours or a shoreside family member's, especially in the case of a recurring problem. Business: if a phone buys you the relative freedom of time on the water, get the phone. Security: a recent addition to the phone "reason" list. For some, a feeling of isolation is a good thing; for others, it's worrisome. With a phone, you can enjoy the solitude without being isolated, so—get the phone.

If you want to use modem or fax with your laptop, then the cellular phone is a necessity.

• You can maintain emergency contacts by having a pager. They're simple and inexpensive; if someone needs to contact you, they call your pager number; the pager displays *their* number; you can go to a shore phone and return the call. Service is available by city, region, or the entire country.

Alternative to VHF?

Cellular phones have the advantage of private conversations, but they should be used as a supplement to VHF communication, not as a substitute.

For emergency calls, a cellular phone call goes out to only one person; VHF goes out to everyone within hearing range.

VHF radios can be used to locate your position. Not so with the cell phone.

Other boaters wanting to assist in an emergency situation would have difficulty communicating with you through a shore-based third party.

LONG-RANGE RADIO

If you plan only coastal cruising, the VHF radio, with or without an added cellular phone, is all the communication you need. If you plan to do serious offshore cruising—or you *want* the long-range communication capability—then you should think about a single-sideband or ham (amateur) radio.

Where VHF might have a 25-mile range, SSB and ham can send and receive worldwide, transmitting via skywaves bouncing between Earth and the ionosphere.

SSB

SSB is one answer to long-range communication. It has both radio and telephone capabilities and receives the long-distance weather reports. You can call other boats anywhere in the world. SSB also has the safety feature of 24-hour monitoring by the Coast Guard (2182 kHz). Through a connection to the boat's GPS receiver, the SSB can send a distress signal that includes your location. (Call the FCC at 1-800-322-1117 for license information.)

You can place or receive telephone calls through the High Seas Operator, or use ATT's High Seas Direct, which provides direct access to phone lines worldwide, without operator assist. It works by connecting an ATT modem and handset to the SSB radio. Calls are dialed normally, starting with the user's ID number. (Call 800-392-2067 for information.)

Ham Radio

While SSB is an excellent radio choice, it is just a radio. Ham, or amateur radio, is a club, a hobby, a family interest, with husband and wife often both licensed hams.

You'll hear boaters say they'll meet on the "waterway net," a daily broadcast where boaters exchange weather reports, file float plans, receive position reports about other boats, and provide emergency help.

Until recently, knowledge of Morse code was necessary to get a ham license. Now, one category of license—Technician Class—does not require code reading. If you *want* to learn the code, you can still use a battery-operated gadget to tap, tap, tap your letters, like the telegraph operator in the old movies, or computer software will beep at you in code. The program SuperMorse will even concentrate on those letters that are giving you the most trouble.

Call the FCC for information on licensing—800-322-1117—or write to the American Radio Relay League, Newington, CT 06111, for general information on amateur radio.

Satellite Communication

If all those options aren't enough for you to call home, there's always satellite communication. Its range is around the world; you use a "normal" phone; you get voice, fax, and telex capability; and all you need is a giant boat with giant power capacity and plenty of money. It is probably beyond the needs of most recreational boats, which is not to say it is out of reach.

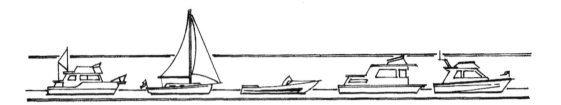

7

Tending Bridges

People who are new to small-boat travel worry a lot about low bridges, with "low" defined as anything the boat can't get under without opening the bridge structure. As with other aspects of cruising, knowing what to expect—and planning for possible scenarios—gives you a head start on easing the concerns.

Yes, there may be a few hairy times: wind or current will try to push you where you can't go; the bridgetender may be asleep, out for coffee, or otherwise unavailable and non-communicative (we watched a morning exercise routine one day); a dredge is waiting to come through from the other side, dragging its pipeline and peripheral gear behind. But these are the maybes, not the probablys. Most bridge transits go smoothly if you follow a few simple procedures.

Depending on the local custom, you'll signal with a horn or you'll call the bridge-

tender (try Channel 13 first) to request an opening. The bridge goes up, you go through, and the bridge comes down. Easy. Only a 10-minute delay, tops. Keep that picture in mind as you read about the *other* pictures.

SECTIONED SPANS

Whether you're cruising a river or a waterway channel, you'll find different types of bridge structures with different machinery to operate them. On a lucky day, you'll be pleasantly surprised to see a brand-new, high-level fixed bridge where the chart still shows the older, low-clearance span.

Bascule Bridges

Most common are the bascule bridges, which work on a seesaw principle. The section of roadway that crosses the water is actually separated from the rest of the road so it can move. It may be split down the center span and also on each side; the two half sections each tilt up at the center, clearing a central path for boats to move through.

A few bascule bridges have only one moving section, and of these, not all raise to a completely perpendicular position; so of course, you should favor the side with the most clearance.

(Occasionally, a normally double-opening bascule will be undergoing repairs, and only one side will open. The bridgetender usually notifies boat traffic when this is the case, so boats can pass through more carefully, one at a time.)

• In general, bascules open faster than other types, once they get started. Some will surprise you by how fast they can move.

• When you see the first separation starting to show between the jaws of the bascule, you can start moving forward, carefully judging the bridge's progress along with your own.

Swing Bridges

These operate like the bridges you set up with the model train set. As their name indicates, swing bridges turn on a pivot point, stopping when fully open in a position parallel to the navigation channel.

At some swing bridges, boats pass through on both sides of the opened section, for two-way traffic. With others, only one channel is maintained, and when this is the case, there will be times when the bridge swings *toward* you as it opens.

• Watch for the first sliver of an opening between bridge and road before starting to move close, and go slowly anyway; swing bridges don't win any speed-opening awards. Be cautious and patient, especially when the bridge is opening toward you.

Lift Bridges

With a lift bridge, that portion of road or railroad track that crosses the water lifts straight up, still in its horizontal position.

As with any bridge, it's difficult to judge the height; the bridgetender has a better view, and (presumably) will give you plenty of clearance, even if the bridge does not lift to its full height. (How many pleasure boats need 85-foot clearance?)

Recently, the tender of a lift bridge in Norfolk called to say he was in the process of lowering the bridge, but only to 65 feet, so we should come ahead. Though 55 feet would have been plenty of clearance, it still required a certain measure of faith to proceed while watching a bridge descend.

Pontoon Bridges

A few pontoon bridges are still in use: two in Washington and one on the Atlantic Intracoastal Waterway. The portion of the road that crosses the water sits on floats. To open, underwater cables pull the floats off to the side, at a right angle to the road position. Besides waiting for the opening, you must also wait for the cable to drop to be sure the underwater passage is clear.

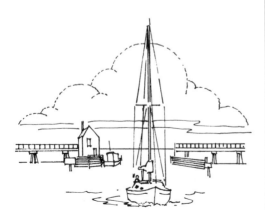

These bridges may be slow to open, but they are a bit of nostalgia to see, and a definite photo op.

Railroad Bridges

Since railroad bridges are necessary only when trains run, and since trains *don't* run all day long, many bridges stay in the open position most of the time. Most of these are operated automatically; long before a train actually arrives (at least 20 minutes) you would hear sirens and see light-flashes and sometimes signs, and then the bridge would come down. At least, that has been our experience. It is highly unlikely you could be surprised by a suddenly descending bridge.

Sometimes, a railroad track will parallel a road less than a quarter mile away. When both cross a river or waterway channel, their bridge openings are usually synchronized so you will not get stuck between the two, where you may have very little maneuvering space. Before you start mentally berating the highway bridgetender who seems to be ignoring you, look beyond. If you see a neat row of slow-moving piggyback trailers, find something to do while you wait.

BRIDGE CLEARANCE

Studying your projected route on the chart will show you how many bridges cross your path, and which of them might cause a delay in your scheduling. Chart notations will tell you what kind of bridge to expect, and also its closed clearance.

Signs and Gauges

Restrictions for some bridges are posted on a sign placed a half mile or more away from the bridge, presumably so you don't have to get on top of the bridge structure before being able to read them. Unfortunately, these signs are not always updated;

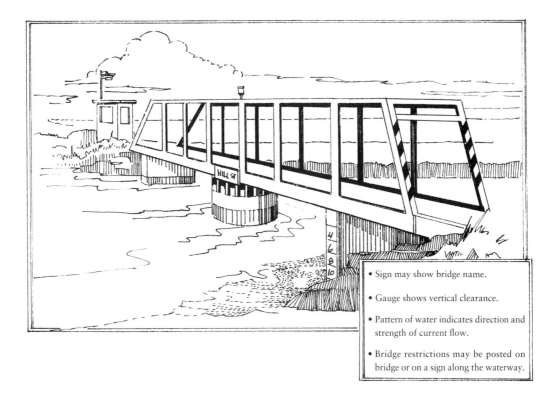

- Sign may show bridge name.

- Gauge shows vertical clearance.

- Pattern of water indicates direction and strength of current flow.

- Bridge restrictions may be posted on bridge or on a sign along the waterway.

don't be too surprised if the sign indicates no restrictions for the time you arrive, but the bridgetender ignores you anyway.

Many bridges have clearance gauges attached to the base of the bridge. As water rises or falls, its level gives you a clear picture of the clearance at that time.

- Bridge clearances are shown on charts, but certain variables must be considered when reading these figures. Tide naturally affects the clearance daily and sometimes, wind can also change the water depth noticeably.

- If your mast height is close to the charted clearance, you may want to wait for a lower tide, which can mean a 1- or 9-foot difference—or more—depending on your geographic location and the phase of the moon.

- Besides the clearance gauge, many bridges have a familiar blue-and-white

phone sign indicating the tender monitors 16 and 13, and a smaller green-and-white sign showing the official name of the bridge. (It may have changed since the publication date of your guidebook.) Though not a real sign, water flowing past the bridge supports will tell you which way the current is flowing, and how strong it might be in mid-span.

- A radio conversation mistakenly carried out on Channel 16 once confused a lot of people. One boater warned another that a sign on shore indicated the next bridge had a horizontal clearance of only 40 feet. "Clearance" triggered "vertical," creating a temporary panic among listeners. In fact, the sign meant to explain that only one side of a bascule bridge would open, so boaters would not have full across-the-channel (horizontal) clearance. (Check chart notations for *both* clearance figures.)

Restrictions

• A bridgetender might not open a bridge just because you ask for an opening. If the tender determines that your boat could clear the closed span *if* antennas or fishing gear were lowered, then you'd best lower them and go through without an opening. (Or else, wait for a taller boat and sneak through with it.)

• Most restrictions at bridges are for recreational boats only; government and commercial vessels go through anytime. If you're already waiting at a bridge, you will probably be allowed to go through with one of these privileged boats, but always ask the bridgetender first so you'll know when to go, and so you won't see a bridge starting to descend just when you're too close to back down.

• When traveling any waterway, check charts and guidebooks daily for the number of bridges to get through, and note their restrictions. You don't want to leave at dawn or rush like mad to make miles, only to wait an hour or two 6 miles down the way. The good news: In many places, more old opening bridges are being replaced by fixed 65-footers. Bad news: Sometimes, municipalities leave the old ones functioning anyway.

• Look for BRIDGE-DEX, a set of four laminated sheets that provides information on bridge restriction from Norfolk to Port Isabel, TX. Call 1-800-531-1014.

• In southeast Florida, the Intracoastal Waterway still has many bridges that must be opened for sailboats—37 bridges in a 90-mile stretch of waterway. Understandably, from the shore perspective, many of these are on restrictions—half-hour, third hour, or *only* hour—and it's impossible for most boats to time the bridges to avoid long waits. After a number of frustrating trips through this section, one captain found the solution: go through at night. The opening restrictions usually apply to daytime hours only, so there's no waiting. The waterway in this area is lined with homes and condos, all well lit, so there's none of the usual concern about traveling after dark. Another coincidental benefit is very little traffic in a place usually stuffed with boats, all going somewhere too fast.

• Most bridge restrictions are on a reasonable half-hour or one-hour schedule; even those with two-hour rush-hour closings may open once in mid-restriction. In a few places, you must call ahead to request an opening (a few bridges in New York, New Jersey, and on the Potomac River; also on Puget Sound and some places in Canada). Here's where you need current guidebooks as well as charts.

Do-It-Yourself Height Adjustment

Some sailboats are actually equipped to lower their masts, but fortunately, bridgetenders don't expect them to do so at every bridge; it's a bit more involved than lowering an antenna. It *is*, however, a grand asset on those occasions when a bridge may be "down" for days due to malfunctioning machinery.

If a sailboat's mast height is only slightly higher than the official clearance, there are various ways to heel the boat (thereby shortening the overall height). (1) If you only need a few inches, get all the weight on one rail. (2) Run the boom out at a 90-degree angle; have crewmembers sit as far out as they can. (3) Tie the dinghy onto the end of the boom and load it up with people-ballast. (One boatyard helps sailors get under a 49-foot bridge by lining one deck with 5-gallon barrels filled with water.)

How will you know if you're heeled over far enough? On a length of line, mark off the desired clearance—if the bridge is 50 feet, mark off 49, or whatever margin you want. Attach a weight to one end of the line, and tie the other end to a halyard at the measured mark; when you hoist the line, the knot will stop at the masthead. As the boat heels, the weight becomes a plumb line. When the weight touches the water's surface, you should clear the bridge.

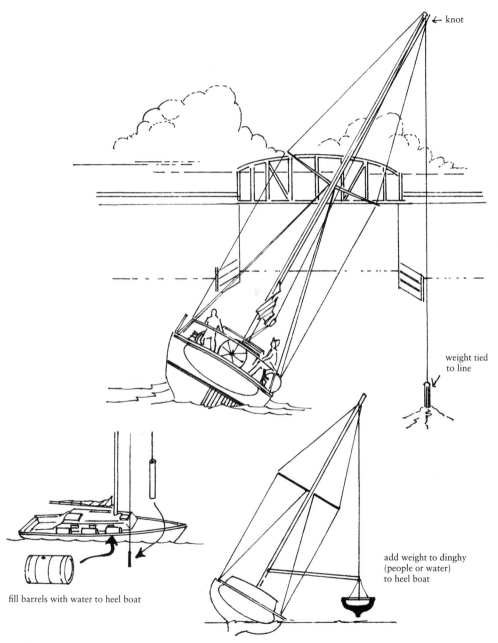

← knot

weight tied
to line

fill barrels with water to heel boat

add weight to dinghy
(people or water)
to heel boat

When you put weight on the boom to heel the boat, use a halyard at the end of the boom to hold the weight.

COMMUNICATION

Charts usually don't show the names of bridges. Guidebooks do, though they may not be up-to-date, as bridges occasionally are re-dedicated. In many places, the name is shown on a sign tacked onto the bridge, so if you get close enough (or your binoculars are good) you can read it. If you cannot find a name anywhere, look at the chart and use the name of a nearby town or island name. Unless a bridgetender is feeling contrary, you'll probably get an answer, including the correct name of the bridge. (If you're using horn signals, the problem does not exist.)

Contact

When you can reach the bridgetender on Channel 13, the opening request is an easy call. Just say, "Hobucken Bridge, this is *My Boat* (trawler/sailboat/motoryacht/ferry), southbound, standing by for your next opening." The bridgetender may respond by saying when the bridge is scheduled to open next.

If there are no restrictions, you'll be told to "bring it up." You will, the bridgetender will, and that's it; you'll soon be on your way. (You may hear the bridge sounding the five-blast danger signal as the bridge is coming down.)

• After you've gone through, the bridgetender may call you, to ask the name of your boat. If the transom lettering is clear, you won't be called much; if the lettering is arty or faint, you'll be called a lot.

• Even though a bridge is already opening for three or four boats, notify the bridgetender of your presence, by horn signal or by radio: "I'm the fifth boat, northbound, requesting opening." The bridgetender will be happy, and you'll be safe.

No Answer

When radio calls bring no answer from a bridgetender, and you see no red flags or signs that might explain the silence, get out

the horn and sound the correct bridge-opening request: one long, one short. If there's still no answer, keep sounding. If you're in the right location, a shore person will soon tire of hearing all that noise and will telephone—or walk to—the bridgetender's house to alert the tender of your presence.

• Keep a horn handy whenever you're around bridges. You may need to notify somebody fast of a dangerous situation; radios are nice, but only when someone acknowledges the call.

• A bridgetender may answer your sound signal with the repeat signal if it's okay to open, or with five short blasts if it's not. Not all tenders respond this way.

Don't Call

Before you call a bridge to ask for a special, non-scheduled opening, think how foolish (self-important) you will sound to the bridgetender and everyone else who monitors the channel.

"I had to slow down for all this boat traffic and so I was late for the regular opening." (Should the bridgetender care?)

Or, "You don't have much land traffic on that bridge; why can't you open it for me?"

Without meaning to answer that question, it is true that road traffic may not be the primary consideration in restricted bridge openings. Many bridges are not exactly new; limited openings may save their machinery for a few more years. Instead of feeling put upon because of restricted opening times, be glad they operate at all for recreational traffic. With the obvious exception of big river channels, most waterways are not jammed with the commercial traffic for which the channels were made.

COURTESIES

When you're waiting for an opening, it's polite to wait in the order of arrival. But it's sensible for the sailors to wave the power-

Waiting for a bridge opening, sailors usually signal powerboats to go first.

boats ahead, since they'll just pass later, on the other side, causing an extra slowdown for both passer and passee.

Waiting Lines

Powerboaters generally move right up to the bridge, having confidence in the boat's machinery to keep them hovering safely. Many sailboats do not stay stationary; understandably, sailboat captains are less inclined to wait too close to the bridge for an opening.

Bridgetenders often ask all the boats to move up, suggesting you may miss the timed opening if you stay too far back. Try to find an acceptable medium, where you don't feel threatened, but you don't look like you're still a half mile away. (Remember, it may take 5 or 6 minutes to cover that half mile, and bridge traffic will not be pleased.)

The perfect waiting spot is close enough so you can zip through as soon as the channel is clear, but not so close that excess current can push you too far too soon. It would be nice to say, "Err on the side of caution," but here, again, judgment is required. We've seen bridges close before the last boat got through, because its captain miscalculated distance or time.

• Most sailboats have a hard time "holding station." Only on rare occasions can a sailboat stay in one place, with just the exact amount of power to counteract current or wind influences. Try turning around, pointing bow to wind or current; it's usually easier to stay in mid-channel. Even powerboats with a twin-engine advantage sometimes get pushed out of channels by winds and currents.

• Whenever you have a longer-than-5-minute wait, check the chart for depths on either side of the channel in the bridge vicinity; if you must drift, you can be careful to avoid shoals. Most other waiters will probably be considerate, but that doesn't mean they know how to control their boat, so try to maintain a safe distance.

• Often (not always) you'll hear a horn or siren when the bridge is about to open.

Usually, you can see the traffic gates; when they go down, you know the bridge will open shortly. "Shortly," however, varies from bridge to bridge, depending on the type of structure, and the condition of its machinery (and maybe the condition of the person in control).

• Once the first boat is going through the opening, there's no more reason to hold back. Close up ranks fast.

Right-of-Way

Some bridges can take two-way traffic with plenty of room to spare. With others, it's safer to stick to a single lane of one-way traffic.

On rivers, boats traveling with the current have right-of-way over those traveling against. The same logic applies to any waterway, but don't expect everyone to acknowledge that. Also, because of their size and unwieldy shape, commercial boats can't maneuver as well in narrow places; their alignment going through a bridge is critical. Pleasure boats should stay out of the way until big boats clear the bridge. (Radio is most helpful in such situations; monitor or call on Channel 13.)

Bridge Tips

• Bridges are not a place for speed or big wakes. Often signs are posted, just in case someone doesn't know this: "no wake" speed through all bridges. (Sailboats, be wary if a speeder is in the area when you want to go through a bridge. This is the worst place for a pendulum roll.)

• Even if no specific time restrictions are posted, a bridgetender may decide to wait for some other boats to catch up to lessen the number of openings, especially when other boats are clearly within sight. It's their prerogative; fewer openings save wear on the bridge even as they allow smoother land traffic. (If you *were* the land traffic, it would make perfect sense to you.) Try not to be upset by such delays. If a 10-minute time-out in your boating day is a problem, you haven't adjusted to boat-time yet.

• Whether current is with you or agin' you, as you get closer to a bridge, it will be noticeably stronger, and when you get between the bridge supports, it will be *most* strong. With some boats, at some bridges, you may have to wait for slack water or a favorable current. (In the Great Lakes, you don't have the option of waiting for changing

Boats traveling with the current should go first.

current flow

tidal current; it may take a very long time to go a very short distance.)

• Most cruising boats keep an anchor "at the ready" as a matter of general precaution whenever traveling a river or waterway channel. If you don't, you should, to keep you away from a bridge in case your engine fails at an especially inopportune time.

• Some bridges will not open if the wind climbs above whatever speed has been established as that bridge's danger limit. And no amount of discussion—or phone calls to supervisors or Coast Guard—will get the bridge open, so save your transmission. Practice patience or resignation. Drop an anchor and read a book. And be ready when the bridge *does* open, even if it's an hour before dawn.

• When you have perfect conditions for sailing down the waterway—flat water, wind just abaft the beam, and you're loving every minute of the quiet—you really don't want to be bothered with the engine just to go through a bridge. And if you could depend on the wind holding perfectly and the bridge lifting promptly and there's no other traffic for you to worry

about or disrupt, then it might be okay to ignore the engine. Reality, of course, intrudes. The wind won't hold steady once you're between the supports. If current's against you, and/or you don't have enough momentum, you could move sideways into the bridge abutment. With all sail up, you can't see properly in close quarters. And how often do bridges open exactly when we expect them to? At least turn on the engine for backup. And probably roll up the jib so you can see where you're going. Or not going. There's no Coast Guard rule about it, but there may be local regulations; it's one of those common-sense things in any case.

• Some people offer favorite tips for judging distance of—and above—mast height, but don't believe them. Unless somebody climbs to the top of the mast and watches at eye level as you go through, it is really hard to know if you'll clear.

• In an area of considerable tide, the vertical clearance at a fixed bridge will change with the tide. If your mast height is too close for confident clearing at high tide, wait a few hours rather than risk damaging any masthead fittings.

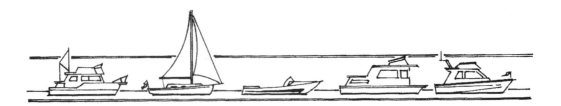

8 Mastering Locks

Locks are wonderful inventions: simple in principle, but impressive in engineering and construction. Without locks, our rivers would still be giant canoe trails, with rapids and waterfalls carrying adventurous voyagers to sea. With locks, giant boats carry commerce and work crews, and small boats carry happy boaters out to see the sights.

When transiting any lock system, you must marvel at the construction. Even one lock seems a mammoth undertaking: dig a lock chamber, put gates at both ends capable of keeping water out (and in). Give the natural water flow a route to travel (over the dam and into the "pool") and engineer a way to fill or empty the chamber in 10 or 30 minutes, many times a day, taking along a bunch of boats for the ride.

While locking systems were built for industry and commerce, recreational boating derived the benefit of cross-country travel.

The East Coast Intracoastal has one lock on its main route, and two in the alternate Dismal Swamp Canal. There's one lock in the Canaveral Canal that connects the Intracoastal Waterway to the ocean, and five along the cross-Florida Okeechobee Waterway. Seattle has the Ballard Locks to link Lake Union to Puget Sound.

The Erie Canal has 34 locks in its 330-mile length, plus eight more in the Oswego Canal connecting to Lake Ontario. Many of the locks front lovely park settings, a welcome place to spend the night after a day of locking (some of the lifts are high, and some days, you do get tired). Even the huge locks on the Mississippi River or the Welland Canal will take pleasure boats, though in locking schedules, recreational boats are low boat on the water totem.

Boaters hear some bad reports about the ride in locks. Like most scare stories, the

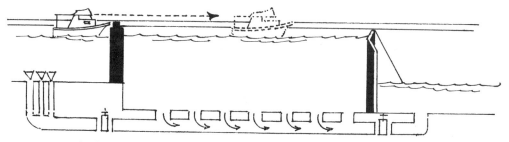

Boat enters lock chamber filled to match high-water level.

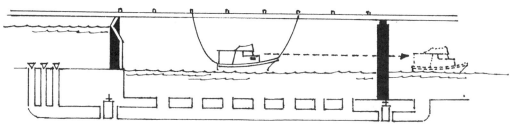

Water is drained from lock to match low-water level of next stage.

bad rides are the exceptions, and like most scary situations, awareness and preparation are good prevention.

LOCK APPROACH

When nearing a lock, call the lockmaster or use a horn signal (two long, two short, or whatever is used locally) to announce your arrival and request a lock-through. If you get a radio response, ask which side you'll be tying to, so you can get lines and fenders ready. If there's no radio response, wait till the green light shows you it's okay to enter. (Watch the lock gates, too; when they start to open, the green light will follow soon.)

• At some locks, recreational boats may announce their arrival at the lock by pulling a line that hangs down to small-boat level at the end of the lock fenders; apparently, the "lock bell" rings in the lockmaster's office.

• If there is a lot of commercial traffic in the river or waterway, the workboats will lock first. You may have a long wait, unless the lockmaster can make room for you, sometimes rafted off a tug or barge.

• Where there's a lock, there's a dam. Study the chart or river map to see how the two are situated; then be very careful to avoid the side of the waterway that carries water over the dam.

• As you enter the lock, water may still be disturbed from filling or from door-opening, so be prepared to counteract any sudden swings.

• Don't be too anxious to get close to the lock when waiting for it to open; exiting traffic may need a lot of room to maneuver. (Signs will usually indicate the area to keep clear.)

Enter lock slowly; watch for disturbed water.

READY

If you were not told ahead of time where to tie up, you'll learn as you enter, which may force a speedy line-and-fender switch. (Many people are prepared with lines on both sides, so only fenders need be moved.)

Lines and Handlers

You'll need long lines at bow and stern. Each line handler should also have a fend-off pole (boathook or mop handle) and a pair of tough gloves that won't suffer from contact with a grubby lock wall.

Lines should be twice as long as the lock is deep.

Fenders

Put on the fattest fenders you own. If you're allowed to use bags filled with hay, they're handy for extras, and their cushioning can save a hull side from scarring.

Old tires always seemed a good idea (from the boater's perspective) but are no longer allowed; when they fall overboard, they sink, and could create problems with the water-controlling mechanism.

Rules

• The order of locking importance:

1. Government vessels

2. Commercial vessels (passenger, tow, fishing)

3. Pleasure boats

• As in any situation where crew may be moving around deck quickly, everyone should wear a PFD.

• You may see signs instructing you to turn off engines while in the lock, but we've not seen this regulation enforced; some captains like to use the engines to

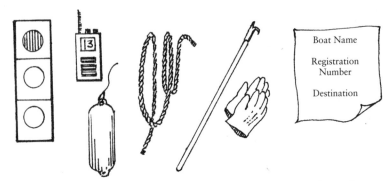

Call on 13; wait for green light. Be ready with lines, fenders, gloves, boathook, and boat information.

help keep the boat in place. Nevertheless, if the locktender requests it, consider it more a directive than a request.

• Know your document or registration number, in case the lockmaster asks. You may also be asked where you've been, where you're going, and what the boat's draft is.

• Turn off radar, for the safety of locktenders.

TIE-UP

In some locks, you won't need your own lines; the locktender will hand you a line already attached to a bollard, or you'll grab one that's hanging down against the lock wall; after locking, you toss it off, or he'll haul it up, depending on whether you locked up or down.

Sometimes you'll be told where to tie, other times you can choose your own spot. Most often, lines will be passed around bollards, bow and stern, and two people will control the lines, releasing or taking in as the boat moves up or down.

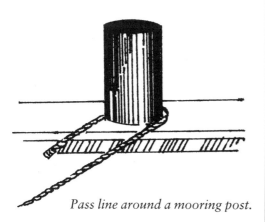

Pass line around a mooring post.

Floating Timber

Some locks have a floating timber (or bollard, or bitt) which is set into a recess in the lock wall, and floats up or down along with the boat. Position the boat so the timber is amidships (centered fore-and-aft); pass the lines around the timber, and hold the boat close to the wall.

Stationary Pole

A stationary pole is also set into a recess in the wall. You pass your two lines around the pole, and hold them snug; they slide up or down as the water level changes; if both lines are kept tight, the boat cannot swing bow-out or stern-out.

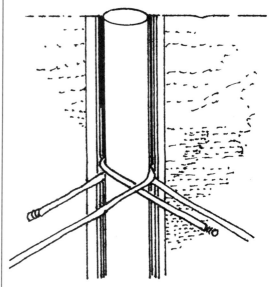

Ladders

A ladder extending the full height of the lock provides another tie-up. Bow and stern lines are turned around a rung of the ladder (*not* tied); as the boat moves, the crew switches lines, "walking" up or down the ladder to the next rung. Switch lines one at a time, so you're always attached with at least one line. Always ask the locktender if ladder use is okay; in some places, it's not.

• If you're tied alongside a straight lock wall, a fender board could be useful, but if you're using a ladder or timber, the board might get caught in the recessed wall.

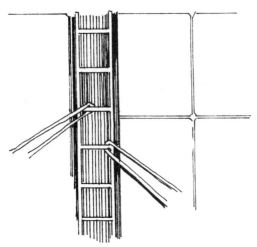

Use ladder to "walk" lines up or down.

• Occasionally, traffic is busy, and you'll be rafting to other boats. This is not a problem in most cases, but in locks with a high lift, the water turbulence flips boats around more, so everyone needs to be more careful, watching that fenders stay in place.

LOCKING DOWN

This is the easiest way to travel, but it's also the messiest. Easy because when water is exiting from the bottom of the lock, it is *not* creating eddies and waves to toss the boat around; most messy because the lock walls are naturally most wet.

When you enter a downbound lock, you'll tie to a lock wall that is low, just like a seawall along a waterside park. Probably, one end of the line will be cleated on the boat; crew holds the other end. (Depending on the tie-up method, you'll flip the lines over bollards—which may be called buttons—or around a cylinder or a ladder rung.)

When everyone's in and secure, the lock gates close, and soon, your boat is easing down the wall as the water leaves the lock. One person controls the bow line, one the stern line, each releasing more line as required by the falling water level.

Try to keep the boat close to the wall, but not rubbing hard against it. (Your fenders should be in position to protect the hull side when it does touch.) At the bottom of the lock, the gate at the "exit" end opens slightly, so water in the lock can level out with water outside the lock. That accomplished, the water is reasonably settled; when you see a "Go" signal, haul down your lines, and leave.

• Don't just cleat one end of the line and hold the other loosely; it is surprising how quickly the boat can get away from you even in such a seemingly basic situation. Cleat the one end securely, then turn the holding line around a cleat, to give yourself some leverage.

• Down-locking moves you away from most of the wind that could push the boat around—another reason why it's an easier ride.

• Often, locktenders are very chatty, and you can learn something about the town/waterway/restaurants/tie-up spot or what kind of fish "they" caught yesterday. Take advantage of those times to gain some valuable local knowledge.

LOCKING UP

This is the intimidating part, especially in those locks that lift you 40 feet or more. The gates open and as you enter, you look up, up, and up at a sheer lock wall. (The good news is not all "up" locks lift you that far; many are in the 10-to-20-foot range that you eventually file in the "no problem" category.)

In some locks, lines are waiting for you, hanging down from bollards "up there." You position the boat where you can comfortably grab and hold two lines, one at the bow, the other at the stern. When no lines are waiting, you'll pass *your* lines up to the locktender.

Make sure your fenders are well situated; put on your hand-protecting gloves, park your fend-off mop handle nearby, and wait.

Same routine; when all boats are tied up, the lock gate closes.

In "up" locks, you must be ready for some turbulence. It's not bad in all locks, but be aware of the possibility. As water comes into the lock from below, little whirlpools rise to the surface, and sometimes grow into bigger whirlpools of swirling, foamy water. It is first noticeable in the front of the lock, and flows back (something to remember if you have a choice about where to tie up).

Problem Prevention

Two common problems to watch for: In the first situation, the bow gets caught by current and tries to swing out, away from the wall. If this is not corrected fast, the boat could end up stern-to the wall, where the lack of fenders will have a damaging effect on your transom.

First, be sure the wheel is centered, so your own rudder doesn't add to the problem. To prevent the bow-out, both line handlers must keep tight control of their lines. If both allow the boat to drift backward too far, they have not kept proper tension on the lines; the longer the bow line, the more difficult it is to hold the boat parallel to the wall. Once the current catches the bow from the wall side, the boat starts to move away from the wall.

In the second scenario, the bow is pushed *into* the wall, and unless you are well fendered forward (not a usual fender location), the boat may be scratched as it rubs the lock wall. To prevent this, the stern line must be kept tight enough to keep the boat snug to and parallel with the wall.

• Another reason "up" locks demand more attention: besides the swirling water, you may be lifting *toward* the wind, and if it's blowing hard, it will add another influence.

• For fending off, don't use a telescoping boathook in the fully extended position; you might bend it beyond repair.

LEAVING

Eventually, all the water motion slows, then quits. You'll see the exit gates open slightly as the last level of water flows in or out; then the gates open wide and you can see the new outside level.

The lockmaster signals when you can leave the lock. If you have locked through with a commercial boat, it will probably leave first, and you will need to be extra careful, as the big prop wash will start a whole new bunch of swirling currents for you to counter. Exit as you entered, at idle speed.

• In Seattle, sea lions and salmon often lock through with the boats. In Florida's Okeechobee Waterway, you may lock through with a manatee or two; when it's time to leave, *they* go first.

SPECIAL LOCKING

• In those locks where there is little actual water exchange, you may not be required to tie up at all; just hover in neutral in the middle of the lock. Naturally, this would not happen with a lot of boats in the lock, but with only one or two, it's a possibility.

• A few locks change water level so little, the flow is controlled by the gates rather than the underwater structures. Initially, the appropriate gate is opened slightly, and water starts to flow in or out; as the level inside gets closer to the level outside, gates open more and more till finally the water quits moving.

• How a singlehander manages locking procedure depends somewhat on the size

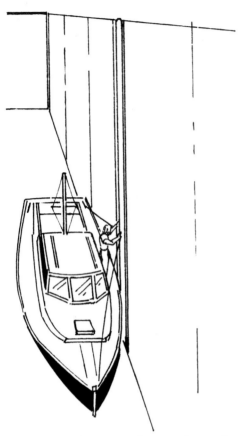

of the boat. With a smaller boat (perhaps up to 25 feet) it's possible to use one long line; cleat it aft, flip it round a bollard, and hold it at the bow, releasing or taking in line as needed to keep the boat centered on that bollard. Or, pass bow and stern lines around a stationary pole, and control them from a place amidships.

Larger, heavier boats might get caught with one end being pushed away from the wall while the other end is getting crushed against it. Try cleating one end of a long line aft; flip it round a bollard, then pass the loose end through the center of the cleat, so any pull on the line will come from the stern. Take the free end of the line to your position forward, where you can release (or take in) both lines as needed. (We've seen people try to cleat both ends of both lines, then run back and forth releasing a few feet at a time. This seems chancy at best, dangerous at worst.)

A singlehander passes bow and stern lines around a stationary pole and holds both from amidships.

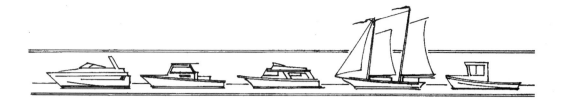

9 Dodging Danger

This chapter might better be called "Mariner's Murphies" because it describes a bunch of things that could go wrong, go wrong, go wrong. Maybe none of them will ever disrupt your boating day, and if that's the case, be grateful for your angel, or karma, or aura.

Where glitches are concerned, boating life is no different from ordinary life, and on those days, anything that can go wrong, will. Read about some common problems now, and sometime down the waterway a vague memory might help you undo the attempt to ruin your day.

CHANNEL VISION

Channel markers—reds on one side and greens on the other—line such an obvious path, it seems impossible a boat could go wrong. But boats do, literally, go wrong, in a variety of ways.

The easiest "wrong" is caused by sleepy-steerer syndrome: Not paying attention, you proceed confidently past a mark, forgetting only which side of the mark you are supposed to pass. You are reminded quickly, hopefully by a depthsounder's rapidly descending digits. Avoiding this one may be a simple matter of more caffeine, earlier. (Or, let the morning person steer.)

Centerline

• Sometimes, red and green marks do not appear opposite each other, but instead are placed at alternate half-mile intervals. If you have trouble judging the channel width, aim roughly mark-to-mark; you'll be running a slight zigzag course, but it will not make a big difference in your ETA (estimated time of arrival).

• Watch the depthsounder. Once you know the average depth of channel center, a noticeable departure from that depth warns you to scoot sideways and look for deeper water.

• Don't pass too close to waterway markers, especially the large, lighted ones. They are firmly planted in some way, and you do not want to find out how.

• When you are sighting marks forward and aft to check your lineup, position yourself along the centerline of the boat. Sitting off to either side will change your perspective.

• Where lighted marks are set up for safe night travel, it's equally sensible to follow them by day, too, staying well away from the interim daymarks, which may be set in the shallower side limits of the waterway channel.

• Do not cut the corner at a lighted daymark. The interim daymarks indicate the sides of the channel as you travel from lighted daymark to lighted daymark.

Side Sets

Another go-wrong with a lot of variations happens when the captain neglects to guard against a side set, caused by either wind or current. The boat slowly wanders to the side of the channel, then *outside* the channel, until the keel abruptly finds the side limit of the safe channel.

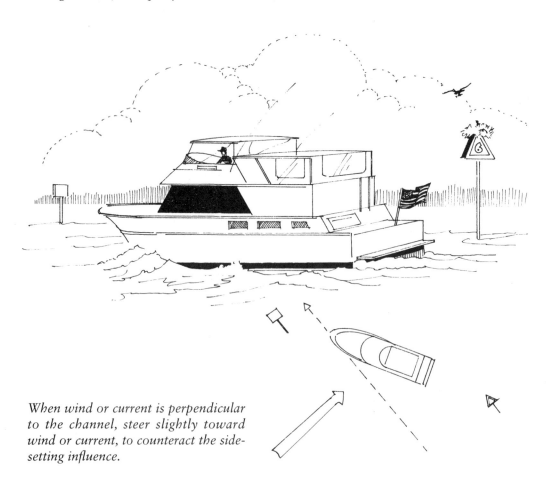

When wind or current is perpendicular to the channel, steer slightly toward wind or current, to counteract the side-setting influence.

Avoiding this embarrassing (and potentially damaging) situation is easy, if you remember to look behind the boat frequently as you pass marks. A side set will be noticed quickly if markers no longer appear to be aligned. You can correct the offsetting tendency by "crabbing" up the channel: steering slightly toward the opposite side of the channel to counteract the direction of drift. (If you should over-crab, and touch bottom on the high side, the wind or current will help get you off.)

• To stay in mid-channel when a cross current is running, try to pick out a shore feature that visually aligns with the channel; note its compass bearing, then try to maintain the same bearing as you head toward it. Naturally, if you can find two objects that make a range, so much the easier.

• Steering on charted range marks is the best way to follow a channel, inspiring confidence that you've not strayed from the safety of center. But sometimes, you must steer by "backward" ranges; the marks are set for boats going in the opposite direction, so you must turn around and watch behind you instead of ahead. When you're looking back and steering forward, it's easy to turn the wrong way. A bit of a snake wake won't send you out of the channel as long as you correct in time; it's more frustrating than dangerous.

• When following "backward" ranges, have another person face aft to watch the range marks, and give you steering directions by the basic finger-point method. Pointing helps prevent confusion on the part of the aft-facing person, who might accidentally give backward port and starboard commands.

• If markers seem to be moving sideways rapidly (relative to background scenery), it's time for more coffee; it is really your boat drifting off to the side.

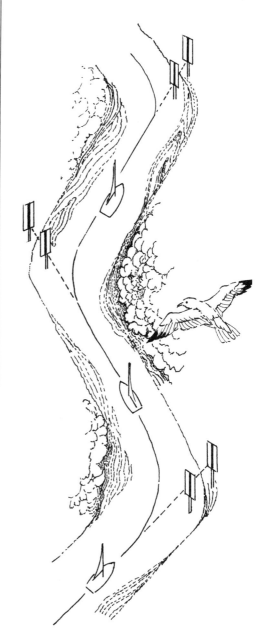

Steer on range marks to stay in mid-channel.

More Channel Notes

• When following a big-ship channel, pleasure boats can often ride just outside the channel buoys, rather than stay inside and become a traffic hazard. Check the chart, and watch the depthsounder. You can always duck back in if conditions warrant. (A few examples: Norfolk Harbor, Charleston Harbor, Delaware Bay, New York Harbor, Puget Sound, and much of the Chesapeake.)

• Sailors taking advantage of some wind along a marked channel must be watchful of what's behind the jib. Rubrails are no match for large, steel-platformed waterway markers.

• When traveling any waterway, watch for an apparent transposition of buoy colors when two marked systems meet. The obvious colors may seem backward; study the chart, and locate "your" marks.

• If you come to a place where markers for two or more channels are all visible but not clearly lined up (from your viewpoint), take a minute to figure an appropriate compass course to your next mark. This is much better than guessing wrong and ending up planted on a dividing shoal or rock.

READING THE WATER

Besides depending on an elaborate system of markers and lights to guide you through the water, you can get a lot of information from the water itself, if you're an observant navigator.

Water in Motion

• Where two currents meet, the water takes on a disturbed pattern like little wavelets jumping up and down.

• A line of weeds or foam often marks a wavy separation line at the place where two currents meet.

• When bypassing an inlet that is at a right angle to the channel, watch for an abrupt side sweep as the tidal current (inbound or outbound) catches the hull. Often, you will pass these places crabbing

at a considerable angle. Sometimes, you can tell ahead of time which way you'll be pushed by watching the angle of heel on a floating buoy.

• Any noticeable disruption in the overall wave pattern indicates an obstruction. (More about this later in the chapter.)

Clear Water

If water is swimming-pool clear, you are able to see all the problems that navigation channels avoid: here a rock, there a shoal, a grassy patch in between. The waters of the Bahamas, and, to a lesser degree, Florida's Keys, are famous for their clarity, making the usual navigation aids unnecessary. Why mark a channel you can plainly see (once you know how to *read* what you see)?

• Initially, you worry about going aground when you're still in 20 feet of water. Then you get overconfident and you plant your keel. Until you can match color with depth, leave the depthsounder on. And practice reading on a rising tide.

• Pale beige with only a hint of a green overlay is grounding depth. Deep blue is deep water. Between the two are variations on the blue-green theme.

• Coral heads show dark, often almost black. A brown color may be either grass, or rock ledges.

- Lighting is important for depth perception. Having the sun behind you is best for reading water, though it's not always possible to position yourself for that benefit. Polarizing glasses help a lot, and height improves visibility.

Shallow Water

A depthsounder is not required equipment, though it would seem a good idea from a safety standpoint. Once you're in the habit of using one, it becomes a valuable navigation tool. It is your first warning of an off-course track, and if you're watching carefully, you usually have time to correct the error before it becomes a real problem.

- When you're running along a coastline, the depthsounder will tell you if you're angling in closer than you intended. If you're running down a narrow channel, the depthsounder will show you if you start to drift over too far to either side. When you want to anchor, the depthsounder tells you where it is safe to do so.

- You may see many "spoil" areas noted on the chart, usually, though not always, shown as blue (shallow) water. These are places where dredged material has been deposited; that's why they're so close to the navigation channel. Don't go across a spoil area, even if "someone" says there's plenty of water there. Sometimes, there isn't.

- Powerboaters should watch their wake, for their *own* benefit. If the boat seems harder to steer, check your wake, and if it seems higher than usual, you may be getting into shoal water. Slow down; the boat won't squat down so far, and you may clear the shallow spot.

FIXED OBSTRUCTIONS

A marked navigation channel should be an unobstructed path for boat traffic, but the assumption doesn't make it so. Fishermen place pots and nets and traps. Signposts and bollards hide broken beneath the surface. Mother Nature adds a rock or a tree stump.

Fishing Snags

- Lobster, or crab trap (pot) markers often find their way into navigation channels. And outside the established routes, trap markers may cover an alternate course with an irregular checkerboard of obstacles.

The markers themselves won't bother you—the floats are usually Styrofoam or soft-plastic bottles—but the line connecting them to the underwater traps.

When passing either the stray floats or a marker maze, note the direction in which the floats are being pushed (whether by wind or current) and pass them on their downwind (down-current) side. This way, you are past the end of the connecting line, so there is no possibility of accidentally catching the line on prop, rudder, or keel. (See illustration on page 88.)

- If you try to pass the float on the high side, you may be amazed at how quickly you and the float close, despite your best efforts to steer clear. The same wind or current that pushes the float is pushing you, and you have a lot more surface to push than a small float or bottle.

- At low tide, the line will be most horizontal, closest to the water surface for a longer distance, most apt to be caught by a passing anything.

- Be equally cautious at times of extreme high tides. If the trap setter did not use a long enough line, the float may be partially submerged. Watch for dome-shaped bubbles, or a telltale V in the water.

- In Maine, you may find two floats on one pot: a long leader connects the main float and a smaller float called the toggle. If you pass between the two floats, you will get snagged.

Pass trap-marking floats on the downwind or down-current side.

• If a sailboat starts to feel sluggish shortly after going through a patch of pot floats, it's possible the keel snagged one of the pot lines. Spin in a circle (if motor-sailing, put the engine in neutral in mid-spin) and the pot may drop off.

• If your prop picks up a pot line (or any line) you will have a "fouled propeller," and the resulting wrap will probably shut down the engine. You *might* be able to pull the line off without going swimming.

With the boathook, snag a portion of the line and haul it up to the boat where someone can hold it taut. Then you (or the mechanic among your crew) go into the engine compartment; with transmission in neutral, try to turn the shaft by hand, or with Vise-Grips, or whatever might work. As you turn, the person holding the line keeps tension on it; if you're very lucky, the combined tension and turning will unwrap

the line. (If nothing moves the first time, try turning the shaft the opposite way.)

• If you're boating in an area noted for an abundance of crab or lobster pot floats, you may want to consider some snag-avoidance techniques. In Maine, for example, many boaters use a prop basket, a cage-like attachment that keeps stray pot-lines away from props, thereby preventing a dreaded wraparound.

• Consider adding a weed cutter, which attaches to your shaft. SPURS is one brand of weed cutters; call 1-800-824-5372, extension 100.

• If you see a bunch of sticks, or tree branches, standing upright in the water, they could be there for a few different reasons. Many tall sticks in fairly regular rows are probably the support structure of a pound net—a big fish trap. Don't go near the sticks. They may be marked by flashing amber lights, or they may show only reflective tape.

• A few short sticks probably mark the limits of leased clam or oyster grounds. Here, there's no net to worry about, but since clams and oysters live in shallow water, stay outside the boundary if you can. It's also important to avoid disturbing the beds with prop wash.

• A gill net is a wall of netting set underwater, stretched out and anchored or staked at each end. There are two kinds: with floating nets, the top of the net is just under the surface, and a row of floats will show the length of the net clearly. The below-water nets are usually set low enough for small boats to get over, but it's always better for cruising boats to go around rather than across. In some places, they're marked with double floats on each end.

• Channel nets are funnel-shaped, similar to the kind of net shrimp boats drag, except without the "doors." They need a lot of tidal current flowing to keep them open. You often see them around inlets, where tide is strongest. Usually, you'll see a boat (or boats) *with* the net, which may be marked with big barrels striped with reflective tape.

• When you see a "fish haven" on the chart, it might be a good place to fish. In one of the earliest recycling efforts, old ships, almost-useless junk, and maybe a bunch of old tires were deposited in assigned locations to become artificial reefs and provide homes for fish. Charted depths do not usually change enough to bother recreational boats, but the Coast Pilot advises caution when "passing over or anchoring in the vicinity."

• "Fish trap" areas are also charted. Since these locations are approved for fish traps, boats should stay out. There may be nets or traps under the water, anchored or staked in such a way that a boat of moder-

ate draft might not clear them. The boundaries of fish trap areas should be marked with yellow buoys.

Submerged Snags

• Charts note the position of submerged pilings; even if there is no additional note saying "position approximate," you should assume that to be the case and give the location a wide berth.

• If you see a lot of broken-off tree trunks along a shoreline, it's a safe assumption there may be more of the same along the water side of the shoreline as well, hidden from view perhaps by a change in water level. Move cautiously, if you need to pass near the shore, or if you're thinking of anchoring in the area.

• Many boaters ignore a marked channel in places where the chart shows good water outside the channel as well. While charted depths are probably reliable, the off-channel areas may not be maintained in any way, so snags may not be spotted and removed. Obviously, it's a "your choice" situation, but consider all the variables when making the choice.

• A V-shaped pattern in the water indicates an obstruction; the V trails down-

current from a snag that might be a single branch, or the top of an entire tree stuck in the bottom.

• A more circular disruption in the water pattern might be caused by a submerged rock close enough to the surface to force a change in the overall flow.

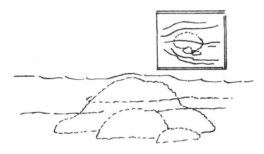

Flotsam

Floating debris is a problem anywhere, but more so in a confined channel. If you see a leaf or twig in the water, your first reaction is to overlook it—except it might still be attached to a significant portion of the original tree. The same holds true for a tiny pointed stick just breaking the surface; it could be the topmost sliver of an entire log.

• If a log is floating horizontally on the surface, there may be nothing to warn you of its presence till you're almost too close to avoid it. Deadheads—"waterlogged" logs—do hide underwater.

• A single, visible square corner might be part of a harmless cardboard box, or it could be a section of a house roof. Worst of all is the sight of an inverted boat hull. (If you should see any such major hazards in a narrow channel, report it to the nearest Coast Guard station.)

• Other things float by too often: coolers, Styrofoam cups, barrels, bottles and cans. One of the smallest, but most damaging items is a plastic bag (or a piece thereof) that may decide to take a ride into the boat's water intake (make sure your engine cooling intake has a water strainer).

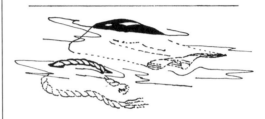

• A small length of line seems innocent enough, until it finds a boat propeller to wrap around (and break off a blade.)

• After a tug passes you, slow down till there's considerable space separating you from the tug. The tug's prop wash will find all the loose debris in the water and bring it to the surface, where it may surprise the next unsuspecting boater with dirt or damage.

• The purpose of mentioning these items is not to frighten, but to show why you need to maintain a good lookout at all times; other boats are only part of the looking-out-for picture.

OTHER BOATS

Fishing Boats

• Everywhere in the Chesapeake, you'll see crabbers zigzagging along as they tend traps. It's hard work and getting harder: fewer crabs, more pots. Some of the boats are a treat for the eye—graceful sheers, fantail sterns, looking out-of-place even though it *is* their place.

• Small clam dredges are good for a pre-dawn wakeup call in many back creeks; don't be surprised if they don't let you sleep late.

• In the Gulf of Mexico, along the coast from Florida to North Carolina, and in the Pacific Northwest, you'll see a lot of shrimp boats, both at work and at anchor. When they're working, give them lots of room, as you would any commercial fishermen. It's fun to watch the shrimpers, from a distance. Some days, you'll see hundreds of birds having a convention on a pair of outriggers, lined up

like decoys at a carnival shooting range. On foggy mornings, you glimpse the outlines of nets stretched like wings from the deck of a ghost ship.

• An unusual meeting occurred along the Intracoastal channel in South Carolina; a shrimp boat had just come into the waterway, and its outriggers were still extended. A sailboat was traveling in the opposite direction, and as the two boats met, they *really* met, in a tangle of outrigger and shrouds. Fortunately, no major damage resulted from the too-close passing. (On the West Coast, give salmon trawlers a wide berth.)

Big Boats

• Small boats must always be wary of getting too close to freighters or big tugboats. In narrow channels, the big boats create a strong suction—you can watch the water visibly recede from the shoreline as the ship or tug moves along the channel.

• It's difficult to "keep clear" sometimes. A tug captain will stay as close to mid-channel as he can, not wanting to plant the barges he's pushing, but when there's no water outside the channel, there's no place for you to go.

In some cases, you'll be in a location where you can just turn around and wait in a wider part of the waterway, rather than meet a commercial boat in an especially narrow cut. (Listen to Channel 13.)

• Sailing boats should not get so close to ships that the ship blocks the wind, cutting power and control at just the time you may need it most.

• Small boats shouldn't travel close behind big workboats, for reasons other than the debris. The turbulence caused by a tugboat's engines can extend a long way behind the tow; you'll get tired of steering first to one side, then to the other as your hull gets caught in the swirls.

• In West Coast waters, log booms (rafts of logs) are a common obstacle.

• Chapter 2 describes the official lights and shapes on the working dredges you must pass from time to time. Remember to look for the safe-passing side, but call the operator anyway, to be sure all cables are down.

If you have time to study the equipment, you'll see that the dredge is held in place at the stern by poles acting as giant ground stakes. An anchor is set off the bow, marked by a big spherical float. Cables that control the dredging may run across the channel.

The dredge probably takes up half the channel, the same as it would if it were moving, so don't try to pass too far away from all the equipment. It's safer to pass it closely, as long as the captain knows you're there.

When you do meet a moving dredge, it is a mini-adventure. There is not a lot of turbulence, so it's not worrisome from that aspect, but it is *so* long, and there's so much stuff to keep on passing and passing—the mariner's version of a freight train.

Anchored Boats

• When you're running through a bunch of anchored boats, think about where the anchor lines are. Unless it's flat calm (when boats wander at will), the boats will be hanging back from their anchors; it's obvious which direction the anchor is set, so that's the direction you want to avoid. Don't pass close in front of anchored boats, and you should clear the lines. If you do pick up a line, try the removal technique described earlier in this chapter in the section on crab pots.

An exception to the front-watching caution occurs when two anchors are set Bahamian style—both from the bow, with one line extending forward and one line aft. You'll still see the direction the anchor lines lead, so you'll still know what to avoid, but you will have two lines per boat to watch out for.

• Be alert for recreational fishermen in channels. Boats should not anchor in navigation channels, but some people who spend a lot of time on boats regard themselves as fishermen rather than boatmen, so they're not bound by boaters' "shoulds"— or so they think. Since fish

Don't pass too close to anchored boats; your prop might snag an anchor line.

92

Section Two—Boating Skills

apparently like to spend time in channels too, they are logical places for the fishermen. Try to maneuver through a weekend maze without catching either a fishing line or an anchor line. Consider it good training. On good days, you may even get some fish.

CHANGING TIDES

• Tide tables are wonderful collections of numbers. The expected times and heights of tides are predicted for a certain number of primary stations. Correcting figures are given for hundreds of secondary stations. You adjust the time for Daylight Savings when necessary, and the rest is simple math: add, subtract, or multiply for a percentage.

• Tide tables are probably as good as they can be, but don't be too surprised if they're not exactly right all the time.

• Some days, tides may be considerably lower than the prediction. Get into a habit of observing the water levels daily. Unless it's from wind influence, a drastic drop in water level doesn't happen overnight; usually, you can see it worsening daily.

• When passing through an area with iffy depths to begin with, be extra careful if it has been windy. A few days of strong wind can alter the expected tidal rise as well as the usual low-water level.

• Even in the tideless Great Lakes, a persistent wind can change the water level by 2 feet.

• Unusual barometric pressure can lower water even more.

• If you don't have an up-to-date tide table, listen to the NOAA weather on VHF radio; in some areas, tidal information for a few primary locations will be broadcast along with the forecasts. Local

TV stations in coastal cities also give tides with their weather report.

• If you watch carefully every day. you can make your own good estimate of what should happen when. Note when the water is still (slack) and when it starts to move, and which way.

• Naturally, the accuracy of this estimating depends on where you are; if you're traveling along the East Coast, it's fairly easy to see what's happening. If you meander inland for a while, then come back to the coast, your estimates may not be as reliable. Don't guess in areas where tides vary greatly, as in Puget Sound.

• Most locations on the East Coast have two high and two low tides every day, so something is changing roughly on a 6-hour schedule.

• Using tide tables alone to estimate times of maximum current flow is an exercise in frustration. Current does not just stop flowing when it reaches extreme high or low; it levels out for a while. One guess says tide rises or falls most (so it flows the fastest) in the third and fourth hours between high and low. Tidal current tables can help with current predictions, but if there is a river current on top of the tidal current, it's anybody's guess.

Odd Gotchas

• Boaters should report any lights-out, off-station buoys, shoaled-in channels—whatever is a problem for navigation. Radio the nearest Coast Guard station if it's an immediate problem; or write to the appropriate Coast Guard District with any general suggestions.

• Watch for signs along the shore that warn of underwater cables and pipelines, and obey the DO NOT ANCHOR notice.

• Get the latest chart you can buy, but

don't count on total accuracy. We've found a bridge on a new chart when the bridge itself had been gone for 10 years. No publisher can keep accurate charts without accurate depth information, and *nobody* can keep up with shifting sandbars. (That's why so many inlets are not even charted; the buoys are shifted as the bottom shifts.) Don't go full speed ahead into an anchorage, just because the chart says you should have 10 feet of water.

• When your charted travel line takes you through a charted Danger Zone, check your Coast Pilot to see why it's dangerous. You'll read about firing ranges, bombing target areas, rocket launching, or other unfriendly activities. But you would not be surprised by an unannounced practice attack: When such activities go on, you'll see flags or lights or patrol boats; you'd probably have heard about it on the VHF if you were paying attention. My favorite chart note refers to an entire river. It says, simply, "Closed to the public."

• While in-the-water snags are the most common gotcha, sailors in narrow creeks

must watch overhead, too. It's not often that a sailboat would be in such a confined place, but it does happen occasionally. We've heard of sailboats touching tree limbs in the Dismal Swamp, though the only personal experience we have was in a very narrow creek where a tree tie-up was the only way to moor.

• There may be times when you want to follow a side creek to find fuel or a mechanic, or just to explore. If your chart quits before you want to stop, try to call the Coast Guard, or a local marina or boater, to see if any bridges or power lines will be in your way.

• While the Coast Guard establishes vertical clearances for bridges, the Army Corps of Engineers sets the heights for power lines. The height of a utility line is based on the height of the tallest fixed bridges in the area. The more voltage a line carries, the higher the line will be set to prevent any arcing of power to an aluminum mast.

• If you're confused about a channel, or need help with an entrance, look for a local boat to give you some local knowledge. But, *follow* a local boat *only* if you know its draft matches or exceeds yours.

• Read a list of boat collision statistics, and you wonder how such accidents could happen. Night and fog are two big factors. Boats run into jetties, daymark platforms, docks, bridge supports, rocks and reefs, even seawalls and shore. Mistaken location, obviously, is the cause of such collisions, and simple inexperience, too often, is the reason for the mistaken location.

• Misguided "blind" faith in an autopilot is another example of an accident waiting to happen. Always, always, always maintain a lookout, lookout, lookout, to watch for the immovable objects *and* for other vessels.

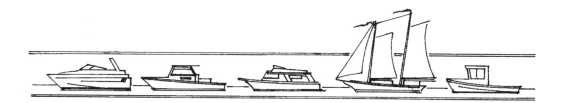

10

Touching Bottom

It's easy to put a boat aground. You miss the chart note about a spoil area. The wind sets you onto a shoal or rock. You read the chart upside down. Confusion about a mark is not resolved early enough; when the confusion is settled, so is the boat.

Luckily, most groundings damage only the crew's egos. If you're in a no-tide area, ungrounding can probably be done with the help of an anchor, a winch, and/or a friend. If grounding happens in the tidal zone when the tide is rising, the water will soon give you an assist. If, however, the tide is falling, your chances of floating anytime soon may also be on the way out; it may already be too late for speedy action.

NO TIDE

When you know there's no tide to come to your rescue, you should be more careful about how fast you go into strange places. If you go aground at idle speed, you have a good chance of backing off.

Engine Power

One of the most common grounding scenarios is the one that happens when you're feeling your way into an unmarked place—whether to anchor, or just to sightsee a side creek. Usually, you're moving slowly and your depthsounder or leadline is showing a gradual (or abrupt) shoaling; when you *do* ease into a mud bank or bump onto a sandy bottom, you can probably ease back out, using the engine to move backward on the same general course that brought you in. This is the only route you can be sure has adequate depth.

If you're more solidly planted, be cautious with the engine power. One school of thought says if you run the engine vigorously with the prop engaged, all that swirling

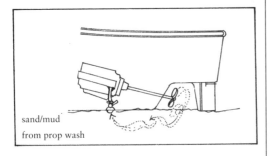

sand/mud
from prop wash

action will dig a hole to help you escape. The other opinion says all that silt will end up in your water intake, thence through your water pump, destroying the impeller and seals as it goes.

• If you went aground abruptly because you were traveling too speedily, try to check for damage to the propulsion or steering system, or to the hull itself, especially if you landed on rocks. Make sure the water intake is clear.

Anchor Power

If you're stuck beyond the prop's power to push, use the dinghy to take out an anchor. Set it in such a way that you can pull the boat toward the anchor, or "kedge off." When the boat floats free, it should swing away from the shoal (picture this as you're setting the anchor). In the interim, the anchor keeps the boat from being pushed farther onto the shoal by wind or wave action.

While you're out in the dinghy, check the water depth around the immediate area. Use a leadline, boathook, mop handle, or hand-held electronic depthsounder. If you find that only the forward section of the hull is touching bottom, you may be able to pull the bow off to one side till it falls off the shoal.

Use the dinghy to set an anchor, so waves can't push the boat farther onto the shoal and you can "kedge" off.

From dinghy, check water depth all around for all possible escape routes.

Shifting Weight

With any boat, weight-shifting some-times helps. To reduce draft at the stern, get all crew forward; or weigh down the tran-som to lift the bow.

• Sailors can try to reduce draft by var-ious heeling methods. *If* you went aground while motoring, and *if* the wind is coming from the *right* direction, you may be able to put up sails to heel the boat and sail off into deep water. Seldom are conditions so obliging, but there is more than one way to heel a boat.

• Swing the boom off to the side, and let the crew climb aboard. (Don't expect the topping lift to handle all the weight; tie the main halyard to the end of the boom.)

• If you're short-handed, hang the dinghy from the boom, and add whatever weight you can.

• Take an anchor out and set it on a 90-degree angle to the boat, roughly posi-tioned abeam of the mast. Attach the an-chor rode to the main halyard, so you can try to winch the boat into a heeling position as the masthead dips toward the anchor.

• People who know about cars stuck in snow try a familiar tactic when aground in a soft bottom: alternate forward and reverse, in an attempt to wiggle the keel off the shoal.

Special Circumstances

The basic how-to sug-gestions work for most full-keeled sailboats and for powerboats with displacement hulls and protected props, but any hull type can have peculiar problems.

• Planing powerboats with exposed props suffer the most damage from a grounding, particularly if they hit bottom at high speed. Often, sufficient damage has been done to prop and shaft that a com-mercial tow is required to bring the boat to a repair facility.

• Smaller powerboats with inboard/outboard propulsion may be able to sim-ply lift the lower unit, then pull themselves off (with the help of an anchor or another boat). If the lower unit is significantly damaged, then another worry has replaced the grounding problem.

• If you have a small trolling motor or a dinghy outboard, and the boat is not taking on water as a result of the ground-ing, you may be able to push yourself to a marina or yard.

• Smaller boats have one big advantage: you can *walk* your kedging anchor out.

• Sailboats with a full keel usually exit as they entered.

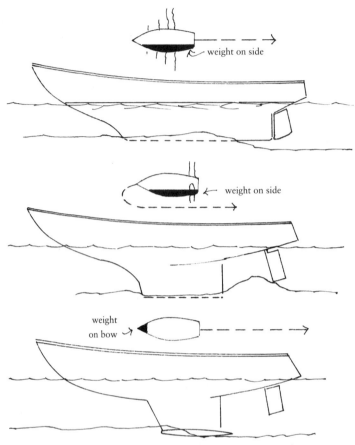

weight on side

weight on side

weight on bow

Shift weight on board to heel boat and reduce draft.

When you see other boats like yours, ask the owners how they deal with the problem; you'll be surprised by some of the strategies people invent. And some of them work.

The standard caution: try not to do anything that adds to the problem, or creates another.

RISING TIDE

If a tide check shows the water's coming in, all you need is patience. Waiting for more water is easiest on you and the boat.

• Sailboats with fin keels *may* be able to pull the bow off to the side, depending on how the keel is stuck. (Don't try to pull a fin keel off backward; you may damage the rudder.)

• Centerboards are easy, *if* you can get the board to move up.

• Owners complain that wing keels dig in like an anchor, especially into soft mud. Some try rocking back and forth and side to side, to break the suction.

It's obvious there are so many variables, each situation may require different un-grounding methods. Learn as much as you can about the underbody of your boat.

• Set out an anchor anyway, to keep you in place until the water re-floats you. Place the anchor upwind of the grounding site, so when water comes in and the boat refloats, the wind will cause the boat to swing away from the shoal and back into deeper water. (If there's no wind, position the anchor so current will push the boat the way you want it to go.)

• Once the anchor is set, make some coffee. Read a book. Watch the birds.

• If you have planted yourself *at* high tide, you may want to consider calling for a tow. Check the tide tables to see if the next high tide will bring more water rather than less (daily highs are not always the same height). Think about your location, too, and realize you'll be sitting on the bottom for a lot of hours.

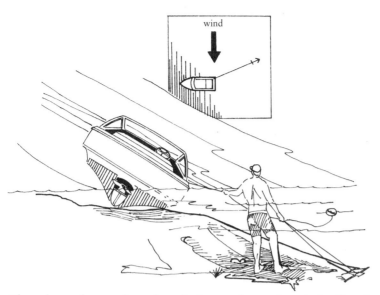

Place the anchor so that when the boat refloats, the wind will swing the boat into deeper water.

HELPERS

There is a popular harbor on the Chesapeake's Eastern Shore where the weekend entertainment frequently revolves around watching newcomers go aground on the one spot in the entire harbor that has not been dredged, is not marked, and is less than clear at ordinary chart scale. The good part, in our experience with the place, was that in addition to the bemused watchers were two who made an effort (successful) to help us off.

Tide was falling, and a couple inches of bottom paint were already exposed by the time our helpers arrived. With the dinghy on the boom and two men riding, the boat slid off the shoal, to the apparent disappointment of the gallery. Thanks once more to the gentlemen from Galesville with the character boat.

• If you see someone obviously aground, resist the temptation to "help" with such observations as "A lot of people miss that mark" or "Better hurry—tide's going out" or "You know, there's a shoal there."

• A small, lightweight boat cannot do much for a larger, heavier boat that is firmly planted, other than to carry out anchors.

• If you think you can pull a boat off, toss a connecting line to the stranded boat; use the weight of a monkey's fist to help throw the line, or do a dinghy-delivery. Rig a bridle arrangement for the pulling line, and try to divide the pulling strain on the grounded boat as well. Pull slowly and

Put a monkey's fist (a tight, round knot) into the end of a line. The weight helps carry the line to its mark.

steadily—no jerking, for the sake of hardware and lines—till the stranded boat comes off. If you're unsuccessful the first time, try tugging from a different angle. When the grounded boat starts to move, watch the towing line and any anchor lines so nobody gets hung up on either. (Before the grounded boat starts to move, the towing line may seem to shrink in diameter as it stretches to its limit. Crew should not stand close.)

• In one such pull-off effort in a narrow channel near Swansboro, North Carolina, we and a Gulf-Star 36 trawler spent a couple of hours taking turns grounding and assisting till the practice finally got too funny to continue. Luckily, the tide came to the rescue of both boats.

• Powerboat wakes are sometimes blamed for bouncing boats out of the channel, but such wakes are welcome when they can lift a boat free of a shoal.

FALLING TIDE

When the tide's already moving out, it's probably too late for ungrounding attempts. As the water recedes, the advisability of any towing assistance recedes with it. Trying to pull a boat off once it is firmly settled in could do more damage than the grounding, hardly a sensible alternative.

Bottom's Up

When the departing tide exposes first the waterline, then the bottom paint, admit defeat and move on to some practical use of your time. With up to 12 hours to kill, you might as well spend some of it on boat bottom maintenance.

• Scrub the bottom; check the prop; check the zinc; check the cutless bearing; check the through-hulls. Pretend you did this on purpose, just for this purpose. When the hull dries, you can even paint

the top couple feet of bottom, at least on one side. (Next time, tilt the other way.)

Peripheral Problems

As the boat settles further on its side, you might have problems other than the cat being unable to walk properly, or leap from seat to seat.

• Listen for the sound of trickling water, and if you hear it, check the sink drain on the "down" side. With the boat hull in its present position, water may be streaming into the drain rather than the other way around. This will not help you get off the bottom. Water is heavy. Foil the trickle by closing the seacock.

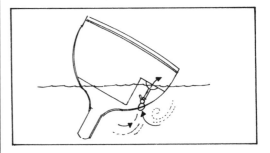

• When the handle of the seacock breaks, ignore it; find the wood plugs you should carry for emergency through-hull plugging.

• If you're doubly unlucky and have gone aground in a fog, you should send the same sound signals as an anchored boat. (If over 12 meters, ring a bell rapidly for 5 seconds at 1-minute intervals, and sound three distinct bells before and after the rapid ringing. If under 12 meters, make some noise every 2 minutes.)

• An exception to the rule about finding deep water by following the reciprocal course of your entry: If you're aground because the water simply flowed out from under you, there *is* no deep water to backtrack into. We learned this the hard way one day, sailing into a place where we'd anchored at least a dozen times before, always with plenty of water. This was a day of extreme low water. As we watched the depthsounder's numbers decreasing steadily in what we knew to be a large area of consistent depth, we were confused, wondering how we could be in the wrong place. We turned toward safe water—we thought—only to settle onto the sand a few minutes later. In fact, there was no safe water for us till the tide changed many hours later. Good part: that was truly an exception.

- In order to be ready when the water returns, you need to know when that will happen. Dangle a line into the water so you can watch the direction of current flow. Watch as the water goes out; watch as it goes slack; watch as it turns around and starts to come in. Cheer.

- Once the tide has turned, can freedom be far behind? Make a plan for anchor retrieval and course return, and make sure everyone knows their part of the plan. As soon as the boat starts rocking again, pull on the anchor line to kedge yourself back into deep water.

DAMAGE CONTROL

- When you're floating free again, check the engine's water strainer to see that it's clear, and check the water pump to be sure seals and impeller are okay. Watch the temperature and the exhaust water for a while.

- Too much engine-revving in reverse could damage the cutless bearing; with so much silt in the water, some of it might be forced into the shaft tube.

- Whenever you've gone aground, especially if it was more than a gentle touchdown, try to look at the boat-bottom as soon as possible, whether by diving or haulout.

- If you feel any strange vibration, or hear unusual noises; if a bulkhead is squeaking or water seeps in from an unknown opening; if anything odd is noticeable, have the boat hauled and checked out by a competent surveyor.

- All these suggestions assume the grounding has not done any immediate, obvious damage to the boat. If you have hit a rock or other underwater structure that has put a hole in the hull, then you have a bigger problem to address. Use whatever you can to block water from entering: cushions or mattress pad, stuffed from the inside; a canvas "patch" on the outside, tied around the entire hull, if necessary, to hold it tight. Then call for a tow to the nearest yard. Naturally, if steering or props are damaged to the point where control is marginal, you'll need to be towed to a haulout facility for repairs.

ATTITUDE IS EVERYTHING

Perfect people never go aground, and caution will keep you afloat. But we must share the thought expressed by our favorite Mississippi tugboat captain: "If you ain't been aground, you ain't been nowhere."

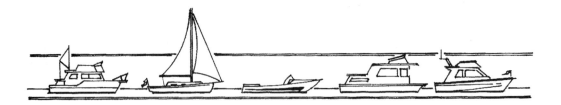

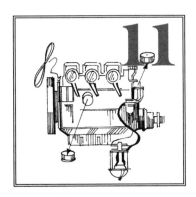

11 Shooting Trouble

Guidebooks for car travelers don't discourage readers with a bunch of trouble-shooting tips, but somehow a boat book seems incomplete without including a few suggestions for dealing with common problems. Not because boat engines are inherently inferior—after all, many of them are "marinized" versions of automotive or industrial engines—but because they have special obstacles to overcome.

It's easy to blame the environment—not the green one, but the engineroom one. A small, enclosed, usually damp space is not friendly to an engine, especially a gasoline engine. Diesels may not share the same level of sensitivity to moisture, but they still find ways to show incompatibility with their surroundings.

When a car engine breaks down along the roadway, most drivers open the hood and wait for help, perhaps speeding the process with a call to a tow truck via CB radio or cellular phone; the problem is thus turned over to somebody else. When a boat engine breaks down along a waterway, the boater, too, can often use the calling and towing option, but this can be very costly and many boatmen choose not to do so, at least not until it becomes a last-resort tactic. These captains would rather help themselves, so most consider engine care and minor repairs as part of the boating experience, if not quite part of boating fun.

FUEL TO GO

Even if your idea of good cruising means never having to tie up to a dock, you must allow the exceptions whenever you need fuel. (Unless you are that rarest of cruisers, the auxiliary-less sailboat, and then you can skip this entire chapter.) For most boats, the fuel dock—anybody's fuel dock—is the most familiar tie-up of all.

Gas Facts

When lead was removed from gasoline for emission control, other additives were put in to restore octane. The gasoline you buy might contain up to 10 percent alcohol. At one time, methanol was also used, but now the second additive of choice is an ether known by its initials: MTBE.

A bit of alcohol in gas was once considered good: it mixes with the water that may be in the tank from condensation, and is then burned off in ordinary combustion, ridding the tank of the water. But too much alcohol in gas is *not* good; it causes excess carbon buildup, and it can weaken hoses. Since premium-grade gasoline has the most additives, it will cause the most carbon. Avoid premium, and buy a mid-range octane—around 89—for the best compromise.

• To help prevent carbon buildup, put your own additives into the gas. Also look for one that prevents gummy gas, especially during the time when you may not be using the boat regularly.

• Fueling cautions are most important for owners of gas engines, for the obvious reason: gasoline is the most volatile fuel, including the gas vapors. You want to keep fumes out of the boat, and prevent any kind of spark.

• When you come to the dock to take on gas, turn off lights, radio, fan—anything that could create a spark. Turn off the galley stove. Close all the ports and hatches and doors; be sure the tank vents are clear. *Don't smoke.*

• During fueling, be sure the hose nozzle is in contact with the fill fitting so there's no chance of a static spark.

• Carry the extra cans off the boat to fill them, so there's no chance for gas to spill and find its way to the bilge.

• When the tanks are full: completely close all fill caps; wipe up any spills; air out the boat; run the blower for 4 or 5 minutes, and then sniff for fumes, especially at the vents, before you start the engine.

Diesel Quirks

The most significant caution regarding diesel fuel is to keep it clean. Most marinas that dispense a lot of diesel don't have dirty fuel, but use a filter funnel for insurance. (Some people add the fine mesh of nylon stockings or cheesecloth inside the standard funnel.)

Keep the spare fuel cans clean, too: don't carry one batch for any length of time. Whenever you fill up, empty the spare fuel into the tank, and refill the can with fresh fuel.

From time to time, take a sample of fuel from your tank to check for any visible contamination. If there's no drain valve, pump out a sample with the oil-changing pump.

• For a time, commercial and recreational boats used different kinds of diesel. The fuel sold to pleasure boaters was low sulfur; it produced less emissions, but it had some disadvantages, too. It was more likely to thicken, or gel, and also it did not provide proper lubrication to injectors and other fuel system components. If this regulation is reinstated, look for additives: one for the lubrication, one to prevent gelling.

• Bacteria can grow in diesel fuel, so foil them with a biocide additive (Biobor is one). Put it in as you fill the tanks, not after.

Fill-up Hints

• Estimate how much fuel you will take on, so you can guard against an overfill. Leave some room in the tank.

- Ask if the pump is a fast-fill (high-pressure) pump, which may be hard to control. Count the gallons going in, so you won't be surprised by a geyser of an overflow.

- For a day on the water, plan to use a third of your fuel each way; then you'll have a third left for the variables of contrary wind, waves, or current.

- Without being obsessive about it, try to keep the fuel tanks topped off regularly; less vacant space means less opportunity for condensation in the tank.

- If you stay in one place for a long time, check the condition of your fuel before starting out again. If it looks dirty or feels thick, add some Sludge and Slime (or comparable product to break up the dirt). Better yet, get rid of the old, dirty fuel by pumping out the tank. When it's empty, pour in some clean fuel and pump that out again, to get rid of as much residual debris as possible. Do it until you feel confident that fuel coming out is as clean as fuel going in, then fill up for your trip. (Before you start this project, check with the marina or yard to find out how to dispose of the dirty fuel. Or ask the yard to do the messy job for you.)

- Check fuel lines and fittings regularly. Change rusted hose-clamps, and if any fuel lines feel soft or develop bulges near the clamps, change them before they fail.

HAPPY INBOARDS

Whatever kind of engine you have, basic checks will be the same. While a few people have uncanny luck with ignoring all engine maintenance, they are most definitely a minority. Most cruising captains establish a daily lookabout—it soon becomes such a familiar habit that anything out of the ordinary practically announces itself.

Before you start the engine, check the levels of assorted fluids: fuel, engine oil, battery water, engine coolant. Test the tension on the alternator belt, and see that all hoses are well attached. Check leak sites for any signs of fuel, oil, or water leaks.

After you start the engine and from time to time during a day of running, watch the amount of water coming from the exhaust, and check everything for leaks again. Do a general look-and-listen; sometimes, a sniff in time may detect a problem while it's still small.

An oil-absorbing pad placed in the oil pan provides an excellent background for detecting leaks.

Fuel Filters

Each engine has its own fuel filter, and each manual will explain how to change it and at what approximate engine-hour intervals. Partly, the timing between filter changes will depend on the quality of fuel you're getting.

On a diesel engine, it's a good idea to fill the new filter with clean diesel before putting it on; you'll have less priming to do. Keep a gallon of diesel handy for this purpose, and replace it regularly, just as you do the fuel in the spare diesel cans, so it cannot get stale.

Oil Filters and Oil Changes

Again, read the engine manual for change recommendations—though changing the filter with every other oil change couldn't hurt.

- Look in an automotive parts store; you may find appropriate filters at a lower price. This is one case where an automotive part can be used without concern about the effects of the "marine environment." An oil filter won't be on the engine long enough to suffer.

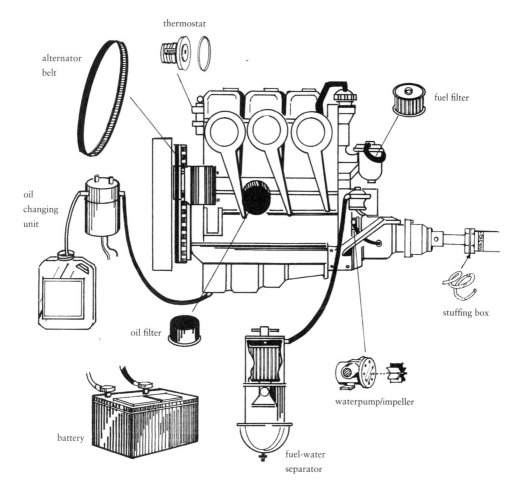

thermostat

alternator
belt

fuel filter

oil
changing
unit

stuffing box

oil filter

battery

waterpump/impeller

fuel-water
separator

Things to check.

• When changing the filter, try putting a plastic bag around it; as you turn the filter to remove it, it's already inside the bag, so spillage is kept to a minimum.

• To change oil, run the engine for about 15 minutes to warm the oil (it will be easier to pump out). Make your oil-changing system as easy as you can, so you won't continually postpone a nasty chore; it's important that you do it regularly. Least messy is the kind of unit that will take oil from the bottom of the sump, rather than pump out the top.

• Carry spare oil, so you always use the same kind; engines do not like new products.

• Use oil-absorbing pads to catch the messes.

• Take a sample of your used engine oil and have it analyzed (MDR sells a kit). An early diagnosis may prevent a premature breakdown.

• Additives are made for engine oil, too; a lot of people like an old standby, Marvel Mystery Oil, which also works for other problems like valves and carburetor needles made sticky by gummy gas.

Transmission Care

Transmissions require very little maintenance: Keep them clean and check for leaks. Watch the level of transmission oil. Normally, you won't need to add any; if the level is down, look for signs of a leak.

Change the oil at least once a year, and be very careful not to overfill, as this may *cause* a leak.

Fuel/Water Separator

If you don't already have a fuel/water separator installed, do it now. Look for one that makes it easy to change the filter. (Some require three hands and a lot of nasty language.) Racor is a popular brand; you can *see* water and sediment in the collecting bowl, so look often, and drain it as often as necessary. An accumulation of dirt will restrict fuel flow, so change the filter element before it clogs.

If you see a lot of water separating into the filter, it may indicate that you forgot to put the anti-condensation additive into the tank. Do so with the next fill-up.

Engine Zincs

If you haven't already read your engine manual cover to cover 15 times looking for solutions to whatever, read it now, specifically to find out where the engine zincs are, so you can check their condition. Consider why they're called "sacrificial zincs," and you'll realize why it's so important to look at them occasionally. Their function is to catch the galvanic and electrolytic action before it gets to the engine's metal.

Replace an engine zinc when it starts to look porous, or when it has shrunk to about half its original size. When putting in the new zinc, don't use any kind of sealant; you want the metal-to-metal contact.

Belt Care

If a water pump belt fails, the subsequent overheating can wreck the engine. If the alternator belt fails, you'll have no electrical power. Watch belt edges for signs of fuzzing or cracking; replace them if you see any indication of wear.

• The alternator belt should be tensioned so the center of the belt can be depressed ¼ to ½ inch (or whatever your engine manual recommends).

• After a few hours of running with a new belt, you may need to adjust tension again.

• If the belt develops a squeak, try a spritz with some WD-40. If the noise persists, get a new belt.

• If a belt goes, and you don't have the spares you should, try pantyhose. (Of course, you'll have them on board.)

Diesel Only

Diesel owners quickly learn the meaning of "bleeding" the engine, though "venting" is a kinder, gentler term. Whenever air gets where it should not, you must bleed/vent the engine.

This happens when you change the fuel filter, when you've worked on the fuel lines, or when you run out of fuel. The general procedure is the same for all engines: Open venting plugs; pump fuel through until clear, bubble-free fuel is flowing; then close the venting plugs.

• A diesel engine does not have to be tuned up as often as a gas engine, nor is the tune-up done the same way; but valve settings can be checked, and injectors should be pressure-checked.

• Watch for any signs of corrosion, or leaks, or deterioration of gaskets.

• Along with clean fuel, marine diesels want lots of clean air. To clean air filters:

remove each filter, and clean it with diesel fuel; blow it clean with compressed air; soak it in thin engine oil.

- The inflatable dinghy's air pump will provide a marginal substitute, but if you can get to a shoreside gas station, use the tire pump to clean the air filters.

Gas Only

Gas engines like to be clean and dry. One's fairly easy, the other's impossible. Clean the engine often; spray it daily with a moisture displacer. And keep a good inventory of those parts that are most prone to failure due to dampness.

Like your car's engine, marine gasoline engines should be tuned at regular intervals to keep them running at their best.

Maintenance Miscellany

- Install a decent light in the engineroom, preferably something movable like a clamp-on, so you can attach and direct light wherever you need it.

- When you add items to the engineroom (fuel/water separator, bilge pump, box for spare oil and coolant), keep everything reachable in order of importance.

- A vent or fan to move air around is helpful while you're working in the confines of a hot, smelly engineroom.

- Label things others might need to find (switches, wiring, hoses); use colored tape or stickers—whatever works.

- Paint the engineroom white. The light will be better (more of it will be bouncing around), and you can readily see leak indicators, whether they be dirty oil spots or rusty water stains.

HAPPY OUTBOARDS

In order to comply with air-pollution regulations, outboard motors are in the process of an industry-wide redesign (except for some four-stroke Hondas, which have been minimal polluters for some time). The reason for the regulating is that older, two-stroke outboards did not burn gas efficiently, sending out too much unburned gas in the exhaust. But the older models with their older maintenance problems will still be around for some years to come.

- If you won't be using the motor for a month or more, use a fuel stabilizer (Sta-Bil is a standard) so you don't end up with a gooey carburetor.

- Don't leave the outboard attached when you're towing the dinghy; you'll just have more to clean. Hoist it aboard with a simple strapping arrangement (ours is made of lightweight nylon webbing).

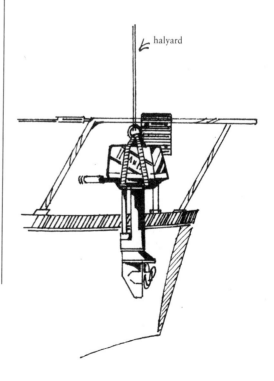

halyard

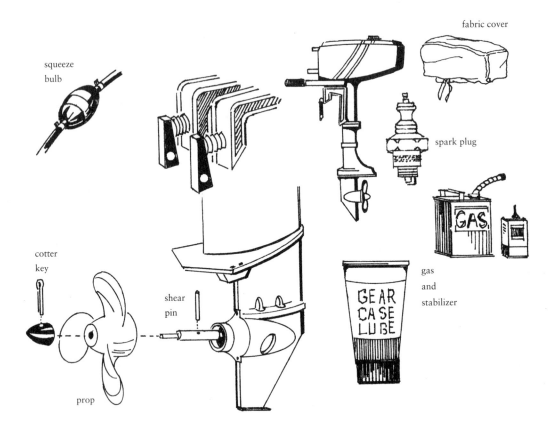

squeeze
bulb

fabric cover

spark plug

cotter
key

shear
pin

gas
and
stabilizer

GEAR
CASE
LUBE

prop

- Keep the gas tanks and the gas clean.

- Keep plenty of the outboard's favorite oil on board, so you always use the same brand.

- Check periodically to be sure the outboard is spitting out exhaust water so it can keep its cool.

- Lubricate the lower unit twice a year.

- Give the outboard a freshwater rinse now and then. Run a small outboard in a bucket of water; get a flushing kit to attach a hose to a larger motor.

- To carry the outboard safely, clamp it onto the stern rail with a small bracket. A teak block on deck saves the deck surface. A fabric cover shields the motor from constant UV and spray; use the same material as the boat's Bimini top or sail cover.

TROUBLESHOOTING

After you've been sitting in one spot for a long time, the first troubleshoot is to see how much stuff has attached itself to the bottom of your boat. A lot of growth on the hull and prop—whether grass, barnacles, or other marine junk—will have a marked effect on RPM and speed.

If you're lucky enough to be cruising where you can actually see something when underwater, grab your snorkel and mask (and wetsuit or drysuit, where necessary) and go for a swim. Check the bottom and prop for growth; check the zinc for disappearance; and wiggle the shaft to see if the cutless bearing is doing its job and preventing most of the wiggle.

If you're not a snorkeler, you can hire a scuba diver.

Engine Trouble

One of the better ideas we've heard is a plan-ahead: find and hire a qualified mechanic who will walk you through the common trouble spots and show you what to do. There's no comparison between watching a hands-on demonstration on your own engine and reading general instructions in a book.

Some engine manufacturers prepare videos showing the required maintenance for specific models. Your private demo will go further into repair work as well.

It's also possible to go to engine school, whether it's a complete course at the local community college, or a simpler manufacturer's weekend seminar. Either will be beneficial as you gain familiarity with the beast.

Though gasoline and diesel engines function in different ways, they share many common problems, so troubleshooting strategies will often be the same.

No Start

If the engine will not start, maybe there's an easy explanation: see if the battery switch is turned on; check for loose or corroded battery cables. Check the fuel gauge or tank; check the fuel shutoff; look for blockage in the lines.

Temperature's Rising

Though longtime cruisers scoff at the concept of raw-water cooling (are they *still* doing that?), it is really not such a rarity. The simpler system, it draws water from lake/river/ocean, sends it through cooling passages in the engine, then dumps the hot water overboard, usually combined with exhaust gases, out the exhaust pipe.

Its disadvantages: passages will clog up eventually with salt and other deposits carried by the water. Salt water starts to crystallize at just over 160 degrees, so the engine must be run cooler, which is less efficient, at least for a diesel. With salt water flowing through engine metal, there's more possibility of galvanic corrosion.

The other temperature-control system is called either a heat exchanger, or freshwater cooling. With this self-contained system, water is mixed with a commercial coolant, and the same mixture circulates through the engine over and over. After a trip through the cooling passages to control engine temperature, the coolant water is hot; it must be re-cooled by going through the "heat exchanger" (out with the hot) before going back to the cooling passages to do its job again.

Raw water cools the engine coolant and is discharged overboard. Advantages: The water passing through the engine is always free of contaminants; many people use distilled water so there's no possibility of mineral deposits. With no worry about salt, the engine can run hotter, more efficiently.

Freshwater cooling systems have their share of breakdowns, too, though most owners rightfully point out it is easier to replace a cooling system than an entire engine. Use the proper mix of water and antifreeze (or whatever combination of water and protective additives you choose to use).

• If the engine overheats, you have a long list of possibilities to check out. For starters:

Blocked water intake

Bad water pump/impeller/hose

Defective thermostat

Broken or loose belt to water pump

Fouled prop

Low oil level

Clogged engine passages

Clogged heat exchanger

• When you first start a marine engine, always make sure plenty of water is being discharged with the exhaust.

- To see if the thermostat is working, remove it and drop it into hot water. If you can watch it open up when water is hot, then close down again later as the water cools, you know it's working.

- Besides spare parts for the raw-water pump (impeller and seals), take along a whole spare water pump. If you have a problem, put on the new one, and you're ready to go quickly. Later, when you have the time, fix the original as a spare, and get more parts.

- The engine coolant pump must generally be replaced as a complete unit.

- If you don't already have a strainer on the water-intake line, put one in. It consists of a metal mesh tube inside the filter housing; you can remove it to clean out the grass, algae, cigarette butts, whatever.

- Sometimes, in some places (Dismal Swamp, Okeechobee Waterway, Kissimmee River, inlets of Puget Sound), the water is covered with algae: light green stuff floating on the surface. Though it seems to be on the surface only, some inevitably gets into the strainer, and can sneak through the mesh to clog up the thermostat or worse. Always clean out the strainer right after you've gone through such an area.

Oil Pressure's Falling

If oil pressure shows low, turn off the engine and try to trace the cause. It could be something fairly simple, like somebody put in the wrong grade of oil, or easier yet, you just need to "fill 'er up." Other possibilities within the realm of self-help: engine overheating or a stuck pressure-relief valve.

An oil leak sends the same shut-down signal. You may not be able to fix it, but try to slow the leak by whatever temporary patch method works. Run the engine slowly, replacing the amount of oil that continues to leak; you may be able to take yourself to a dock for a more thorough investigation and repair.

Oil Level's Rising

If the pre-start oil check shows oil level higher than it should be, chances are the oil doesn't look oily anymore. Look closely at the oil on the dipstick. If its color is an opaque, milky gray and its consistency is closer to glue than oil, you have a case of water-in-the-oil, a messy and potentially damaging problem.

Don't start the engine. Prepare for a lengthy cleanup session. Use your oil-changing kit to pump the goo into containers for disposal. Pour clean diesel fuel into the oil-fill; then pump it back out, to help clean out the gray oil. Do this as many times as it takes, till the outcoming diesel fuel is clear. Then refill with real engine oil, and start the engine. (Change the oil a couple more times soon, to be sure the consistency—viscosity—returns to normal.)

How did the water get there? If you're in a sailboat, water can come into the exhaust system with a following sea, if the standpipe doesn't have a high enough loop to prevent such a backflow. In any boat, it can be caused by a bad head gasket.

- To prevent a water backup through the exhaust: Put an anti-siphon valve into the exhaust line in front of the place where the cooling water flows into exhaust manifold. Place it on the centerline, and as high as possible. If you already have a valve, check it often to see that it's open and not clogged with salt or scale.

Shifting Problems

A shifting system does not usually break down all of a sudden; it has probably given you warning for a long time, with a harder-to-move shifting lever, or a longer-than-normal pause before the transmission engages. Don't ignore these signals on the hope-they-go-away theory. Transmission problems create the frustrating scenario of the person at the helm shouting directions to a crewmember who is balanced precariously over the engine, manually switching gears, *if* commands are heard over engine noise. The only good part is that such heroic acrobatics do work, in an emergency situation.

To brake or not to brake? Only your transmission manufacturer knows for sure. When a boat is sailing or being towed, should the prop be allowed to turn, or should the shaft be stopped? Opinions go both ways. Some people think a free-wheeling shaft causes excess wear on the transmission and the cutless bearing. If you choose to brake a manual transmission, you can stop the turning by setting the shift lever to reverse. (This does not work with hydraulic transmissions, since you cannot shift when the engine's off.)

Stuffing Problems

A stuffing box is one of those check-daily things, since excess water inside the boat makes it sink. Despite its importance, many people are only vaguely aware of its function, which is basically to keep most of the water out, while letting a small, controlled amount in.

The propeller shaft fits inside a stern tube to exit the boat; the place where the stern tube fits through the hull needs to be practically waterproof, and this is what the stuffing box does. The box is really a cylinder that sits around the shaft, "stuffed" at the boat end with a flax packing material. The finishing fastener is a large nut that can be tightened against the packing, to seal the assembly against a steady water flow.

A small amount of water, however, should get through; a few drops a minute (when the shaft is not turning) keeps the shaft lubricated so it can turn freely.

Gas Engines

• When a gasoline engine won't start, or quits almost immediately, first check the carburetor, where gas and air are mixing in perfect burning proportion. If you smell gas, you've probably left the choke out too long, and the carburetor is flooded. Wait a few minutes and try again. If the mix is heavy on gas, the engine will smoke a lot just before it quits again (a gas-heavy mix is called "rich"). If the mix has too much air, the engine will sputter and gasp before it quits.

• If you decide the gas parts are okay, your other choice is electrical, which most people assume is the problem in the first place. Check spark plugs for a carbon loadup; clean them, replace, and try again.

• Eventually, your search brings you to the distributor (unless your motor has modern solid-state ignition), every mechanic's best friend: all those little parts, each waiting to malfunction just because of a little dampness. If the engine knocks, stalls, misses, or generally acts cranky, blame it on the points (or the timing). If it's extra hard starting, then misses and dies, blame the distributor cap.

• Keep the ignition system as dry as possible. Spritz often with a moisture displacer. Bring lots of spares.

For Diesels Only

• If the engine won't start, and you've already checked the battery/fuel tank/fuel lines, see if any air has gotten into the system. Hope it's not a bad injector.

• If the engine starts to drag down or run rough, it could be caused by bad fuel or blocked lines, or a dirty air filter. You may have wrapped something around a prop blade—and, of course, it could be the bad injector possibility you're trying to ignore.

• If the engine stops after only a few seconds of sputtering warning, you may have a blocked fuel line (the old bad injector), dirty air filter, dirty fuel, or *no* fuel. Try not to run out of fuel; not only is it embarrassing, but the engine may have pulled sediment from the bottom of the tank in its frantic search for fuel, and now you'll have a cleanout problem.

• When you do run out of fuel, air gets into the fuel lines and you must "bleed" the engine—get rid of all the trapped air—before it will work properly again. Engine manuals give specifics; you must open vents along the fuel system, hand pump fuel till no more bubbles are visible, then close the vents.

• Alternative to bleeding: spray WD-40 into the air intake as you start the engine, and continue spraying until the real fuel takes over. (Usually, the engine will run on the WD-40 until it picks up diesel fuel.)

• Exhaust smoke helps diagnose problems. Black smoke suggests improper combustion; the engine cannot burn all the fuel it's getting, so some of it goes out as un-burned carbon. The cause might be a faulty fuel pump, a restricted air filter, or an overload brought on by a dirty bottom, a failed prop, or excessive auxiliary equipment.

Blue smoke comes from the burning of engine oil. The engine may have been run at low or idle too much; it doesn't get hot enough to work properly.

White smoke could be unburned fuel, or water vapor in the exhaust, which could be from dirty fuel or a bad head gasket. And don't forget the possibility of a bad injector.

Catch-All

• A sickly engine can cause some roughness, but a hull-shaking vibration probably means a badly damaged or fouled propeller. You don't have to hit something to wreck a prop; wrapping something (like polypropylene line) does a good job, too. See Chapter 9 for suggestions on how to clear a fouled propeller.

• If the engine quits while you're running down a narrow channel, drift off to anchor as far to the side as possible.

Be prepared to drop an anchor quickly from bow or stern.

- Replace idiot lights with real gauges, so you can see when a change starts to happen, rather than hear an alarm after the damage is done.

- If you can't get the engine started again, see if you can get to a marina; you may be able to use the dinghy to push yourself there. (Of course, if you can sail there, so much the better.)

- If you're motorsailing and heeling a lot, straighten up the boat occasionally so the engine stays properly lubricated.

- If you forgot to restock the supply of spare hose clamps, and you need one, take some wire and twist it like the grocery store's twist-tie for a temporary fix.

- Keep a complete record of fuel purchase and usage; running hours; engine maintenance (products used, dates work was done); all repairs (what was done, by whom, and how much it cost).

OUTBOARD TROUBLE

- If it won't start, look for the easy solutions. Be sure it's in neutral, or "start" position. See if the safety lanyard is correctly attached to the kill switch. Check gas-feeding components: tank, hoses, connections, squeeze bulb.

- If it starts, then quits, it could be any of the above gas-feed items, or dirty gas or the vent plug on top of the tank is closed. Dirty spark plugs (or the wrong kind) will also cause a stall.

- Choke will do the same thing to an outboard that it does to the big engine. Use a rich gas-air mix to start, then stop choke quickly. Too much choke will flood it; wait awhile and start again.

- If choke doesn't help to start it, see if the spark plugs are excessively dirty, or if the wires are attached well.

- If you forgot to put oil in the gas (or didn't put in the right amount), you could damage the engine; bearings and piston walls will have no lubrication. If you add too much oil, you'll have fouled the spark plugs—more smoke. (Don't add oil to gas for four-stroke motors.)

- If the motor smells hot or vibrates more than usual, check to see if any weeds are wrapped around the prop, or stuck in the water intake.

- If you bumped bottom and the motor starts to vibrate, check the prop—you probably dinged it.

- A more severe bumping will break the sacrificial shear pin, which is why you carry so many spares.

MORE THINGS TO WATCH

- If you're planning a long cruise, think about how much electrical power you'll need. You may have added electronics or refrigeration; even with the same items on board, full-time usage will require more frequent recharging.

- Add power through a higher-output alternator, solar panels, or wind generator; or, use a separate, 110-volt generator motor.

- Use only distilled water in the batteries, if they're the fill-up kind.

- Check battery cells with a hydrometer. All cell readings should be about equal. If one is especially low, you probably need a new battery. If all cells are low, charge the battery and check it again.

- Clean the battery posts with a baking soda solution and coat them with petroleum jelly or other appropriate anti-corrosive.

- Keep batteries confined in a box so they can't slide around or fall over. But don't encase them completely in a sealed box; the cover should allow air circulation.

- Don't discharge a battery beyond half its capacity; once it gets too far down, it may not recharge.

- Watch for and replace any wiring that is nicked, scraped, chafed, or flattened by a melted spot on the coating. Then look for whatever caused all of the above.

- You or a diver should check the underwater zinc frequently, especially if you've had any problem with a quickly eroding zinc. A stray current we never did identify took bite-size chunks out of a bronze through-hull fitting—and it happened in the short time span of a couple of weeks.

- For extra protection in marinas, where stray currents are a concern, some people like to use "guppies"—free-hanging zincs that clip onto some part of the boat's bonding system and hang overboard as additional sacrificial metal.

- Keep seacocks sprayed with anti-stick stuff. Close and reopen them occasionally to make sure they are working smoothly.

- Look into the bilge everyday and pump it as necessary. Keep an oil-absorbing cylinder in the bilge, so no oil can discharge into the water. It is illegal to discharge oily bilgewater.

- Make sure bilge pump, hoses, and clamps are all good; you may need them in a hurry someday, and one bad part makes them all useless.

- A diver can also save you a haulout fee by changing a prop, if equipped with a prop puller. On a smaller boat, the job can be done with pliers and breath-holding, though it's not recommended.

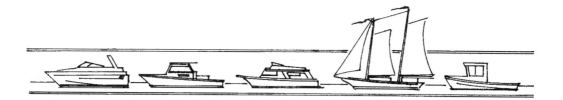

Tying Docklines

Have you ever been to a watermen's festival, where the pros in their workboats play water games for prizes? They usually have some ordinary racing regattas, but one of the highlights is the docking contest. Besides handling their boats as easily as we might handle a wagon, these watermen have an uncanny understanding of wind and tide, knowing how to make each work to their advantage. Such contests are won by seconds—too fast for ordinary folks to try to copy.

The recreational boater who rams the dock or misses it entirely should not feel bad. It takes years of practice to be a perfect docker—and even then it doesn't always work.

BOAT SWING

Your boat has either a right-turning prop or a left-turning prop (or one of each if it has two engines). It would be most convenient if you could choose which turn you wanted on a given day, but that's not the way props work; the boat is set up with one or the other, and owners must learn to deal with it.

Prop-turning direction naturally makes a difference in how the boat maneuvers, especially in reverse. You have probably

If prop turns counterclockwise when going forward, it is "left-handed."

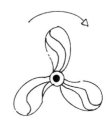

If prop turns clockwise when going forward, it is "right-handed."

pulled in and out of your home port slip and fuel dock often enough to be aware of your boat's prop-swerve habits. You also know too well that single-engine boats do not necessarily back in a straight line, and that no boat sits quietly in place when wind or current wants it to move.

SIDE DOCKING

The best way to learn how your boat handles in docking situations is to go out and practice. Don't use a crowded dock for your first efforts; look for a well-fendered, empty one, or start farther out in the water with a buoy. Approach it from different directions, when wind and current are together and again when they're opposed. You'll learn to judge how much power you need to keep control against current, how much space it takes to come to a stop, how reversing the prop affects your position—all in varying conditions.

Backing practice is even more fun. Try to ignore the laughing and pointing as you go 'round in frustrating circles; stick with it till you feel your action at the wheel actually has some effect on the direction the boat moves.

Line Toss

"Throw me a line" sounds deceptively easy. The problems: the line is too light and doesn't have the weight to carry it the distance. The line is too heavy and you don't have the strength to fling it far enough. The line is a perfect weight, but the wind's very much against you. Or, you just don't know how to toss a line properly.

Before you get near the dock, coil the line neatly in your non-throwing hand (don't let it fall into figure eights—that's a tangle in the making). When you're close to the dock, take enough coils in your throwing hand to give you some weight, and fling them to the dock person. More

loops should follow from the holding hand, so it's safest to tie the end of the line onto the boat before you start pitching practice.

Line Handler's Job

If there's nobody on the dock to take a line, the crew should move to the beamiest part of the boat, holding a bow line and a stern line (or a stern line and a spring line—whichever two work best with your docking plan). Crew should be able to take the two lines, step off the boat, and attach both lines quickly to bollards or cleats in a temporary tie-up. Once the boat is settled down, other lines can be added and all of them adjusted.

(Our normal tie-up uses the stern line and the spring line that attaches to the forward cleat and leads back on the dock. With these two, the boat is usually easy to control.)

• When stepping off the boat for a starboard-side tie-up, hold the bow line (or bow spring) in your right hand, and the stern line in your left. Once you're on the dock, the lines are in the appropriate hands for fast attaching. (Port-side tie-up, do the reverse.)

Helm Maneuvers

Meanwhile, the person at the helm may be juggling forward momentum, contrary current, and beam wind. The plan is to bring the boat in at an angle, then line up with the dock just before stopping. The trick is to determine the exact right time to shift into reverse.

If you're not parallel to the dock yet, that last burst of power can kick the stern out just when you need for it to go in. It's not an easy call, and practice with your own boat is the only way to get the basis for judgment.

Once you learn to dock the boat well, you've made a giant stride in good boat-handling. Stop is much more difficult than go.

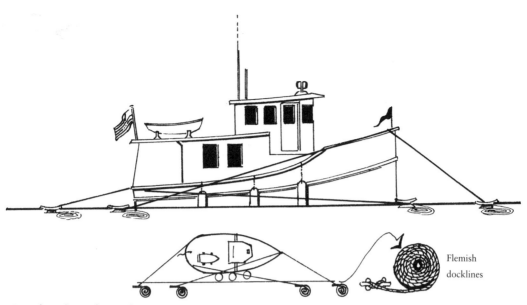

Use four lines for ordinary dockside tieup: bowline, sternline, and two spring lines.

Flemish
docklines

Side Tie

People who teach boating skills may remember the official names of various docklines (each named according to a very specific use, not just because it's a line tying a boat to a dock), but most boaters do fine with the knowledge that four lines can do the job nicely: a bow line, a stern line, and two spring lines. It's quite obvious what the first two do, and a spring line by any name would still be used to (1) prevent the boat from moving forward, or (2) prevent the boat from moving backward.

Docking Helps

• In tidal areas with a lot of fluctuation in water level, look for floating docks. Failing that, you'll have to allow for the changing water level.

• If you dock at high tide, leave enough slack in lines to allow for the fall. Tie them tighter if you dock at low tide; they'll slack as the water rises. This is trial and error at first; it's always best if you can stay on board through one tide change so you can adjust lines if need be.

• Longer spring lines help to adjust for tidal changes.

• Flemish the ends of your lines on the dock, for safety (less chance of a trip-up) and for neatness: Make a tiny circle with the end of the line lying flat on the dock, then turn the line in ever-widening circles; the finished flemish looks like a round mat.

• When coming to a dock, be sure all lines are outside pulpits, stanchions, and shrouds.

• You'll have the most control when docking if you approach against the wind or current (whichever is strongest).

• Coast along a vacant dock sometime going *with* the current, just to see how it would affect a docking attempt.

• If somebody on the dock takes a bow line, ask them *not* to pull the bow in toward the dock; it puts the boat into a bow-in angle, and destroys the parallel docking plan.

• The spring line (tied to the bow of the boat, and led aft on the dock) is sometimes used for a temporary single-line tie-up. If there's not much room at the dock, get this line on first. If the prop swerve is the right direction to push the stern *in*, then the single line and a bit of engine power will hold the boat in place till you can attach the other lines. (Bow spring prevents the boat from moving forward; prop power prevents the boat from moving aft and pushes the stern toward the dock.) This is the docking procedure that works so well when someone else does it.

• If the wind is cooperative, the single bow spring line will hold you to the dock as the wind blows the stern in.

• Don't head for the dock till everything's ready: fenders and lines are on, the crew is aware of the plan, there's room at the dock.

• No screaming. It just makes it impossible to think clearly.

• If at first you're 4 feet away from the dock, don't let anybody jump for it. There's no reason the boat can't make another approach. Turn out, and try again.

• If the usual crew is two people, one should stay on the boat till two lines are tied to dock. Then the second person can get off and retie everything.

• If you own a twin-engine boat, pick a no-wind, little-current day in an un-busy marina, and dock the boat using only one engine. Do it twice: once with each engine. And then do it again, and again, until it's doable. When the inevitable breakdown forces such a docking, you'll have some experience to recall.

• If the wind is perpendicular to the dock, and blowing toward it, line yourself up parallel to the dock and stop a short distance out; the wind will push you the rest of the way.

• Once found only on jumbo ships, bow thrusters are now seen on ever-smaller recreational boats. No doubt a boon to docking, to be able to push your bow sideways at will.

• When you must dock with the wind behind (perhaps in a lock), get the stern line on first and fast.

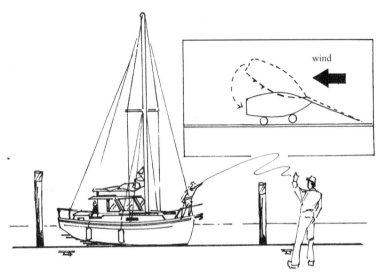

• If a strong current is running at a right angle to the dock, it will be difficult to keep the boat properly aligned. If you can tie to either side of the dock, take the leeward, or you may bounce right into the dock.

UN-DOCKING

Sometimes, boats get "glued" to a dock by wind or current hitting at a bad angle. If the wind almost parallels

If wind is parallel to the dock, a single line forward can hold the boat in place as wind pushes stern into dock.

the dock, you may be able to push the bow out with a big shove and go for it. But, if it's a heavy boat, you won't get enough clearance by simple pushing.

Leave a spring line still attached to the stern cleat and turned around a cleat or a post on the dock. Back the boat; the stern will swing in, the bow out; when you're at a good angle, shift, pull in the line, and go.

If the wind is pushing you against the dock from abeam, leave a spring line attached at the bow (also turned around something on the dock). Go forward, steering toward the dock. The stern will swing out as the bow swings in. When the boat's perpendicular, toss off the line and back away fast. (If the dock is not fendered, you should hang a fender forward, though it could be tricky keeping it in place.) These maneuvers work better with powerboats because their hull shape allows fending in the required places. Sailboats may have too much overhang, bow or stern.

ODD DOCKING

If there's no room at the dock, look for an alternative tie-up.

Moorings
Mooring buoys are usually easy to pick up. Once you've chosen your preferred mooring, slow down to idle as you come near. Determine if wind or current is dominant by looking at the other boats already tied up. If you're the first one in, just stop and watch where your boat drifts. Or, you may be able to read the wind or current by the way the float itself is sitting: is it being pushed noticeably in any direction?

Approach heading into the wind (or current). The crew at the bow should give directions with nice, quiet hand signals. When the boat is in position, nearly bow-over the mooring, the crew signals the helm for a quick burst of reverse; as the boat

Approach the mooring by heading into wind or current.

slows, the crew picks up the mooring line with a boathook and secures it quickly to a cleat. What could go wrong?

Usually, nothing. Occasionally, there is a failure to communicate, or the wind pushes the bow off to one side, or the crew misjudges the momentum and the boat just misses the mark, but a second go-round should not be a problem, especially now that you've had some practice.

• Leaving a mooring is even easier. Drop the line, drift back a short distance till you have a clear path to steer away, and steer away.

Bank Tie

For another alternate tie-up, you'll probably use anchor lines instead of docklines, but you won't need the anchor and you won't be at a dock. Often along a riverbank, you'll find a small cove tucked into the shoreline. It may or may not be big enough for swinging room with an anchor down—or the water may be too deep to set an anchor at all—but with the help of the dinghy, you can carry lines to shore and tie to a couple of substantial trees. Run the lines bow and stern, pulled fairly taut. Here, you'll be safely away from any river traffic, and maybe safely away from shore mosquitoes. (See Chapter 17 for a closer look at river tie-ups.)

Rafting

Occasionally, you will raft alongside another boat (often, this happens at free docks).

Never raft to another boat without permission of the owner, no matter what the docking situation. Use as many fenders as you have; sailboats should watch spreader position so no wave action can bounce them together. If you go ashore, walk quietly and invisibly when crossing the neighbor's deck.

Always walk across the bow of the neighboring boat, never through the cockpit, even if people are below. If boats tie up facing opposite directions, everybody has the most privacy; the rafted boat's crew will walk across the neighbor's bow without it being a detour, and if both groups want to have cockpit cocktail or dinner parties, they will not be seated next to each other.

SLIPPING IN

Six lines will keep you nicely centered in a slip: two bow lines, two stern, and two spring. The bow lines reach out from each

Use a dinghy to carry lines to shore, and tie to trees.

side like whiskers on the cat to keep you centered forward. The spring lines are looped over bollards, and cleated on the boat, to keep the boat from drifting forward or back. (If there is a finger pier, that's the side the spring lines are usually attached, only because it may be easier to reach the bollards.) The stern lines are often, but not always, crossed, to keep you centered aft.

• Most sailboats pull into slips bow first; most powerboats back into slips. There's no right or wrong way to be faced; the prevailing wind may influence direction, or it may be a personal choice.

• With bow in, you have more privacy on the boat; dock strollers cannot peek in and wonder aloud how many she sleeps, or what she goes for. With bow out, it's a lot easier to leave, especially if you pick a departure day when the weather is less than ideal.

• When you tie up in a slip, do it in a way that lets you leave the slip easily. If a mooring line is long enough, loop it around the most distant piling, and bring

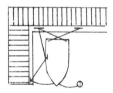

Six lines will keep you centered in a slip.

both ends to the boat. Then you can just pull lines back to the boat when you want to leave.

• When you plan to stop at a marina, call ahead to see if you can reserve a slip, so you can be ready with fenders tied on the proper side.

• If you're buying fuel first, make the docking arrangements while at the fuel dock. There's no need to take up radio time when you'll be there in person.

TIE-UP HELPS

• Many people use docklines with eyes, or loops, spliced into one end. Often, the loop goes around a boat cleat, and the other end goes to shore. But if you cleat the non-looped end of line onto the boat, you can adjust lines without getting *off* the boat (for example, if the tide drops farther than anticipated in the middle of the night, you won't have to go dock-hopping). If the lines are long enough, you can run them from the boat to the dock and back.

• The lazy way to tie to pilings: drop the pre-spliced loop over the piling. If the loop is too small, pass the standing part of the line through the eye to make a larger loop. If you don't have docklines with

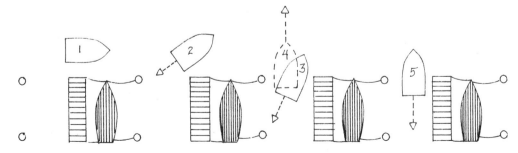

Backing into a slip.

If eye in line is too small to fit over bollard, pull a loop of line through the eye and drop the loop over bollard.

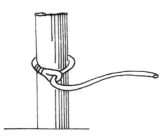

loops, tie in a bowline, leaving as large a loop as you need.

- Nylon line is good for docklines; it has a lot of stretch.

- Expert tie-up types can flip a dockline over a post, making a clove hitch and dropping it so fast you wonder if you're connected to anything. This is a good temporary tie, but if the water's bouncy, it can loosen and jump off short posts. Finish it with a half hitch or two, so it will stay put.

Clove hitch: fast temporary tieup.

- To prevent chafing of docklines, use a piece of hose, or tie some cloth around those places where the lines pass through chocks.

- When you put the unlooped end of a line on a cleat, it should look like a figure eight, with the last loop turned under so tension holds it in place.

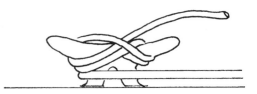

- If you simply drop the looped end of a line over a cleat, it could jump off, with the right combination of wave action and angle of pull. It's much safer to push the loop through the center of the cleat, then bring the loop around both ends and pull the line tight.

- Some boathooks have a grabber on the hook end, which you can use to carry the loop of a dockline over to a faraway piling, drop the loop over the top, then release the grabbing part of the hook. Fingertip control.

- If your fenders have eyes at each end (or a hole down the center), you can hang them vertically (when tied parallel to a dock) or horizontally (when fending off a piling).

- A quick-release snaphook makes for fast fendering, but it's better to tie fenders for long-term use.

- A typical fenderboard is a 4-foot length of 2 × 6, with two rubber pads attached. The rubber faces the boat; the wood faces the dock. You hang the board at an approximate midship position to fend the boat off a piling. (They can be used vertically, too.)

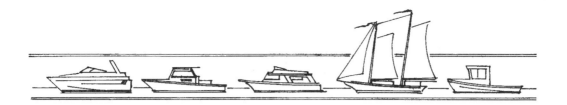

13

Handling Towlines

The battery is dead. The starter fell off. Oil is spraying all over the engineroom. You ran out of gas?

That last one is hard to admit, even though it's a common occurrence. As much as you want to handle your own problems, some things cannot be helped by a quick fix at anchor.

In the olden days, a quick call to the Coast Guard would fix your immediate problem—at least you'd be taken to a repair facility. Today, you have more choices, though that original option is not one of them—the number of Coast Guard boats has not increased in proportion to the number of recreational boats. (The Coast Guard does respond to emergencies.)

In the more common non-emergencies, you might be able to "tow" yourself, or you can call a friend. Even strangers frequently offer to help, which may be good or it may be bad, depending on how much they know about boating and towing. Finally, there is the bite-the-bullet choice: call a professional towing company, a relatively new category in the Yellow Pages, but the logical response to the end of non-distress Coast Guard assists.

SELF-HELP

If you're in a harbor or other protected waters, and you have a dinghy with an outboard, you may be able to move the big boat without assistance from anybody.

Side Tow

This is called towing, even though it looks more like pushing. It may not seem possible, but it works; in our observation, the prize goes to a 6-horse Johnson on a

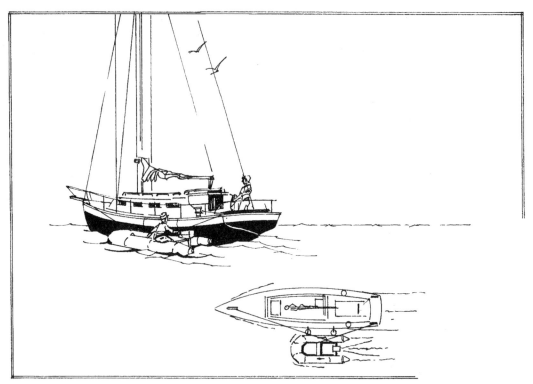

Use the dinghy to move the big boat to a dock.

10-foot Zodiac, pushing a 44-foot Gulf-Star motorsailer in Nassau Harbour. Yes, the captain was wise and waited for slack tide, but it is still an accomplishment.

Tie the towing/pushing boat alongside near the aft quarter. Hang a couple of small fenders between the boats if necessary, but tie all lines snugly so the two boats are tightly connected and will move as one. The dinghy motor will provide the power, but someone should be at the helm of the big boat to help with steering.

Push Boat

You can try real pushing, too. Snug the dinghy bow up to the transom of the big boat, using the shortest possible lines. Again, someone must steer the big boat. As with any towing, getting started is the hardest part. After the initial burst of power, steady, slow progress can usually be maintained.

Towboat

A smaller boat *can* pull a larger one behind, but only within limits, and that does not include the usual cruising boat/dinghy twosome. For other towing, you'll know right away if you have an impossible task. If the engine is set for full ahead and starting to overheat, and the wanna-be towed boat is still sitting and waiting, give it up.

TOWING VOLUNTEERS

Many boaters remember themselves in the "stuck boat" position, and in so doing, they want to help. As long as both captains agree on a plan of action, consider yourself lucky to have a volunteer close by.

The helping boat should pass the waiting boat to leeward, then turn in front of its bow and toss a line. If the water is too rough for accurate tossing, you can tie the

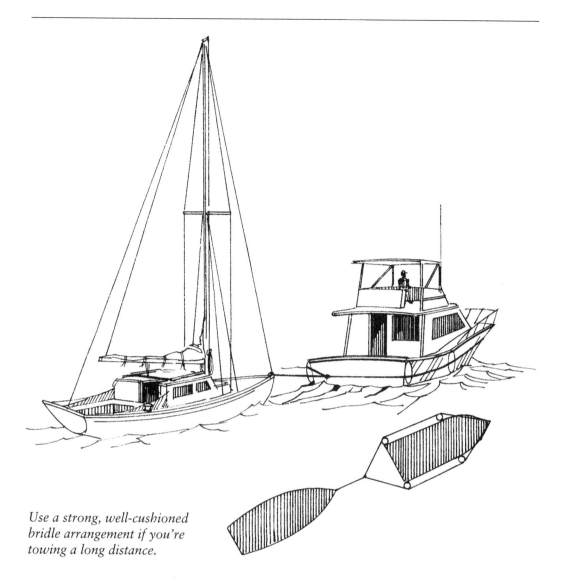

Use a strong, well-cushioned bridle arrangement if you're towing a long distance.

line to a fender, move upwind of the stalled boat, and float the fender-and-line down to a waiting boathook.

The towing boat should make up a bridle arrangement, starting the tow line as far forward on the boat as practical. (If the line is attached to stern cleats only, the strain of the towed boat might make steering difficult.) Depending on how the bridle touches the sides of the hull, chafing protection may be needed.

The towed boat might also use a bridle, so towing strain will be on both bow cleats and possibly on midship cleats as well. (How elaborate these bridle arrangements should be depends on whether you're towing a short way in protected water, or a longer distance in a rough sea.)

Tow slow. There's no particular need for speed, and the faster you tow, the more strain on hardware and line. You can see a towline getting smaller in diameter as it stretches to its limit.

When the towing boat cannot move in front of the stranded boat (as in a grounding situation), towing is often done from the towboat's bow, with the engine in reverse. Hopefully, your mission will be accomplished with a single burst of power, so there's no need to worry about steering and maneuverability during a lengthy tow.

Towing Tips

• Use the radio to communicate, but establish a few easily recognized hand signals anyway, for stop, go, or let go. (Adapt some water-skiers' signals: thumb up, "go"; thumb down, "stop." Wave your arms in a criss-cross pattern for a "let go.")

• When you must slow down, do it gradually, to prevent the otherwise inevitable ramming of the towing boat's transom by the still-forward-moving towed boat.

• Someone should steer the towed boat.

• When towing a sailboat, the towing line is sometimes tied around the mast (but not if it's a small sailboat with a deck-stepped mast).

• If you have any small floats, like the cork floats from fishnets, which might be attached to your dinghy painter, put them on the towing line. Then you won't have to worry about adjusting the line in mid-tow; if it slackens occasionally, it won't sink, so it can't foul the prop.

• Nylon line has the most give, so it's best for a towline. Braid is stronger than three-strand.

• The longer the line, the more it can stretch.

• Try not to adjust the length of the towing line while both boats are in motion. (A scarred knee is a reminder of how quickly rope can burn, and how easy it is to make a "know-better" mistake.)

• If it's absolutely necessary to change line length, slow down to slack the line. Always leave a wrap around a cleat, so you can take in or release line in a controlled way.

• When you're towing a boat in a confined place and you want to make a turn, pretend you're an 18-wheeler and exaggerate the turn so the towed boat can stay behind, not cut a corner and go aground or bump a dock.

Don't cut corners when towing. Make wide turns.

- If you're towing through waves, try to set the towing line to a length that puts both boats on top of a wave at the same time.

- Caution everyone to stay as far away from the towing line as possible. Cleats can pull out, making a slingshot out of the stretched nylon. And if the line is stretched to its limit, it *will* snap, sending two potentially harmful line-ends flying.

- Keep a large, sharp knife reachable whenever you're in a towing situation, whether you're towing or being towed. If you must separate the tow quickly, cutting the line might be the fastest way.

- Someday, when you want to be a worry-wart, look at the way your deck cleats are fastened. If you *don't* find substantial hardware and/or backing plates, change the fastening to through-bolts with washers and nuts used with a wood backing plate. And you might even consider larger cleats, as long as you're going through all that effort.

CALL FOR HELP

When you need a tow and nobody's near, it's okay to call the Coast Guard on Channel 16, and they may coordinate help efforts. They'll call a specific towing company at your request, or they'll put out a Marine Assistance Request Broadcast (MARB). Then you may be helped in one of three ways. A commercial towing company may answer the request call; if you accept its help, you will naturally pay for it. A Coast Guard Auxiliary boat might come to your aid; they will tow you to the nearest marina (or home dock, if that's closer). Other boaters may offer, and if you accept help from any of these, it is on the "friendly volunteer" basis: if they're not licensed, they cannot ask for payment.

Once you have contacted the Coast Guard, you should keep them informed of what's happening: when help arrives, when you've been towed to safety, or if conditions change.

Before accepting the volunteer aid, try to determine if those who offer help are qualified to give it. What seems a simple towing job can develop glitches you never thought of.

Even with so-called professionals, try to determine if the company has the right equipment for the job, or if the crew is knowledgeable. Today, the question of liability is always in the back of somebody's mind: does the company have insurance if some unforeseen problem comes up?

According to Coast Guard regulations, anyone accepting compensation for towing must be properly licensed. And if the Coast Guard calls a towing company, it's a fairly safe assumption the company has the license, and hopefully the rest of the requirements, too.

PRO TOWS

Towing companies monitor the VHF radio; when you need a tow, someone's usually close. Some not only listen for radio calls, but also follow boats along those sections of waterway known to be constantly shifting or shoaling. Having a towboat watch your every move does not inspire confidence in an already nervous captain.

- BOAT/U.S. offers towing insurance as one of its services, so to ensure the quality of the service, they also check out the towing companies. (You'll see a lot of towboats marked with the BOAT/U.S. logo.) While nothing is 100 percent perfect, this is probably as close as you'll get to a guarantee of fair treatment, in service and on the bill.

Among the things checked: licenses, equipment, crew, liability insurance, 24-hour availability, and whether the company belongs to a professional towing association.

• Towing is not cheap (which came first, towing fees or towing insurance?), but when you *need* help, you're in no position to bicker about price. You'll likely pay $100 to $150 an hour, and sometimes additional fees are charged for a "hard grounding" or for rough weather or sea condition. According to BOAT/U.S., the average cost of a tow nationwide was $263 in 1995.

• When a towing company answers a call for assistance, make sure you know what kind of assistance you are accepting before you sign a contract. Sometimes, it will be a set hourly rate; sometimes a pre-established fee for towing from here to there; sometimes an open contract, where the final costs can't be included till the job is actually done.

TOWING OR SALVAGE?

If the boat and crew are not in any immediate danger, then the help you receive is considered simply towing.

But, if the boat is in a position where the helpers are preventing damage to the boat, or danger to the crew, then the help might be considered salvage.

Always establish the kind of help you're accepting before the work begins. Salvage costs more than towing. A lot more.

See Chapter 19 for contract information.

EVERYDAY TOWING

Cruising boats often tow their inflatable dinghy rather than carry it on deck or in davits. For the least strain on the dinghy,

rig a bridle that uses four tow lines: two start on each side of the transom, and two are tied into the towing rings on each side of the bow. Then all four are brought together through an O-ring in front of the dinghy, and the towing line attaches here.

The lines at the bow should keep the dinghy following in a straight line, but the actual pull is on the two lines attached to the reinforced transom. Adjust line length as needed to accomplish this. (Watch for any indication of chafing; if it appears, glue on a sacrificial patch of dinghy fabric.)

• If you're towing a hard dinghy (wood, fiberglass, or aluminum), make sure the towing eye is positioned so the dinghy will sit level as it's being towed. If the eye is too high, the dinghy will ride bow-down; if the eye is too low, the dinghy will ride bow-up.

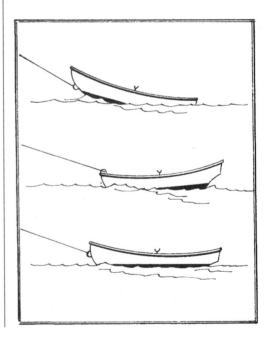

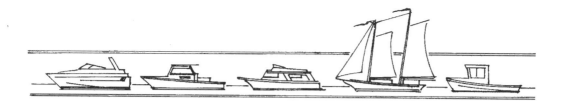

14 Setting Hooks

Of all the reasons to enjoy cruising, anchoring may be the best. It's the total escape land-people dream of, the perfect end to any kind of day. The boat rocks gently in a secluded cove while sunset paints a golden halo over the shore. Wading birds inspect the tide line, and frogs begin their evening chorus.

Even when the anchorage is neither secluded *nor* a cove, the wind is climbing over gray-lined treetops trying to dislodge the anchor, and the approaching thunder keeps the birds and frogs in hiding, it's *still* nice to anchor out. As long as you can trust your anchor.

You can't skimp on anchoring gear, even if you'd rather be docking. There will be days when you won't find a dock, either because of distance between ports or no room at the marina. If you're dependent on a "lunch hook" type of anchor to hold you overnight on a bad night, you will *have* a bad night, almost guaranteed.

When you have the proper equipment, you can match your boating time to your mood. Tie up in town or drop a hook in the boonies. Satisfy your own split personality, or practice the workable compromise that keeps some cruising families together. Just don't expect the teenagers to embrace the idea of isolation or solitude on a steady basis.

ANCHORING GEAR

Ultimately, confidence in your anchoring system comes only with experience "in the field"; you need to go through a few nasty nights just to see how the boat reacts. But a thorough check of what's best for your kind of cruising is a good beginning.

Anchor Designs

It may be aesthetically pleasing to have a matched pair of anchors sitting in their matching bow rollers, but it won't please you in any way if that particular design refuses to hold in a particular bottom. Carry at least two types of anchor, and three is even better.

Danforth. One of the most popular anchors, the Danforth and its copy-cats (including the aluminum Fortress anchors) are deep-burying anchors, so naturally they work great in sand and mud: the more the boat pulls, the deeper the anchor buries. Holding power does not depend on weight as much as with other styles, so they're easier on the anchorer. A Danforth-type anchor may not be able to cut through a grassy bottom, and in rock or coral it may not set at all.

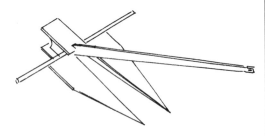

Plow. Another favorite is the plow anchor. A popular brand is the CQR. It buries in sand or mud, except in very soft mud, when it acts like its name, dragging through a soupy bottom as it moves along. (To be fair, *no* anchor sets well in very soft mud.)

The plow buries quickly to do its job, but will come out fairly easily with a vertical pull. Its biggest advantage, however, is that when the boat swings with a shifting current, the anchor turns and resets itself, rather than pulling out.

Bruce. Developed to anchor offshore oil rigs, the Bruce later came down to recreational-boat size. It has the same advantages as the plow: digs in well, resets after a turn, comes up when vertical. The only two criticisms we've heard: sometimes, a large rock gets caught in it, making it hard to retrieve; in hard sand, it would not bury. (But neither would any "burying anchor.")

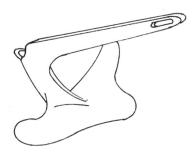

Max. Similar to a Bruce, the Max is made in two versions: a rigid model, and an adjustable one. The "adjusting" changes the angle between the flukes and the shank, so you can adapt the anchor to the type of bottom. (For example, more angle might help the anchor dig into a soft bottom better.)

Luke. This traditional design will hold better than most in grass, or in hard, rocky bottoms. It should be heavier than other

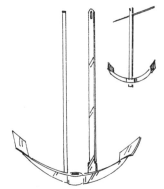

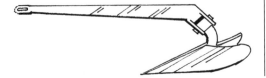

Anchor comes apart for easy stowing.

anchor styles for comparable use. Similar anchors are called Herreshoff, Fisherman, and Yachtsman.

Northill, Pekny. These are also take-apart anchors, so they're easy to stow, and both have good reputations for holding in a variety of bottoms. The Pekny also has different flukes; you change them according to the character of the bottom.

Mushroom. A mushroom anchor can be useful in an inflatable dinghy (you don't have to worry about punctures), and big ones are used for permanent moorings, because given enough time, they will bury deep. But for ordinary, everyday use, they are too heavy, and they can break out when pulled from different directions.

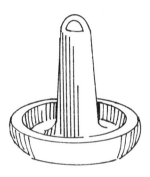

Grapnel. This spidery-looking anchor doesn't do much in mud or sand, but it holds well in rock, where little else will

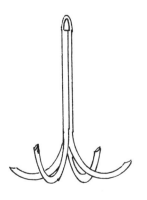

grab. Even if it seems unnecessary for usual anchoring, carry a small grapnel, not for anchoring, but for retrieving things from the bottom. (And one of those "things" just might be another anchor.)

Anchor Rode

Whatever connects the anchor to the boat is collectively termed *anchor rode*. It could be all line, all chain, or some of each. Usually, it's a short length of chain lead used with nylon line.

Line. How long should anchor lines be? Much depends on the size of the boat and the depth of the water you'll be anchoring in. Two lines 300 feet long might be good to have, but a 27-foot sailboat would have difficulty carrying that much. Try for two 150-foot lines; you could tie the two together if necessary. Twisted, three-strand nylon is more elastic than braid, and stretchability is good in an anchor line.

• Ultraviolet affects nylon line, so if you leave anchor line coiled on the foredeck, cover it. A boat-acrylic fabric bag will keep it clean, protected, and neat.

• To help keep anchor lines in good shape, put chafing gear on the line where it goes through a chock; otherwise, the metal will slowly destroy the line. Use short lengths of plastic hose, or tie pieces of leather around the line where needed.

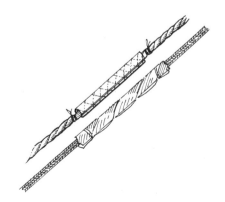

• Every so often, turn anchor lines end-for-end to change the stress end. Later, cut off the worn ends to give the connections new line.

• Replace the lines when they're too worn, or too short. (Save the midsections for mooring lines.)

Chain. Use some chain as part of the anchor rode. The weight helps to maintain the desired horizontal pull on the anchor, and if you're anchored in rock, the chain can't be cut like line could.

For most boats, the chain portion of the rode should be 15 to 35 feet; 8 feet would be an absolute minimum. (Half a boat-length is a conservative minimum.)

If you decide to use all-chain rode, you should use a snubbing line, too. Take a short length of nylon line; with a chain hook, attach one end to the chain just above the place where the chain breaks the water's surface. Cleat the other end of the line to the bow cleat, pulling it tight so the chain goes slack. Now, when wave action bounces the boat, the pull will be on the stretchy nylon line, not on the heavy, nonflexible chain—much easier on the boat.

Attach snubbing line to chain with chain hook.

Rode Marks. Mark your anchor lines for length. You can buy real markers—plastic tags that tie onto the line at regular intervals—but at night, you need a light to read the numbers, and the light will destroy your night vision. Other daymarkers include colored tape, or bands of color painted with acrylic paints. Both need to be redone from time to time.

Better than any of the above are markers you can "read" at night—not by sight, but by touch. Tie a piece of small line around the anchor line at regular intervals. At 20 feet, tie a line with one knot in the end; at 40 feet, put two knots into the small line; at 60 feet, tie in three knots; at 80 feet, four. Then start over.

Another way—use bands of leather sewn around line. Cut slits into the loose end of the leather so it is divided into strips, like fringe: one strip at 20 feet, two strips at 40 feet, three strips at 60 feet, four at 80, and start over.

Chain can be marked with white paint for daytime; for night, use the same knotted line or tiny, nylon cable ties in combinations of one, two, and three.

• Naturally, you can mark the line at 25-, 50-, and 75-foot intervals, or whatever seems most convenient to you.

Connections. To attach anchor line directly to anchor (with no chain between), put a shackle on the anchor, and tie the line to the shackle. Use a bowline, but instead of the usual loop, take an extra turn through and around the shackle. Or, use an anchor bend.

For a more permanent connection of line to anchor, put an eyesplice around a thimble, and use a shackle to connect the thimble to the anchor.

To connect the line portion of rode to the chain portion, use a thimble and shackle; to connect chain to anchor, use a shackle.

To prevent a shackle pin from accidentally backing out, wire the pin to the shackle so it cannot move.

• Cruising boats usually carry two anchors on deck, on an overhanging bowsprit or anchoring platform with separate rollers for each. Lines may be stowed in a forward anchor locker.

• Most boats sit better to an anchor if the line comes straight off the bow, rather than through a chock on the side. A more direct, front lead might help to minimize the tendency to "sail" at anchor.

• Up to a certain size, anchors can be handled by hand, but an anchor winch, or windlass, is a real back-saver. Manual windlasses still require some effort by the crew; electric models are push-button easy.

• With a chain rode, use a chainstopper so chain cannot escape. This fitting locks chain in place, removing strain from the windlass.

• Anchors are lost because the bitter end of the anchor line was not tied to the boat.

FINDING AN ANCHORAGE

When you start looking at the chart for a likely anchorage, try to find two or three possibilities; it's always nice to have alternate plans. The chart gives you a good start by showing depth and bottom composition; also study the character of the land around the anchorage, so you'll know whether to look for trees or marshland, cliff or sand beach.

Protection

For the most protection, look for a separate side creek, or a good-size indentation in the shoreline where you will be well away from any traffic. When you find a likely spot, find the nearest compass rose to see how the anchorage will be in present wind conditions; if there's a strong wind, you want to anchor where trees will give you protection, not where the wind will blow you toward shore.

In areas where shores are steep and/or mountains are close by, "williwaws" may occur. These winds come straight down off mountains, even in calm weather.

If it's a hot, muggy day, you'll prefer a place where you have a chance of capturing any little breeze that might be stirring.

Depth

It's desirable to anchor in fairly shallow water, so that less scope will be required; you and all the other boats will stay in smaller swinging circles. (*Scope* describes the amount of anchor rode you should release to anchor safely in a given water depth. Determining correct scope will be explained later.) Don't forget to allow for tidal changes, when anchoring and when entering. You may enter on a high tide and clear a bar that would stop you at low.

The bottoms of choice are sand or mud, except for really soft mud, which allows the anchor to drag right through it. If the bottom is hard or rocky, you'd need a non-burying kind of anchor. Grassy places also resist the commonly used burying-type anchors.

Read the chart markings, and when you get to the anchorage, use the leadline to be sure the bottom matches your expectation.

Entering

When you get to the first possibility on your list, enter on a compass course from a recognizable starting spot (or make up a range, if you can find two usable landmarks). Then write down the bearing so you can exit on the reciprocal course.

Sometimes, a side-setting wind or current won't let you stay on one heading, especially when you're trying to enter slowly. You must find a compromise: enough power to keep you aimed properly without going so fast you can't back down speedily if the depth-sounder shows the entrance has shoaled.

- The ideal way to approach an unknown anchorage is at low tide; you can see a lot of the shoals and bars, and if you do go aground, the incoming tide will lift you off. Timing seldom works out so ideally in the real cruising world.

- When traveling in areas with two high and two low tides daily, there will be approximately 12 hours' difference between similar tide stages. The late-day water level (when you arrive) and the morning water level (when you leave) will be close.

- The first boat into an anchorage should get the best spot, but don't be surprised when the next boats to arrive anchor close to you rather than choose another area of the anchorage. There is no explanation for this phenomenon.

- If you see other boats in an anchorage, and you know their drafts, you will enter more confidently.

- If you've anchored in a location that will be rough if a predicted weather front arrives, don't wait for the front; move early. Later, you may not be able

to move at all. If that means re-anchoring every few hours as wind clocks around an island, do it. Consider it good anchoring practice, and good insurance.

BASIC ANCHORING TECHNIQUE

You've found a good anchorage—tree-lined shore, sandy bottom, perfect depth, and most important, you made it through the unmarked entrance. Now all you need do is establish the perfect place for the anchor.

Choosing Your Spot

Pick your spot carefully. If other boats are already anchored, remember that boats on chain will probably have less scope, hence a smaller swinging circle, as will boats with two anchors set. A larger boat on a single anchor will probably require more space. Try to allow for those times of slack water or no wind, when boats will not swing in the same direction.

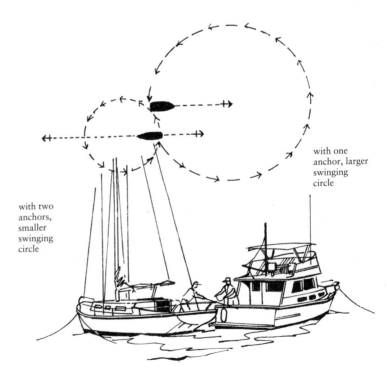

with one anchor, larger swinging circle

with two anchors, smaller swinging circle

Some boats "sail" at anchor—multihulled sailboats have very little hull below the water to hold them in place, so they don't stay in place. Shoal-draft powerboats with lots of windage also move a lot, so try to avoid being close to any of these movers and sailers.

When you find a vacant spot, make a broad circle in the approximate area you might swing, checking the depth all around. Take tide into consideration, too; if you're anchoring at low tide, it's not a problem, but if you anchor at high tide in a place with a 7- or 10-foot tidal range, that's a significant difference. Be sure your circle will be deep enough everywhere when the tide falls.

Dropping the Hook

Determine whether wind or current is the strongest influence, and anchor to that. If other boats are anchored, just see how they're faced and follow suit. If nobody's there, stop and drift for a minute and see where the boat wants to go, then anchor facing the opposite direction.

Steer the boat upwind (upcurrent) to the center of your circle, and stop. Lower the anchor, and drift or back down slowly, releasing rode as you go. Let the line pull taut occasionally, to see if the anchor is digging in; then release more line as you drift backward more. When you've released the desired scope, cleat the line and let the anchor settle in as you come to a stop. Then, use the engine to back down and check the set—not with a tiny bit of power, but with a substantial, steady reverse pull. If the anchor cannot resist this pull, it will not resist strong wind gusts, either.

Pick a reference on shore, and watch to see if your position changes relative to it. If the water is churning forward and the boat is not budging, your anchor is set.

Once the anchor is set to your satisfaction, look around and make some mental notes of your position as it relates to shore objects, marks, and/or other boats. Even if you swing at anchor, you should be able to check your position later, to be sure you're staying in the same place.

• Scope determines the length of anchor rode you should use. The most common recommendation when anchoring with line is to allow for a scope of 7:1. The "1" in the equation is the distance between the place where the anchor line connects to the bow of the boat, and the bottom. If water depth is 10 feet, and distance from surface to anchor chock is 5 feet, then "1" is 15 feet. So: $7 \times 15 = 105$ feet, the recommended length of your anchor rode.

• In bad wind, increase scope to 10:1.

• Boats anchored on all-chain rode can use a 4:1 or 5:1 ratio.

• When anchoring at low tide, be sure to allow ample scope for the times of high tide.

Sailing Stops

As mentioned, it's not only sailboats that sail at anchor; many powerboats have a lot of sail area, too, and they do *not* have the counterbalance of a deep and/or heavy keel. When the wind pipes up, the boat starts off on a speedy tack, and when it reaches the end of the line, an abrupt jerk brings it around to head the other way. Trouble is, those jerks can also pull out the anchor.

Anchor-pulling isn't the only reason to discourage sailing at anchor. All boats do not sail around in unison like some overwater ballet. Yours may be going back while another is going forth, and there may not be room in the anchorage for this kind of random wandering.

• Using all-chain rode keeps some boats facing forward; apparently, the weight of the chain is enough to stop the tacking.

• Sailboats often set a *riding sail* (a small sail well aft) to keep them centered; it works for powerboats, too.

- Catamarans use a bridle with lines tied to each hull.

- On a trawler, try running a bridle from the bow to a cleat at the aft quarter.

- Experiment with tying the helm in different positions till you find one that works with your boat.

- Using two anchors also helps; see the section on the Bahamian moor on page 138.

Backward Anchoring

On a steamy summer night when the water's mirror calm and you feel only the hint of a breeze, anchor from the stern to catch whatever air might sneak in through a back hatch or doorway.

Retrieving the Anchor

With a single anchor, retrieval is simple: Power up slowly as crew hauls in line. When you're on top of the anchor, a vertical pull usually breaks it loose. Hoist and stow it.

If it's really buried, you may need some extra pulling power. Cleat the line short, then use the engine to power slowly forward. In this tug-of-war, the engine usually wins, but if the anchor still won't budge, try pulling from different directions; if it is hooked on something, you may find the right unhooking pull.

In an attempt to avoid this situation, some boaters use a tripline. This is a sep-

arate line attached to the top of the anchor. The length of line should be about equal to the water depth, so when the line is attached, the end will reach the surface and be positioned above the anchor, where you will tie it to a small float. Now if the anchor gets stuck, you will have a way to pull it up straight, hopefully clearing it of whatever was holding it.

If you are hopelessly entangled in some cable, wreck, or other unseen thing, buoy the anchor (tie a small fender or other float to it so you can find it later) and go look for a diver.

Anchoring Tips

- Use more chain with a plow anchor than with a Danforth. When you drop a plow anchor, you want the weight of the chain to hold the anchor more parallel to the bottom, creating the desired horizontal pull to dig in the plow.

- One technique we have found useful is to use less chain with a Danforth. If the anchor can be held at more of an angle to the bottom, the flukes will dig in, not just skid along the bottom. Drop the Danforth till it touches bottom; release a little more rode, but keep tension on so the anchor

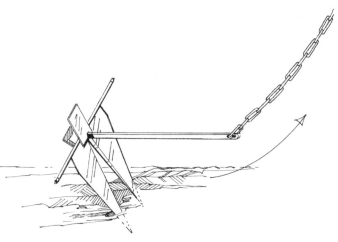

remains partly suspended and the flukes start to dig in.

• With any anchor, once you feel it start to grab, release more rode, but keep slight tension on it. This helps the anchor set, and it keeps the boat backing straighter.

• Always use power—engine or sail—to be sure the anchor is set properly. The toss-and-hope school of anchoring may be popular, but it does not inspire confidence among surrounding boaters.

• With a moderate wind (and no current), all boats in an anchorage will sit the same way, and it's fairly easy to keep them apart; the "You swing, I swing" theory works as long as boats use approximately the same scope. But with *no* wind and no current, boats drift every which way, and may bump. At least it's a gentle bump.

• In a side channel or creek, tidal current will influence the way you sit to anchor, regardless of wind direction. If you have a choice, look for a bend where wind and current are close to a right angle to each other. Set the anchor as close to the bank as safety allows; the boat will swing with the tide, but the bow should stay aimed toward the wind, so you won't end up stern-to-wind, which can cause a noisy night.

• If you're anchored in clear water, hop into the dinghy with a glass-bottomed bucket and go check the anchor. If all you see is chain and a bit of anchor top, you're well set. If it's swimming weather, you can dive on the anchor for an up-close look.

• Keep a bucket handy with a line attached for toss-and-fill, or install a real deck-washdown system. You'll want to clean off mud from the anchor and chain.

• If bad weather is predicted, set out foul-weather gear, boots, and flashlights so that when you wake up at 2:30 to a howling rainstorm, you're semi-prepared to do something.

• After dark, take some bearings on your position, relative to any lights in the area—marks, house lights, dock lights, anchor lights.

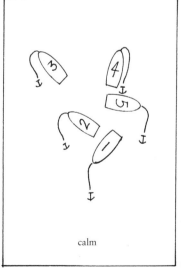

anchors in same position

Anchored boats do not always swing the same way.

TWO-ANCHOR ADVANTAGE

If a boat enters an anchorage where wind and current are coming from the same direction, anchoring with one anchor is easy; upwind is upcurrent, too. Drop the anchor, and the boat sits to both wind and current. But, later, the wind dies and the current switches direction. The boat moves with the current, running over its rode, now pulling on the anchor from the opposite direction. The anchor might pull out, but even if it stays there, this can cause an uncomfortable ride.

If the boat was anchored by the two-anchor system known as the Bahamian moor, it would just turn with the current; no pulling, no fouling.

Setting the Bahamian Moor

The Bahamian moor is known for its usefulness in an area of strong, switching current, but it's a good anchoring system anywhere swinging room is limited. With two anchors properly set, your boat will swing in a circle with a radius only slightly longer than the boat length.

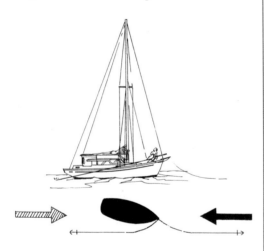

The two anchors are set 180 degrees apart along the general line of current flow. Both are led from the bow; the boat sits between the two anchors with equal scope on both. The bow stays essentially in one spot, while the stern swings around as the current switches direction. The boat hangs first from one anchor, then from the other.

You can set the two anchors in different ways:

1. Drop one anchor as you move upstream slowly; continue forward,
watching the line carefully to make sure it doesn't foul your prop till you've traveled double the distance of your intended scope; drop the second anchor; then fall back to the midpoint, and snug both anchors.

2. Drop an anchor forward, and fall back twice the distance of the intended scope. Drop the second anchor, and pull or power the boat up to the midway point, watching the line carefully.

3. Drop an anchor forward, as usual. Then use the dinghy to carry out and place the second anchor. This gives you the best control over placement of the two anchors.

• When anchoring in a river where wind and current are opposed, you may drop the anchor in a likely spot, but the boat wanders off to sit at a right angle to it, instead of dropping back. Worse, it may run right over the line; the boat is in front of the anchor, and the wind is blowing at the transom. With two anchors, you can control this situation, too. (See Chapter 17 for more on anchoring in rivers.)

• If the weather gets bad, you can still release more scope, as long as there's room in the anchorage to do so. You can release on one anchor only, to increase scope in one direction, or you can release both, for a very wide bridle. When the weather settles again, pull up to the original position.

• When you anchor in a narrow creek, with shore on one side and a shoal on the other, it would be hard to stay centered with only one anchor. With the two anchors set along the centerline, only the stern will swing, so the boat stays essentially in the middle of the safe water.

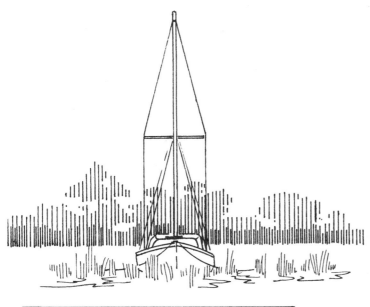

- Another way to separate the lines is to use the dinghy as a push boat, and turn the big boat around in the appropriate circles (at slack tide) to unwind the twist.

- The second worry about two-anchor use is fouling the prop on one of the lines. Leave a bit of slack in the lines so the boat can swing over the "aft" (slack) line; if the line is down far enough in the water, it cannot catch the prop.

Boats with full keels seldom have trouble with the Bahamian moor, but spade rudders and fin keels sometimes get caught for the same reason props sometimes foul: not enough slack in the line.

In a narrow creek, set two anchors along the centerline, so the boat doesn't swing into the shallow shoreline.

Double Trouble

The corkscrew effect of twisted lines is the main problem with the two-anchor system. You can avoid it most of the time, but occasionally, they will twist.

To minimize the chances of a wrap, set the anchors along a line slightly offset from the current flow, so the boat will swing back and forth on the same side of the lines, rather than turn a complete circle. (Also try running both lines out the same chock.)

- To undo a twist, leave one anchor line coiled on deck (instead of having both disappear into the anchor locker). Pick up the coil, and pass it around the other line till they separate.

Other Doubles

If you're just not comfortable with an anchor sitting behind the boat, you can at least discourage the tendency to sail at anchor by setting two anchors forward in a wide V. This has the secondary advantage of dividing the strain on two anchors, lessening the chances of a pullout in bad weather. Also, in a crowded anchorage, setting a second anchor off to one side may keep you away from another boat.

If you must anchor in a very narrow channel, you want to keep yourself as far off to the side as possible, so bow and stern anchors may be necessary. Set the two anchors parallel to the shore, one cleated forward and one aft, with the boat sitting between two taut lines.

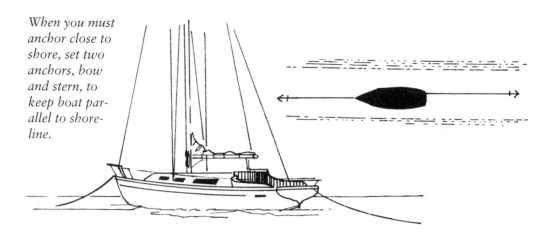

When you must anchor close to shore, set two anchors, bow and stern, to keep boat parallel to shoreline.

ANCHOR LET-GO

When the weather starts to deteriorate, you start to worry about the size of the anchor in relation to the weight of all the stuff you've put on board. As the wind screams and waves build, you realize this may be just too much for your everyday anchor. And the next thing you know, your anchoring gear is sending you signals.

Dragging Anchor

When the anchor starts to move, you may feel a slight shudder as the chain bounces along the bottom. If you feel that irregular motion, get on deck fast if you're not there already. The next signal is more than a warning—you feel the boat suddenly drifting beam-to the wind, a sure indication the an-chor has let go, and you're towing it, backward, through the anchorage.

If you can see the anchor line, you can start the engine to help you control the boat, but watch the line carefully to avoid a wrap.

When the anchor drags, the boat drifts beam-to the wind.

Reset Attempts

Unless your immediate concern is fending off other boats, try to reset the anchor. First, let out more rode, snugging it a bit now and then to see if the anchor is digging in. If it will not grab, try a different anchor. Experienced cruisers always have a second anchor ready, especially when weather is bad. Drop anchor number two, and hope it likes the bottom better than the first.

This is why you always carry more than one type of anchor. There's no point in dropping a duplicate of the one that won't hold. If the second one doesn't grab either, you'll have to pull both in, and try again. Move to a different location in the anchorage—sometimes, 20 feet makes a difference in bottom-holding ability. Or, look for a place where you have more room to swing, so you can increase scope.

Engine Help

When no anchor will resist the weather, your engine can help. Set the anchor with a lot of scope. After you have drifted back to the end of the rode, keep the engine at idle and steer into the wind, keeping the strain off the anchor. If you begin to creep slowly toward the anchor, just shift to neutral for a few seconds, and when you drop back again, switch to forward again. Everyone on board should take turns at the helm; this gets tiresome, but it does keep you in place.

Communication

Communication is a problem at night, which is when you usually have an emergency. You can't see hand signals unless you turn on deck lights, and that destroys your night vision for watching what you're doing.

Some people work out light signals—flashes from a small light—which is okay if you're very careful to flash at an angle that would be visible. At night when you're in a small panic, that's not easy to do. "Walkie-talkie" headsets are also suggested, but also not something you think of when the an-chor is dragging. Deck-stomping may work for a few basic messages: One stomp, "go to starboard." Two stomps, "go to port." Three stomps, "stop." Mostly, people work together by experience; the person at the helm watches what the anchorer is trying to do, follows their lead, and tries to help. Unfortunately, only previous experience can bring the required familiarity.

Talk about possibilities ahead of time; make some what-if plans, and try to stick with them when what-if happens.

Worst Case

A boat drags down on you, or you drag on another and you're in a collision situation. Since neither boat would be speeding, the impact itself is usually not serious, but if boats get tangled together by fouled anchor lines, they can continue to pound into each other.

First, get some fenders between the boats and tie them as parallel as possible, so they aren't rising and falling on different waves. If one boat's keel is stuck on the other's anchor line, you can try slacking the line; it may drop free. If it's necessary to let go of an anchor, tie a fender or other buoy to the line so you can retrieve the anchor later.

Prevention and Suggestions

• One way to increase an anchor's holding power is to use a *sentinel*—a weight connected to the anchor rode. This makes the pull on the anchor more horizontal and may prevent a dragging situation.

• The sentinel hangs from the anchor rode, usually about midway between boat and anchor; a separate line attached to the sentinel lets you stop it wherever you choose.

• Many cruising boats carry a storm anchor, but, curiously, few use them. Calling it a storm anchor seems to signal a *big* storm, for which you'd have days of warning and time to get ready. The anchor is usually hidden deep in an inaccessible locker; if you need it quickly, you can't get to it.

• This quirk falls into the category of human nature (boater's nature) that will probably not change, foolish though it may be. However, if you *are* the exception, set the storm anchor. Sleeping is much nicer than steering the boat all night.

• Anytime you're maneuvering the boat when an anchor line is down, be very cautious not to foul the prop.

• On some sailboats, the anchor line might get wedged into the space between the rudder and the keel; you must try to push it down and out. From the dinghy, you may be able to reach the line with a long boathook; or you may have to wait for a morning swim.

• If a boat has dragged and its crew is having trouble reanchoring, another boat may offer a temporary raft, or tie them along behind. It's not a good idea to stay this way overnight, but it's a nice gesture and it gives the crew a chance to regroup.

• If you drag anchor a lot even though you're careful to set it properly, you probably need a bigger anchor. Overkill in this area is not a bad thing. This *is* insurance for you.

• Some anchor-dragging winds come and go quickly with a squall line or an isolated thunderstorm. But on those nights when the wind continues to shriek all night, you should probably consider anchor watches. Otherwise, it's certain nobody will sleep. With a watch, somebody might.

• Favorite anchor-dragging story: We were anchored in a side creek off the lower Mississippi, and just after dawn, a friend's boat began drifting slowly backward, bound for "the river." A few minutes of panicked shouting brought the sleepy sailor on deck, and after a slow as-

sessment of the situation, he assured us all that "It's okay. I'm not dragging; I'm just leaving early."

Attitude is everything.

LIGHTS ON

Don't forget to show a proper anchor light, or you may get fined—or worse. A powerboat's anchor light is easily seen by approaching boats. Sailboats have a problem: The only light that fits the rules will be at the top of the mast (the only place where 360-degree visibility is possible), but a light at cabintop level is much more visible to other boats. A circular fluorescent would be nice, fitted around the mast in two semicircular halves. Until someone invents that, many sailors leave on a cabin light or a cockpit light in addition to the real anchor light.

Don't forget to turn the anchor light off in the morning. A lot of battery power gets wasted this way.

Obeying the rules, we turned on the anchor light atop our tented pontoon boat when anchored in one of the lakes of the Kissimmee River chain. Within minutes, we heard a steady pounding on the canvas and wondered where the rain had come from. The "rain" of course, was not water, but hundreds of bugs hitting the fabric, attracted by our proper anchor light. There should be exceptions to all rules—perhaps a citronella anchor candle.

RAFT-UPS

On good days, you'll raft up with other boats, for lunches, for dinner parties, for songfests, even for Thanksgiving dinner. When sailboats raft, they must be careful to stagger the position of spreaders, so there's no danger of bumping if one boat dips down when another tips up.

That kind of bobbing is not likely to happen, anyway; boats do not usually raft

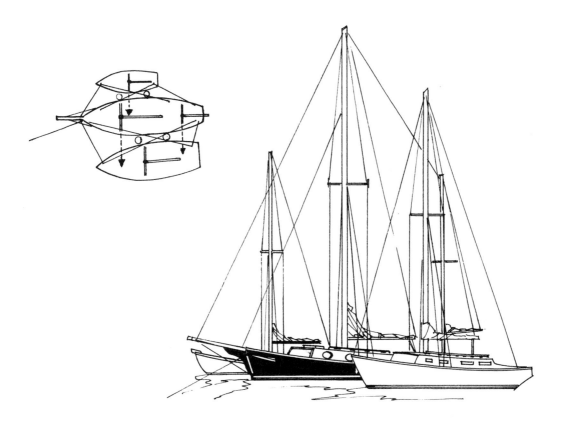

unless the weather is very settled. Boats should be tied snugly together, with plenty of fenders between. If they do bounce, they usually do it together.

If only two or three boats are rafted, they may all hang from one anchor; but as the raft grows, more anchors should be added.

In very protected places on very quiet nights, boaters may stay in the raft, though personal preference may suggest you break up the raft before sleep time.

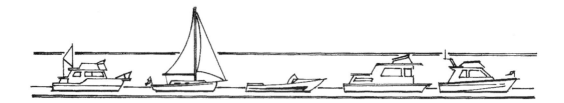

15

Using Caution

Parents worry about the safety of their children. Children worry about the safety of younger siblings or pets. Friends worry about each other. But few people direct that worry toward themselves.

Everyone knows accidents happen, but we all gamble on "not-to-me." Maybe that's better than the opposite extreme—worrying so much it's impossible to enjoy anything—but better than either attitude is finding the smart middle ground.

If there is anything good about boating mishaps, it is that they are mostly predictable—not on an individual basis, but on a list of possibilities. The smart boater will research those maybes and plan ways to deal with ordinary problems and more serious emergencies.

BE AWARE

Some "common sense" considerations are done—or not done—before you get on the boat.

Float Plan

Filing a float plan sounds very formal or official, and when you see the suggested float plan form, it *looks* very formal and official, which is unfortunate because it probably discourages the very thing it is trying to promote. If you don't want to bother filling in all the blanks, at least call a friend. Ask them to make a note of who's on board, where you're going, when you expect to be back, and whom to call if you don't show up within a reasonable time after your anticipated return. (Remind the friend of the boat name, just in case.) Then *don't forget to call* when you arrive at your destination.

Drink Plan

Many cruising boaters enjoy cocktails, whether they're watching for a green flash at sunset, waiting for the show of northern lights, or enjoying the dock party at a marina. But drinking while running a boat is as wrong as drinking when driving a car; it's foolish and it's illegal.

Statistics are clear: half of boating fatalities involve alcohol. Even seemingly small amounts of alcohol have a greater effect on judgment and coordination when you're mixing drink with sun and wind and boat motion. Save the alcohol for sundown, and enjoy days on the water with clear eyes and a clear mind.

Health Check

Just as you shouldn't go boating through an alcohol haze, so you shouldn't go anywhere if you're totally exhausted. Don't try to keep to a travel schedule that doesn't allow ample time for rest and recuperation. If you've just finished a long night run or a two-day trip, your sleep pattern is no doubt badly interrupted. You may think you're alert, but sleep deprivation plays bad tricks on your mind. You surprise yourself with the things you say and do when you're exceptionally tired. Try to be honest about your frame of mind and your physical condition. A lazy day in port is much preferred to a wrong decision or a misjudged position.

If you're prone to seasickness and are planning a day's run offshore, don't try to be brave and do without the prevention pills. You'll do yourself and everyone on board a bigger favor if you take the medicine. It's not a condition that is readily controlled by positive thinking; once you're sick, it's too late to take the pills, and you cannot help with boat operation or chores. Check with your physician or pharmacist to find a preventive that works for you.

Weather Check

Probably the biggest influence on your boating day—good or bad—will be weather. Wind direction can dictate whether or not you will cross a sound. Wind speed can determine whether or not a bridge will open. Rain will challenge the most enthusiastic traveler if the boat has no enclosed steering station. Listen to the VHF reports. Watch TV news for weather map overviews. See Chapter 18 for hints on reading the sky.

BE EQUIPPED

Of course, you'll have the required equipment—all the stuff the government says will help keep you safe. And it probably will help, but why stop with minimum gear? As you read this chapter, put yourself in the problem or emergency situation, and make a list of things you'd like to see in the picture. Then take the list to the boat store. Where safety is concerned, redundancy is good.

Federal Requirements

To satisfy federal government safety requirements, these items must be on board:

Personal flotation devices

Visual distress signals

Fire extinguishers

Sound-producing device

Navigation lights

PFDs. Personal flotation devices (life vests, by common description) must be Coast Guard approved, in good condition, unwrapped, and easily accessible. The boat must carry one PFD for each person on board, and each one must be properly sized for that person. In addition to the wearables, any boat over 16 feet must also carry a throwable flotation device.

flares

whistle

wood plugs

life jackets

PFD

radar reflector

liferaft

watermaker

safety harness

lifering

emergency ladder

first aid kit

Safety gear.

Choose the PFD style that best suits your use. Will you always be in sight of shore, or will you make frequent overnight passages? Five types exist:

Type I, offshore life jackets, are designed to turn an unconscious wearer face-up, certainly a good feature. Their problem is that they're bulky and uncomfortable.

Type II, near-shore buoyant vests, will also turn the wearer face-up. These are more comfortable than Type I, but less buoyant.

Type III, flotation aids, are most comfortable, but less buoyant than Type I, and the unconscious wearer could end up face-down in the water, hardly in keeping with their intent.

Type IV, throwable devices, are not for wearing; these are the cushions, life rings, and horseshoes.

Type V, hybrids, are special-use items, like sailboard vests and float coats. They have some built-in flotation, and more can be added by inflation with a CO_2 cartridge.

The Coast Guard has recently approved inflatable PFDs. Inflatables have long been popular in Europe; many people choose them because they *are* so wearable—not awkward and confining. If you'll wear one, buy one.

- Don't shove PFDs in the seat locker if they're wet, especially if they're wet with salt water. Give them a good freshwater bath and dry them in sunshine.

- Check the general condition of all PFDs from time to time. Rotting straps or rusted hardware won't help you. Mildew can make fabric so brittle, it breaks rather than tears.

- Wear your PFD and go for a swim, so you see how well it works to keep you upright.

- Bright colors are good. You want to be visible against water and sky colors.

- Three out of four people who die in boating accidents were not wearing PFDs.

- Attach a small strobe light to each PFD, right next to a whistle. Both can be lifesavers.

- Besides keeping you afloat, a PFD gives you some protection against cold.

- If your cruising takes you into cold-water places like Alaska, British Columbia, Maine, Nova Scotia, or Minnesota, you may want to add appropriate exposure suits to your survival gear.

- If you fall overboard without wearing a PFD, here's an idea that can be a real lifesaver, proved most recently by a crewman who fell off an oceangoing ship and stayed afloat more than 24 hours.

type I

type II

type III

type IV

type V

Coast Guard–approved PFDs now include inflatables.

The overboard crewman removed his trousers, and used them as a flotation device. To try it: Close the end of each pant leg with a knot, and zip the fly. While treading water, hold pants by waistband, swing them overhead, and pull the waist section quickly down into the water. The pant legs should now be filled with air. Your body will rest against the part of the pants that are underwater. This makeshift PFD can keep you afloat for several minutes, depending on how tightly woven the fabric is. Whennecessary, flip them overhead to refill.

Raising and lowering arms is a distress signal.

Visual Distress Signals. You need three visual distress signals for day, and three for night, in any combination of items approved by the Coast Guard for day or night use.

By day, a flag showing a black ball and black square on an orange background is an eye-catcher. Or send a smoke signal: orange smoke from a hand-held or floating "pyrotechnic device." Use these only when you see a boat or plane; if the wind is over 10 knots, the smoke will disperse quickly.

For night, red meteor flares cannot be mistaken for anything else. Again, use a flare only when you see another boat's lights, and know there's a real chance of its being seen.

Send an SOS in light flashes from a strong, focused-beam flashlight or spotlight: dot-dot-dot, dash-dash-dash, dot-dot-dot.

For day *or* night, red parachute flares are easily seen, if anyone's close by. If you choose red hand-held flares, handle them very carefully.

Besides these required signals, many others are recognized as a call for help:

- Open flames in a bucket, burning where most visible on deck
- The code flags "November, Charlie"
- Dye marker, any color
- Upside-down flag
- A person raising and lowering arms

Fire Extinguishers. Depending on the size of the boat and the size of the extinguishers, you'll need one, two, or three "B" type fire extinguishers. "B" fires are the greatest threat on a boat: these are fires cause by flammable liquids like oil and gasoline, so keep the extinguishers where you'd most likely need them. Assuming there is no fixed system on board, the required number of extinguishers are:

Under 26 feet—one B-I extinguisher

26 feet to less than 40 feet—two B-I or one B-II

40 feet to 65 feet—three B-I, or one B-II and one B-I

Sound-Producing Devices. You'll need to make noise for meeting, crossing, and overtaking situations, and also for sound signals during periods of reduced visibility. Under 12 meters, "some means" of making sound; over 12 meters, have a whistle (horn) and a bell.

Sounds recognized as distress signals: Any sound device sounded continuously; a gun fired at 1-minute intervals.

Navigation Lights. Specific light requirements are covered in Chapter 2. Remember to show navigation lights between sunset and sunrise, and during other periods of reduced visibility.

Note: There are also regulations for proper ventilation and backfire flame control, where applicable. Refer to "Federal Requirements and Safety Tips for Recreational Boats."

Extra Stuff

First Aid. Carry a first aid kit that matches the way you cruise. If help is always a short side trip away, an ordinary kit should do. Marine first aid kits are packaged in water-resistant, non-rusting cases that float, but the contents cover the same kind of basic injuries and problems as home or auto kits.

If you're frequently offshore even for a day or two, or you cruise in remote areas like Alaska or northern Canada, you'll want more extensive supplies. Ask your doctor for recommendations and prescriptions for pain pills and an antibiotic. If any of the crew is prone to a recurring illness or condition, take medication for that, too.

A helpful reference is a medical book that describes illnesses and injuries in a way that can help you decide when something requires professional or emergency help. The AMA's *Family Medical Guide* is a good general reference; *The Onboard Medical Handbook* by Paul G. Gill, Jr., M.D.

(International Marine, 1997), focuses on boaters' needs.

Bilge Pumps. Most cruising boats have one or two installed bilge pumps, electric and/or manual. (If you have only an electric pump, you *need* a manual one as well.) Be-prepared boaters carry an extra bilge pump capable of pumping larger quantities of water than the standard pump. This can be fixed or portable; when you need to use it, attach hoses and feed one to the bilge, the other over the side. (The same pump could be used to fight an onboard fire, too, with hoses positioned to bring water on board rather than carry it away.)

You can also get a special fitting that allows the engine to take water from the bilge rather than through the standard intake; the engine functions as a supplementary pump.

Depthsounder. Though not usually mentioned under the umbrella of safety equipment, a depthsounder certainly belongs. Anything that can prevent a potentially damaging grounding is safety gear.

Safety Harness. While a safety harness was once considered necessary only for round-the-world racers and singlehanded sailors, they're now made in a choice of strapping arrangements, in sizes for the whole family.

Even if the extent of your offshore runs is an occasional night or two, a harness is a wise buy. You don't plan to be out in rough weather, but sometimes it catches you anyway. It's a small item for a lot of peace of mind.

While some people find it difficult to work with a safety line, most prefer to put up with a little inconvenience in exchange for the security. One long-distance cruiser sews heavy-duty luggage handles to the backs of the harnesses, the better to haul a person on board in case of a fall-in.

Fume Detectors. Fume detectors sense propane leaks from cooking or heating stoves, as well as hydrogen from batteries. You might trust your nose for those, but you can't smell carbon monoxide, and it can be produced from many sources: stove, heater, or portable generator as well as the main engine.

If you start to feel dizzy or nauseous when closed up in the boat, *don't* ignore it; let in some fresh air fast. How much ventilation you need for what kind of appliance is impossible to generalize. If in doubt, call the manufacturer.

Wood Plugs. A package or two of the tapered wood plugs that replace a broken through-hull fitting is a really small investment for a really big payback. If you ever need them, they can literally save the boat.

Emergency Stuff

Crew-Overboard Pole. To mark the spot where a person falls overboard, many boats carry a crew-overboard pole at the stern, ready to drop into the water with one quick motion.

The pole is weighted at the bottom, to keep it "standing" upright; an orange flag on top is highly visible because of its color and its height above the water. Some units have a water-activated strobe light as well.

Boarding Ladders. Boarding ladders become more desirable in direct proportion to the size of the boat. Small boats don't need them and don't have room to carry them; larger boats need them.

Even if you don't have room for an ordinary ladder, one very compact model can help you get out of the water and onto the boat in an emergency situation. The Rescue Ladder fits into a small bag that fastens onto a stanchion base; a line (adjustable) hangs over the side, ending just above the water's surface. If you're in the water and you want out, pull the line and a 7-foot

long, webbing-and-rung ladder drops down. You may bump your knees and toes as you climb out, but at least you have something to climb out *on*. (Another idea from the company that makes the Mast Ladder—Capt. Al's—1-800-232-9065.)

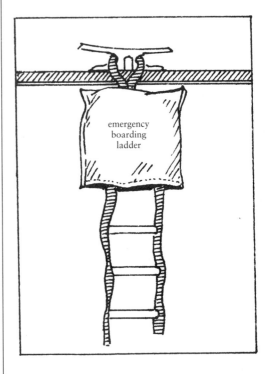

Overboard Recovery Systems. You'll want good equipment for retrieving an overboard person. Both MOM (Man Overboard Module) and Lifesling are popular. Descriptions are included later in the chapter with directions for their use.

Liferaft. If your definition of offshore is running a half mile off the coast, where you're always in radio range of shore and hollering range of fishermen, then a liferaft may seem excessive, unless you cruise in the extremely cold waters of the Pacific Northwest.

Offshore cruisers can go to sea with a fully equipped liferaft, including EPIRB (see below) and watermaker, or they can put faith in a sailing dinghy with a more traditional survival kit. And there are a bunch of in-betweens, all of which are beyond the needs of the coastal cruiser.

If you're ever in the market, rafts divide roughly into three categories: coastal (assumes a quick rescue) is minimal; offshore (assumes four or five days at sea) is better constructed; oceangoing (long-term true survival) is best.

Watermaker. If you get a raft, get a watermaker; the two go together. Since people cannot survive long without water, the rest of the survival gear won't be much good without the watermaker. Of course, these things do not really make water; they make pure, fresh water from salt (or otherwise contaminated) water.

A small water purifier by PŪR can produce 1 quart of fresh water per hour. The larger one, famous for providing water to a couple who survived more than two months in a liferaft, can produce 1.2 gallons per hour, more than necessary for emergency use.

Distress Signals and Calls

The Coast Guard will respond to a true Mayday call. Response methods vary. Near shore, a boat will be sent. Farther offshore, a helicopter may be dispatched; and farther yet, a plane, to fix your location and perhaps drop pumps or other equipment.

VHF Calls. See Chapter 6 for detailed procedures for distress calls. Remember, Mayday is used for true distress: vessel or persons threatened by "grave and imminent danger" requiring immediate assistance: fire, sinking, injury, major collision, breaking up after grounding.

Use Pan-Pan for an urgent situation: messages pertaining to a vessel or persons "in jeopardy." (A crew-overboard call is a Pan-Pan call.)

• Attached to some Shakespeare VHF radios, the Mayday Mike sends a request for help (synthesized voice, not you) with the push of a button. It can be interfaced with GPS or loran, so it broadcasts a full message: boat name, numbers, and position. You can override it at any time to speak directly.

• The Coast Guard can sometimes use a radio direction finder to home in on your VHF signal; this gives them a line of position to your boat.

• If you hear a distress call, and you *don't* hear a Coast Guard response, notify the nearest authority your radio can reach. Assist, if you can do so without endangering yourself.

EPIRB. An EPIRB—Emergency Position Indicating Radio Beacon—is the last resort in emergency calling. A battery-operated transmitting device sends out a signal for help, giving the boat's location.

Signals are picked up by satellites or aircraft, and transmitted to appropriate responders. The newest EPIRBs—406 MHz—include vessel identification with the help call, assuming the EPIRB has been properly registered with the FCC (Federal Communications Commission).

Older EPIRBs (121.5/243 MHz) send out a lot of false alarms, and they are not as accurate with their position indication: 10 to 20 miles, as opposed to the 406's 1.5-mile accuracy.

• If you accidentally activate an EPIRB, call the Coast Guard.

EMERGENCIES TO THINK ABOUT
Fire

If you have a fire on board, try to turn the boat so flames blow out of or away from the boat, not into another section of the boat. Use your fire extinguishers: aim at the base of the flame with a back-and-forth sweeping motion. For a typical boat fire extinguisher, discharge time is under 20 seconds.

If it's possible to remove whatever is burning, do so. If the fire is getting bigger, call a Mayday. Put on PFDs, prepare the liferaft or dinghy, gather signaling gear, toss flotation cushions over, and get ready to jump overboard.

Prevention Reminders

• Maintain the fuel system: no leaks.

• Use the blower: no fumes.

• Take care of galley stove and cabin heater: no surprises.

• Watch electrical wiring: no shorts.

• Don't put oily rags in a locker: no combusting spontaneously.

• If you use propane, get a fume detecting alarm. Back it up with your nose.

• Be smart about smoking: don't. If you must, be aware of potential dangers.

• Keep fire extinguishers accessible near those places most likely to have a fire: engineroom, electrical boxes, galley, heater. Rules specify minimums only; extras give you a better chance to put out a fire.

Crew Overboard

If someone falls overboard, everyone on the boat should be prepared to act fast. This is the reason for all those drills. If only one or two people remain on board, they must respond in triple time; there are so many things to do first.

Mark the Spot. Glance at the compass for a reading of your heading, then send the crew-overboard pole over, followed by as many floating cushions as you can get your hands on; the more you throw in, the more chance you'll have of finding the location, and the more chances the overboard person can grab something to hang onto.

(One suggestion is to leave a trail of magazine pages, or anything else that will stay afloat to mark a return path.)

Turn Around. As you are throwing things with one hand, the other can be jotting down coordinates from the GPS or pushing the auto-save button. Then do something about slowing the boat. If you're on a powerboat, you can do it with one hand: throttle down and shift into reverse to stop till you get your bearings. If you're sailing, head up into the wind to stall; either tack back to the position of the overboard person, or douse the sails and motor back (don't start the engine till you're sure all lines are accounted for).

In the midst of all this activity, look back as often as possible to try to maintain a visual connection with the person overboard.

It's hard to see a person in the water, especially with waves, which is the likely condition in an overboard accident. Popular advice says, "Assign a crewmember the single task of watching the overboard person." That's a nice idea, but in the case of a two-person crew, one is now overboard, so it's not an option. If there *are* more people on the boat, someone could broadcast a Pan-Pan.

As soon as possible, turn the boat around and take up a reciprocal heading. Hopefully, you will see the person, a marker, some cushions, or a trail of other floating stuff. When you do spot the person, approach from the side you consider safest; then head into wind and waves to stall the boat.

Retrieval. Opinions are divided and strong over which side to approach a person in the water. Partly, it depends on sea conditions at the time, so it becomes a judgment call. With a windward approach, the

Sailboat heads into the wind to stall quickly, then returns to the overboard person.

boat should subdue the waves somewhat, giving some shelter to the overboard person. Also, a life ring has a better chance of finding its mark. The disadvantage is a serious one: the boat could drift down onto the person in the water.

With a leeward approach, there's less worry about a harmful contact between boat and person, but it's hard to throw the life ring against the wind, and it would be more difficult for a swimmer to help.

When the boat is close to the person, throw the life ring, with line still attached to boat. Once the person is tethered to the boat, go to your prearranged plan for boarding.

Reboarding

Even though the person is now close to the boat, the next step may be the most difficult: how to get the person from the water to the deck.

On a small boat with low freeboard, the overboard person might be able to roll over the side with some help from the onboard crew, but most cruising boats have too high a freeboard for this option. If you're towing a dinghy, it might be worth trying to board it, depending on the condition of the overboard person. If it was a quick fall-in and fast return, a dinghy entry might be a possibility.

If the person is still strong and alert, a ladder may be all that's necessary, either a standard boarding ladder or the emergency fall-down steps described earlier. (In certain conditions, the swim platform might be the best place; the person can hang on till onboard crew can rig hoisting gear.)

Lifesling. Another recovery device is the Lifesling, a horseshoe-shaped harness. Once the boat has returned to the overboard person, drop the Lifesling with its attached tether into the water, and steer the boat so a circle of line closes around the person in the water, to deliver the Lifesling. The person puts it on, and the rescuer hauls the victim alongside. Use hoisting tackle (not included) to bring the person out of the water and onto the boat. (With the right tackle, a single person should be able to hoist the victim aboard.)

Sailboats can use the main halyard (take it to one of the sheet winches) or the boom vang. Powerboats can rig a block and tackle to the cabintop or wherever they will get the proper height. (An anchor windlass might be used for some added muscle in the hoisting arrangement.)

• If you have no boarding ladder, tie stirrup loops into a piece of line and hang

MOM. One recovery system has been in use for years; you'll see the compact MOM—Man Overboard Module—on many a stern rail. Originally, the MOM held a marking pole and horseshoe ring (both automatically inflated when released). The pole increased visibility for an accurate return; the life ring, of course, held the overboard person afloat. The most recent version, MOM 9, includes a small raft that is used to help lift the victim on board.

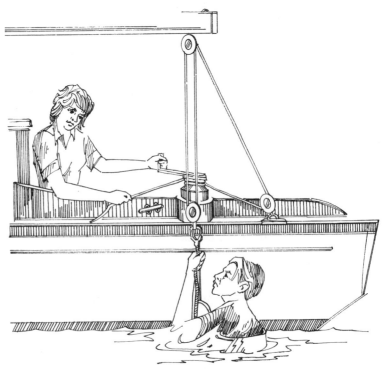

On a sailboat, use the vang for hoisting tackle with Lifesling.

it over the side—anything to help the person get some footing.

- If more than one person is on board, all should *stay* on board, unless the overboard person is weak or injured, and needs help to put on the life ring.

- If it's absolutely necessary for another person to go into the water, wear a PFD and safety line.

- Practice overboard retrieval with crew taking turns directing the procedure.

- Prevention:

  Keep a good nonskid surface on decks.

  Watch lifelines for any cuts or rust spots, and replace the lines as soon as such spots appear.

  Use the head, not the rail. Half of boating fatalities involve alcohol, and it's said that half of drinking men who drown are found with their fly open.

  Wear a harness and a tether, especially when working on deck in foul weather; check the material and hardware on harnesses often.

  Don't leave the cockpit without telling crew—even if it means an early wakeup.

  Attach a whistle and personal strobe light to your PFD.

  Tie netting, or weave a pattern of line, onto lifelines, to close the gap between line and deck.

Hull Damage

If you hit a rock or other immovable object, it's possible the boat has been holed; at least in that circumstance, you'll know the cause of a leak. But sometime, you may see the water, without any such apparent cause. Start looking: check all through-hull fittings and their connecting hoses; watch the place where the shaft exits the hull; look at the head.

This is the reason you carry an extra, large-capacity pump. This may be why you have a set of wood plugs; if a through-hull is broken and cannot be closed, hammer in a plug.

You can use the engine to help pump water out of the boat, by taking the intake hose off its through-hull and putting it into the bilge. (Put a screen on the hose end or set it into a colander, or make some precaution to keep bilge debris out of the engine's cooling system. And don't forget to close the seacock first.)

If the hull is damaged, stuff the hole with whatever fits: rags, clothes, pillow, anything to stop the water entry. If necessary, put a tarp over the exterior of the damaged spot, and tie it as snug as you can around the hull. This should stop most of the incoming water so the pumps can keep up with the rest.

We recall—not fondly—a sailboat race from Chicago to Michigan City, Indiana. The green-gray sky threatened tornadoes, but instead released a deluge of frightful lightning and hail. In the half hour it took the storm system to pass, seven boats were struck by lightning. One boat had six through-hull fittings when the race started and six through-*holes* immediately after the storm. The crew was able to fix each with a wood plug and continued to sail into port. (Not so easily fixed was the hull, which looked like it had been the target of shotgun practice. It was pockmarked along the entire length, and fiberglass had stripped away from the rudderpost in sheets.) Nobody was injured; all boats made it to port safely.

Worst Emergency

Not much can prepare you for a collision with another boat. If it's minor, check all crew for injuries, then look at the damage and do what you can for temporary repair. If it's a major collision and sinking is imminent, get PFDs on everyone and turn to your abandon-ship plan, the true last resort.

If possible, send a Mayday from the ship radio; otherwise, use the hand-held from dinghy or liferaft. Activate the EPIRB if you're offshore. Grab your emergency bag with the survival kit or other abandon-ship gear. Launch the liferaft or climb into the dinghy, but stay tied to the boat as long as possible; it will be more visible to rescuers.

MORE SAFE THOUGHTS

• Be realistic about the kind of weather your boat is designed for, and don't go out when you shouldn't.

• Autopilots have given recreational boaters a lot of freedom—maybe too much. It's easy to get too comfortable with the robot steering, and not keep a proper lookout. Most especially at night, look, look, and look again; scan all around the boat, so you can watch the progress of each light from the time it comes into view.

• When overnight trips are just an occasional thing, there's no point in trying to stick to a 4-hour watch schedule. Each crew will need some rest; work it out by who's the day person, who's the night owl. (We like 2½-hour watches—enough time to get some good rest when you're off, but not so much that you get sleepy when you're on.)

• Cruise with another boat (or more); there's lots of security in having help at hand, and it's fun. But don't follow a leader blindly; always be your own captain.

• Be sure new crewmembers learn where the safety equipment is, and how to use it. This includes fire extinguishers, radio, distress signals, PFDs.

• If you capsize in a small boat, stay with it. If the water is cold, climb onto the capsized boat; huddle together to stay warm.

• Mount the life ring or overboard retrieval system near the steering station, so it can be released as quickly as possible.

• You'll hear disagreement about the effectiveness of radar reflectors, but if there's a chance that one might improve the "visibility" of your boat, it's worth hanging one up. Commercial captains say these help a lot.

• Get a Seal of Safety: request a Coast Guard Auxiliary Courtesy Marine Exam. This is not a test. It does not cost money. Call up the local Coast Guard Auxiliary group, and ask them to look at your boat. If they do, and you pass, you get the seal (with a picture of, who else, Safetee Seal).

The exam is a nice idea. It includes a check on all required equipment, naturally, but the Auxiliary adds a few extras that can only make you a better-equipped boat. Call the Coast Guard Safety Hotline for the number of your local group: 1-800-368-5647 (in Washington, DC, 267-0780). The hotline also handles product-recall information; you can get answers to questions regarding boating safety; and you can comment on Coast Guard boarding procedure. If you prefer, mail your questions or comments to: Commandant (G-NAB-5), U.S. Coast Guard Headquarters, Washington, DC 20593-0001.

• Learn about hypothermia. When a person falls into cold water, body temperature may drop to a dangerous low, causing not only severe chills, but a physical and mental slowdown that can lead to coma and death.

If you should fall into cold water, try to retain as much of your body heat as possible. Keep your clothes on; cover your head if possible. Try not to swim far; you'll lose body heat. If you're alone, bring your knees up to your chest in the Heat Escape Lessening Position.

Once the overboard person is back on the boat, start rewarming by wrapping in blankets, or by huddling with another person to transfer body warmth. Don't apply heat to arms and legs, but it's okay to use hot water bottles on head, neck, chest, and groin. Don't massage, or give a hot bath.

• For a pamphlet on hypothermia, write: BOAT/U.S. Foundation, 880 S. Picket Street, Alexandria, VA 22304.

• For a list of boating courses in your area, call BOAT/U.S., 1-800-336-2628. Courses are taught by U.S. Power Squadrons, the U.S. Coast Guard Auxiliary, or the American Red Cross.

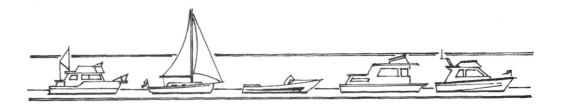

16

Riding Waves

Weekend boaters and coastal cruisers should not have to face a survival-testing gale; with all the weather warnings available to mariners today, people have plenty of opportunity to come in out of the storm, or preferably, before it.

But anybody can get caught by a squall line; winds frequently climb higher than forecasters predict; and it's not impossible for wind to completely shift its expected direction. The sea conditions brought by these fast-moving fronts won't be as extreme as those of a long and nasty storm system, but the problems will be the same, as will the strategies for dealing with them.

Because different hull designs react differently to the same outside influences, boat handling depends as much on judging current conditions as on steering and speed control. Only experience can provide this sea sense, but in the interim, read about and watch what others do, and see what applies to you.

WAVES

Years ago, we heard ocean sailors claim they'd never seen waves like those they encountered on Lake Michigan. Later, we realized it was a statement, not a comparison; it's an apples–oranges conversation.

Ocean waves are mostly long swells; you're not so aware of their height because the boat can ride over them rather than pound through them. Lake waves build high, with a short distance between; the shallower the water, the shorter the wave distance.

158

Meeting Waves

Anyone who has tried to make headway against a short, steep chop knows the frustration. Each wave knocks back your forward movement till you feel like a child on a rocking horse: lots of motion but little of it forward.

When confronted with this kind of wave pattern in some bay or sound, go anchor somewhere and wait a few days till the waves settle and you can enjoy the trip. If you cannot wait, you'll have an easier ride if you go forward in a series of short tacks, so you meet the waves at a slight angle rather than bow-on. Both sailboats and powerboats should do the zigzag; it won't be a speedy trip, but it will be a more comfortable one.

Similarly, if a strong current opposes a strong wind, the water will be a strong mess.

The Gulf Stream is a good example of how current affects waves. Admittedly, this ocean current knows how to exaggerate. You leave Florida and find an ordinary ocean swell; you get into the Gulf Stream, and if wind is from the "wrong" direction (contrary to current), aquamarine hills start to build, with valleys too narrow to slide down and up easily. If the wind picks up, the hills are flecked with white foam, looking downright unfriendly. Perhaps unique to the Gulf Stream are waves that not only build high and steep, but also come at the boat from two different angles, a true example of the phrase "confused seas."

The main reason boaters find themselves in the Gulf Stream when they should not be there is because they got tired of "waiting for weather." They took a chance, and it was a mistake. But now comes the confusing part. Why not turn around? The boat goes both ways, and a backtrack when you see it's obviously a wrong day for a crossing is much preferred to pounding your boat and your crew for another 5 or 6 or 10 hours.

If you listen to the wait-for-weather caution—and heed it—you can have a beautiful sail across gently rolling water; you can even cross a mirror-calm sea. It can happen.

Weather prompted an unusual transit of Lake Erie, one which we now remember as a favorite. We wanted to head west, but the wind was *from* the west, strong and persistent. After a few waiting days, impatience overcame good sense and we left Buffalo. Our intended destination was a U.S. port along the south shore of the lake, but instead, we went to Canada, because that route was *possible*. For the next week, we crisscrossed the lake, visiting an American port one day, a Canadian the next, each tack making some progress along our original westerly course. Eventually, we won: the weather changed.

Running with Waves

When you and the wind are going the same way, it's a sleigh ride for any boat, as long as the wind does not get so strong nor the waves so large as to make steering difficult.

Broach Avoidance. Running before a strong wind and following sea, you also run a risk of broaching: the stern tries to swing to the side, you lose steering control, and if the boat turns broadside to the waves, it will roll badly. Slow down till you feel you have control again.

If your intended course would force you to run with a beam sea, it's safer to do the short-tack routine on this heading, too. Sailboats get some relief from rolling thanks to the damping effect of the sails and the deep keel, but it is not a comfortable boat-to-wave position for any boat, and it could be dangerous.

Wave Speed. Powerboats should adjust boat speed to match wave speed. If you go too fast, you'll ride up on the back of the wave ahead. If you go too slow, the waves will catch you from astern and threaten to broach you.

Getting Pooped. When the boat gets pooped, water pours in over the transom. It happens when a following sea catches you, and the wave decides to go over rather than under the boat. Usually, the wave crests, and you'll hear the splash just before you feel the water.

While sailing in Mississippi Sound one brisk autumn day, we had a good sailing wind pushing us at hull speed. With no warning, a muffled whoosh filled the cockpit with water—green water, with not a bit of foam or spray. While this was a gentle example of getting pooped, if high swells astern threaten to do the same thing, run the zigzag downwind, too. Slow down if you can, but maintain steerage.

INLETS

In bad weather—especially with an onshore wind—many boaters prefer to stay out in deep water rather than face an inlet, particularly one that is unfamiliar, and is *not* a guaranteed deep, big-ship channel. This is not a bad idea.

Entering an Inlet

If you choose to enter, try to come in at a time when tide is slack, or near the end of flood. (An ebbing tide flowing out against the onshore wind will naturally confuse the water even more.)

Call the closest Coast Guard Group for some local advice. Close the hatches, and head in slowly; if you can match the speed of the waves, do so. Try to ride the back of a wave, with the crest staying ahead of the bow. Stay as close to center-channel as possible; if a wave catches your stern and shoves it sideways, you'll have enough room to correct. Probably, there will not be a lot of boat traffic to worry about.

- Be especially careful not to take any shortcuts, even if you've done so before. The safest path is the direct course from the sea buoy, and that's the one you should choose.

- Look behind often to check any side set; many inlets have submerged jetties, and boats and rock piles do not go together.

When entering an inlet in rough water, try to match the speed of the waves.

• Shoals just outside an inlet cause breaking waves in rough weather (see chart note "breakers"). Try not to be intimidated; expect to see them, and keep your eyes on the clear channel. Once you're committed, it is too dangerous to turn around.

Bottoming Out

Accidents can happen under these conditions. If an inlet is shallow to begin with, steep, rolling waves will make it more shallow in wave troughs. Combine that with a low tide, and a boat with even moderate draft might bottom out—hit the bottom while in the trough of a wave. Even local knowledge cannot always judge the peculiar combination of conditions that would lead to such a disaster; don't attempt a shallow inlet in rough weather.

Exiting an Inlet

When you exit an inlet, you may be surprised by the conditions you meet. Even if the weather has cleared and the wind has subsided, a leftover swell builds into a pattern of steep, short waves as it comes near shore. A danger here is in burying the bow

In a shallow inlet, a boat could hit bottom in the trough of a wave.

as the boat dips down the back side of a wave. Go as slowly as you can while still maintaining some headway. These waves will be a problem only till you clear the cut and get into deeper water.

FAST-MOVING STORMS

If the gray band along the far horizon is now threatening to cover the sky overhead, start checking your stowage. Anything not fastened should move to a wedge-in position, as low in the boat as it can go. Pay special attention to cameras and binoculars; you don't really want to test their shock-resistant cushioned coatings. Clear the decks of everything that's not required for running the boat.

Before the storm hits, check the chart to see if you're close to any shipping lanes, and if you are, set a course for a hasty retreat on the downwind side, so you can't get pushed into them.

The same holds true for an offshore buoy. While it will confirm your location for after-storm navigating, it might also be the objective of other boats in the area who wish to stay found. Too many boats converging on the same mark in poor visibility with the added glitch of wind and rain is not a good or safe scenario.

If you're offshore when the storm arrives, it's usually best to simply run, or drift, with it. Thunderstorms seldom stay in one spot very long, so you will not lose a lot of miles, and it's so much easier than trying to hold a particular course if that heading happens to be straight into the wind. Keep track of the course you steer; when the cloudburst quits, you can resume a course to your original destination, with clean hull and decks. In inland waters, you must judge where the safest course lies.

Since many thunderstorms come about as a result of two weather systems meeting, you cannot be sure how many times the wind may shift in mid-storm. Many sailors prefer to drop sail until the front goes through, rather than get caught by contrary winds and flailing sails.

STICK-AROUND STORMS

Most coastal cruisers will be in port long before winds and seas build to problem proportions, but in the unlikely chance you get caught in a nasty weather system, you should think about boat speed in terms of less rather than more, moving in steps from slowdown to almost stop.

Heaving-To

Though heaving-to is regarded by many as an old-fashioned way to deal with rough water, it still works for many boats, so why not try? Its purpose is to retard boat movement; the boat will make very little forward progress, but at least it doesn't go backward.

A powerboat should aim into the wind, or just slightly off, and put the engine at low RPM—only what's needed to maintain position.

A sailboat heaves-to by setting the rudder to "steer" into the wind; the jib (probably a storm jib) is sheeted to windward, and the main (reefed) is pulled in tight. In this way, the rudder and main try to push the boat *into* the wind, while the effect of the backed jib is to push the boat *off* the wind. The boat sits in a compromise position, somewhere about 45 degrees off the wind, moving forward very slowly.

Boats with long, straight keels do heave-to more readily than those with short, fin keels. Different boats often need different sail combinations to heave-to properly. Experiment before you need to know.

When a sailboat heaves-to, the boat should move forward very slowly at an angle about 45 degrees off the wind.

Lying Ahull

If heaving-to leaves too much sail for weather conditions, drop all sail and try lying ahull. Tie the helm to center, and let the boat drift with no direction from the helm. The boat will go to a beam-to-sea position; if the waves get too big to do this safely, this is the condition that would suggest a switch to a drogue or sea anchor.

Dragging a Drogue

With following seas, you want some way to counteract the tendency to broach. Dragging something behind the boat will slow it down and keep it tracking straight.

The traditional way to slow down was to tow one or more long lines behind the boat, but modern-day drogues are made specifically for their function: to limit speed and to ease steering, thereby reducing the chance of a broach. Their rounded cone shape and open-weave design allows some water to flow through.

Sea Anchor

You set a sea anchor off the bow just like an ordinary anchor; its purpose is to stop all way, and hold you in place in the middle of deep water, just like the ordinary anchor holds you in place in a shallow bottom. A sea anchor is shaped like, and often called, a *parachute;* they are sized for different sizes of boats.

• Sea anchors are designed for use off the bow because boats can take seas better on the bow than the transom; the bow offers the least amount of resistance because it has the least surface facing the sea.

A sea anchor holds the boat in place in deep water.

- When a sea anchor is set, the boat will drift only slightly: less than 1 knot.

- Sea anchors are used on all types of boats: sail, recreational powerboats, commercial fishing boats.

- The recommended size for a 35-foot boat: diameter of 12 feet. Recommended size for a 50-foot boat: diameter of 18 feet.

- The rode should be 10 to 15 times the boat length; follow the anchor manufacturer's directions for suitable components and attachment methods.

- If you carry a sea anchor, practice using it before you need it.

- Side benefit: if you lose the engine, the sea anchor can help you stay in place till you can fix the problem, or get a tow.

POWERBOAT ANTI-ROLL DEVICES

Most boaters would like to minimize rolling; it's not a favorite motion. Sailboats can set a sail to counteract the pendulum effect, and powerboaters have a few choices: they can rig a steadying sail, use flopper-stoppers, or add stabilizers.

Steadying Sails

Many people say steadying sails are of marginal use, because they are too small to provide a noticeable damping effect. Many boatowners who own a steadying sail have never tried to use it, so have no opinion about it. But those who *do* use them seem satisfied that the sail helps to dampen roll "some." Even if it's not the 90 percent claimed by stabilizer manufacturers, every percent less is a help.

Flopper-Stoppers

Flopper-stoppers do a good job of minimizing roll, with a combination of masts and outriggers and a paravane, or "fish" that they tow just below the water's surface on each side. As the boat tries to roll to one side, the resistance from the opposite fish pulls it upright.

Unfortunately, their use is limited to slower boats—displacement-type hulls. Because the flopper-stoppers involve a lot of strain on the structure, it is difficult to add them to an existing boat.

Stabilizers

These ingenious add-ons create their own force to counter the wave force that is trying to roll the hull. Fin stabilizers have been used on big ships for a long time; they eventually came down to recreational-boat size, if not price.

SAILORS' SUGGESTIONS

• Sailors know they should shorten sail early, but they seem reluctant to do it *too* early. Who will know?

• When you finally acknowledge that the oncoming storm is not going to veer away, start your list of storm tactics. Shorten sail. Do it before the rain starts; afterward, it's too difficult to see, and you may have already damaged something.

• If it's sail-shortening time, it's also deck-clearing time. If anything's loose, inside or out, it shouldn't be.

• Get out foul-weather gear, PFDs, and harnesses.

• "Up in the puffs, down in the luffs." (Steer toward the wind when velocity increases, steer away when it slackens.)

• If you're running downwind, rig a preventer and/or vang, to discourage a dangerous jibe.

• In a following sea, sailboats move slower than the waves, so wave crests should pass beneath the hull.

• As wind speed increases:

Shorten sail, heave-to.

Go to bare poles, lie ahull.

Drag a line or drogue.

Set a sea anchor.

See Chapter 18 for weather-watching information.

17 Running Rivers

River travel is unlike any other water travel. From one view, it is the most protected—quiet countryside, confined waterway, and in some rivers, a new anchorage every few miles. From another perspective, it's the most dangerous—shallow water, unmarked sandbars and dams, and especially, commercial traffic. You hear about four-stackers—super tugs with four engines pushing a hundred barges; they can't see you and couldn't stop if they did.

Well, you heard right, but that doesn't mean you can't take a river trip; it just means you approach it with a different set of cautions.

First, the big tugs are found only on the big rivers. While the Mississippi and its larger tributaries still transfer tons of cargo, the TVA lakes of the Tennessee River are a cruiser's paradise. Other rivers may start their inland route as industrial through-ways, but soon become scenic waterways.

There's still a lot of riverside that is not shadowed by condominiums. You can find farms and walkaround towns—a true cross section of rural America—seemingly out of touch with today's world, though perhaps on purpose. The United States and Canada have thousands of river and canal miles to explore. And you don't need an oceangoing boat.

River travel is fun, and it's interesting—a bit of history, science, commerce, and folk art, all seen from a water's-eye view.

MAPS

NOAA charts are used for some larger Western rivers (Snake and Columbia), but other river systems use river maps, usually sold in groups as a book: the Illinois River is covered in one book; the Mississippi in two, etc. (Call the area Army Corps of Engineers for information.) These maps show the safe channel, plus markers, dikes, and some shore features, but they do not show depths, a source of frustration for the traveler who likes to wander off the main channel. A depthsounder and leadline are invaluable in these constantly shifting waterways, and local knowledge can be a big help. Talk to locktenders, bridgetenders, local boaters, and then proceed with extreme caution anyway.

MARKS

Familiar red and green buoys or daybeacons will mark the channel, lighted with red and green, just like their coastal counterparts. Rivers add a crossing mark: a diamond-shaped daymark to indicate the place where the navigation channel crosses the river. Following the natural flow of water, the deepest water is at the outside of bends, so the channel weaves a course that favors first one side, then the opposite. Range marks might also be used to guide traffic across.

Instead of the diamond shape, a crossing mark might be literally a cross—a couple of boards making an X.

To help you keep track of your progress, there may be mile markers posted along the shores. Where there is a lot of current, these markers help you determine your speed early in the day; you may be able to revise your docking or anchoring plan based on more miles made good.

DEPTH

The water level in most rivers changes seasonally: deeper with the spring floods, shallow in the dry seasons. (However, we have seen the lower Mississippi rising 2 feet a day in late November—not normally a flood season—so nothing's guaranteed.)

Controlled Depths

In a river that is controlled by a system of locks and dams, water level can change overnight without help from nature. Besides seasonal differences, water levels may be adjusted for drainage, or for mosquito

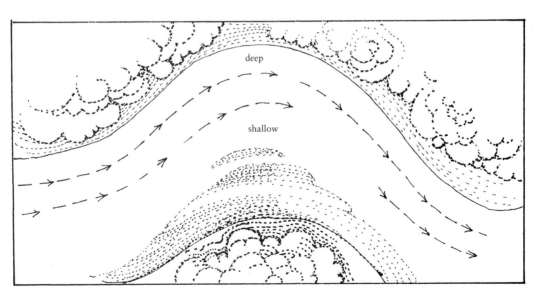

In rivers, water is deepest along the outer curve, where downstream current runs strong. On the opposite shore, shoals build out from the inner bend

control. When you're cruising one of these rivers, you must pay attention to pool levels and planned changes. If the information is not posted on signboards along the riverbank, ask towboat captains or lockmasters. It's important to know when the water level is expected to change; it may influence your docking/anchoring plans, and it will affect overhead clearances.

Reading Depths

Since river maps do not provide water depth information, you learn to judge where the deepest water is by the way the river flows. The downstream force is strongest on the outside bends; the water maintains a deep path by carving away at the bottom. On the opposite side, along the inner bends, the slower water leaves behind sand and silt to build up shoals. Give these points a wide berth; the shoaling will usually be gradual, so you should be aware of it early enough to alter course.

Maintaining Depths

Dikes or wing dams have been built all along the Mississippi to keep water flowing in the desired channel at the desired depth. They're not high dams; they're purposely kept low so they don't obstruct flow during times of high water. Older ones were a combination of wood pilings and stone, but now most are all rock: more permanent, more dangerous if the boat finds one. But they *are* mapped, so at least you're aware of the places to avoid.

- "Revetment" describes the material and the method used to stop the river from undercutting the banks. Left to nature, after the river created the deep-water channel on the outside bend, it would continue its carving, removing mud, earth, and sand at water level till the bank had no more support. The top would cave in and the dirt, vegetation, and trees fall in, putting unwanted fill into the river bottom and unwanted debris into the water.

To hold riverbanks in place, they are stabilized with *revetment*—blocks of concrete reinforced with wire that also ties them together like giant building blocks.

- If you travel down the Mississippi, look for the places where levees are

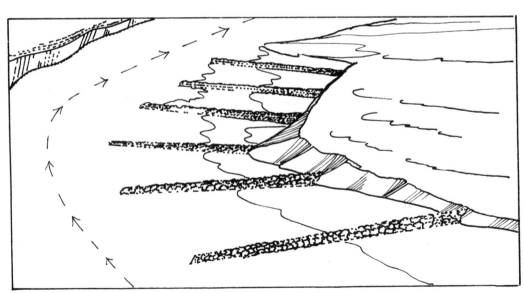

Dikes or wing dams keep water flowing along the desired channel.

marked with "record" water heights. The marks are as high as a sailboat mast is tall. It is difficult to visualize the river rising that high; if you manage to picture that, you next wonder how the levee could possibly hold all that water in.

• When you receive information about water level at various points along the river (whether from signposts or radio broadcasts), you can plot those stages at a series of points along the way. You'll see the pattern of a crest as it moves downstream, and you can judge if the water will be rising or falling in a place you may be considering for an anchorage.

CURRENT CONSIDERATIONS

River current will affect your travel just like tidal current, and with some rivers, you'll have to deal with *both* kinds. If you're headed inland up a large river in a sailboat or slow-moving trawler, look for a favorable tide, or you will go nowhere fast (and you could sit still for a long time, even at cruising RPM).

In some rivers, average-size sailboats with average-size engines cannot go upstream at any speed. The biggest and best example of why not is again the Mississippi. Its current ranges from 1 to 6 miles per hour under average conditions; at times of flooding, we've heard it could be as high as 9, though luckily we've not seen that rate. In our 27-foot sailboat, we traveled 11 mph over the bottom, about twice the speed the boat was capable of doing on its own. And this was a non-flood time of late autumn.

Changing Speed

Narrower sections of the river will naturally have stronger current, as water is forced to funnel through a smaller opening. Bridges are a noticeable example of this.

If a strong wind has been blowing in the same direction the current is flowing, the current will pick up strength from its ally.

When the wind blows against the current, the velocity may slow down some, but you will not notice, because the water will be churned up in a wind-against-current chop. You will have a very sloppy ride, and in Mississippi mud, the splashes are not refreshing.

• Current will be strongest in midstream, so stay as close to center as you can when moving downstream to get the most boost to your speed.

• If you must turn upstream, travel as close to the bank as depth will allow; in some areas, a counter-current will be noticed close to the bank, but even without that, the normal river current will be slower at the sides of the river.

• Floods can cause water to cover the navigation buoys; if you're lucky, the buoy will be close enough to the surface so the V pattern in the water will serve as a warning.

• With windstorms, floods, and bank erosion, branches and whole trees fall into rivers all the time. If they float, you have a better chance of seeing them; if they get caught with one end stuck in the bottom, you may find one only by hitting it.

• Spring is naturally the worst time for floods, but during our unusual November trip, we were actually stalled a few times by log jams spanning the entire river at a bend.

RIVER TIE-UPS

Some rivers are filled with marinas for pleasure boats, and some are mainly commercial waterways. Personal preference will also influence whether you look for anchorage or dockage, but if you vote for anchor, be sure you're well away from any navigation channel.

Docking

If you're on a busy working river, ask the towboat captains where you might stay. They'd rather find you a safe spot than have you pick a hazardous one.

You may be allowed to tie to a little-used dock or to a barge or log boom overnight, but don't ever do it without asking permission, or you may be surprised by a 3 A.M. transfer as your "dock" starts moving down the river.

• Traveling with a strong downstream current, you become adept at crabbing. If, for example, you want to tie up at a dock down the river, you should start your turn very early; the more the boat turns broadside to the current, the faster you'll be pushed downstream. If you don't start edging over to the side soon enough, you might miss your objective entirely, and be unable to come back upcurrent to the dock.

• Try not to dock in a place where you'll be parallel to the river, because you'll also be parallel to the wakes—not a good idea. (Bow-out is the best position, if you can arrange it.)

• Towboats travel all night. Wherever you tie, be well fendered and well sprung.

Bank-Tie

If you find an indentation in the shoreline that's too small to allow you to swing at anchor, tie the boat to a couple of trees, bow and stern, at a slight angle to the shore. (Use the dinghy to take the lines ashore.)

If you'd rather position the boat bow-out, drop an anchor in the river just outside the cove; then use the dinghy to take a stern line to a tree situated behind the boat. You'll be positioned safely in the center; with bow out, you'll take the wakes at the best possible angle.

A third possibility is to tie two bow lines and the stern line to trees. You're still centered, still bow-out.

On an upstream trip during a time of high water, one trawler captain reported tying between two treetops—because only the tops of the trees were visible.

Anchoring

• On some rivers, you can simply pull off anywhere and anchor, as long as you're away from the main channel.

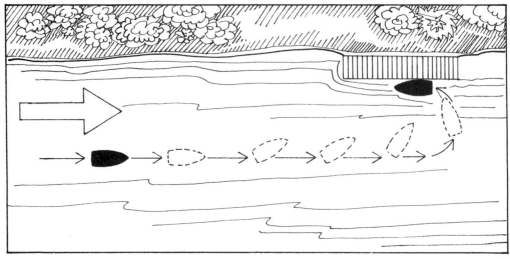

When traveling downstream with a strong current, start turns early.

- On the big rivers, you'll be safer anchored in a side creek, or behind an island; otherwise, you'll suffer from flashing spotlights and bothersome wake rolls all night.

- You may be able to anchor behind a sandbar or wing dam.

- If the channel behind an island is deep along its entire length, it may be used as an alternate channel by smaller tugs. If you anchor there, get as close to the bank as draft permits.

- Always enter side channels (including the one that is the backside of an island) from the downstream end, so you can enter slowly against current, not be pushed in *by* current.

- Go well past the entrance of side channels, as shoals build up from the upper end between the river current and the side stream's current. When well past the place where the two join, turn and favor the bank side as you head upstream into the channel.

- If you can't find a place off the main river, look for a spot under a point of land, opposite the wide, outer swing of the channel. If you can line up a light and a landmark, you'll have a good range to enter and leave on.

- Use a bright anchor light.

RIVER TRIVIA

- Keep an anchor ready, in case it's necessary to anchor quickly, perhaps to wait for commercial traffic to pass.

- Lock signals in some rivers are three long blasts, instead of the "two long, two short" of the Intracoastal Waterway.

- The Tennessee River is a lovely cruising destination in itself. Nine lakes were created by the TVA (Tennessee Valley Authority). Largest and best known is Kentucky Lake, situated near the junction of the Tennessee and Ohio Rivers.

- As of May 1994, fees are charged for boats going through New York's Erie Canal. They're not exorbitant; it seems fair to ask boaters to help maintain the locks, since they benefit from the system's remaining open. Boats 26 to 39 feet pay $75 for an "unlimited season pass"; over 39 feet, it's $100.

- The Mississippi is the only North American river to be included in a list of the world's 10 largest rivers: it is third in length, fifth in volume, draining parts of 31 states. From Minnesota to the Gulf, the river is 2,340 miles long.

- Sailors coming from the Calumet and Illinois Rivers can put up the mast after entering the Mississippi, but sailing will not be ideal: too many bends, too many trees for consistent wind. Motorsailing might help fuel consumption a bit, and it's always nice to feel that you have alternate propulsion for an emergency.

- Take extra fuel cans; first, because fuel stops may be far distant, and second, because sometimes you'll have to walk to a shore station to fill them.

- Keep fuel tanks topped off whenever you have a chance; the next marina may be gone.

- Going upstream in May, from New Orleans to Cincinnati (on the Mississippi and Ohio Rivers), a 44-foot trawler used 860 gallons of diesel fuel. For the return trip, going *with* the current, the same miles were traveled with 325 gallons.

- On any commercial waterway, night travel is not recommended for recreational boats. Besides the danger of the night-traveling towboats, you won't be able to see the debris in the water.

- We once saw the river at night. We were passengers aboard a towboat as it towed our disabled boat down the Mississippi. From the height of the wheelhouse, the river channel was clearly outlined, with the loom of New Orleans always ahead. Occasionally, muffled crunching noises would grab our attention, explained by the captain as "wheel inspectors," and finally understood by us to be some of the partially submerged logs we'd been dodging all day, temporarily stalled as they were caught by the tow's 6-foot propellers.

COPING WITH COMMERCIAL TRAFFIC

On most rivers, towboats could more accurately be called "push boats"; they move cargo on barges lashed together to form a massive, floating checkerboard that the tow pushes from behind. When the number of barges in front of one tow reaches 30, 40, or 50, their combined length and breadth warrants watching, for many reasons.

A big towboat may have three diesels, each about 3,500 hp, each turning a five-bladed, stainless steel prop that measures 10 feet in diameter.

Following Tows

Following in the wake of a towboat is not a good idea. Tows don't travel at a constant speed; they must slow down at many bends in order to position themselves properly to make the turn. Even an ordinary 6-foot-diameter propeller will create strong turbulence that extends a long way behind the boat. If you're too close, you'll know by the way your boat keeps trying to steer itself from side to side.

As frustrating as it is trying to hold a straight line against these circling currents, the worst part is watching for all the debris the wheel wash kicks up, which is now trying to kick your boat.

Meeting Tows

"Keep to the right" is not always advisable, at least not where river traffic is concerned. Towboats pushing barges must maintain speed to maintain steerage, and they must stay in the deep-water channel. If the water is deep bank-to-bank, the towboat may be in any portion of it, depending on how the tow must be aimed at the next bend.

Don't try to second-guess the tow captain's intentions. Just call and ask which is the safest side for you.

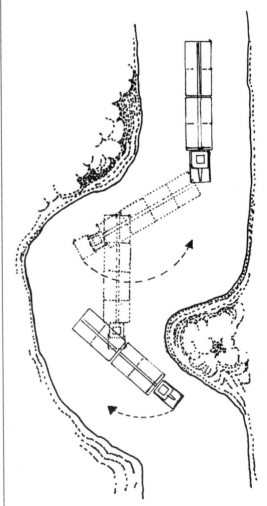

Tugs pushing barges often swing the stern from side to side to maneuver.

One whistle signal: both boats go starboard and pass port-to-port

Passing Tows

If you think you *can* overtake a tow, call the captain and ask if, when, and on which side it would be okay to do so.

Powerboats are asked to pass at low speed. A large wake can start a chain reaction that bounces the barges apart, creating a real problem in a narrow river channel, when only the one towboat must retrieve and retie the scattered barges. This will not make a towboat captain happy. (See also illustration on page 174.)

Talk to Tows

Keep the radio on Channel 13 (scan both 16 and 13). When you hear a security call from a tow nearing a blind bend, you can call to announce your presence and ask which side of the river is safest for you to pass (or whether you should wait where you are till the tow passes).

Passing questions will usually be answered with a statement like, "That's a one-whistle, captain," or "That's a two-whistle." If your understanding of those directions is not yet second nature, keep a diagram next to the helm.

Tow Info

A towboat may be more than 1,000 feet long; it cannot stop in time to avoid your boat, even if the captain sees you in a precarious position, which he may not because of the blind "spot" that may extend hundreds of feet in front of the tow. (Keep clear.)

• A tow can travel 1 mile in 7 minutes. It could take up to 1½ miles to stop a towboat.

• A vessel crossing a river must keep out of the way of a vessel proceeding up or down a river.

Two whistles: overtaking boat passes on port side.

• The downbound vessel is "privileged." (This refers to commercial traffic; recreational boats stay clear no matter which way they're bound.)

• Even a water road can have a traffic jam: barges and tows lined up on both sides of the river, waiting their turn to use the channel. (When the river level is down, or one section has shoaled, the narrowed channel forces one-way traffic.)

RIVER PEOPLE

Having heard unfriendly things about Mississippi towboat operators, we'd planned to be as low-key as possible. Luckily, after only a short time on Old Man River, we found our worries to be unfounded. Two towboat crews were very good to us: one shared Thanksgiving dinner with us; another plugged our shore-power cord into the tow's generator so we could have heat when the temperature dipped to 17 degrees. Towboat crews gave us directions, advice, humor, *and* a 70-mile tow from Baton Rouge to Lake Pontchartrain, including a lock-through assist in New Orleans.

The tow captain would accept no payment for the help, saying "Only payment I want is to know that someday, you'll lend a hand to someone who needs help. That's the way things work on this river."

John Wayne could not have said it better.

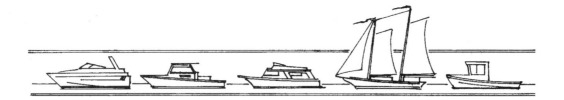

18 Watching Weather

When you're cruising, weather becomes a primary factor in practically every move you make. Should I sail north today? (Not very comfortably, with wind at 25 knots *from* the north.) Can I cross the bay? (Sure; get ready for anti-roll tactics.) How long before I see sunshine again? (How fast have these clouds been moving?)

If you choose the upwind slog or the beam-sea ride, you either enjoy challenging elements or you're on a tight vacation schedule. If you decide to wait out the weather, you're fortunate to have no time frame; most of us move on all the compromise days between awful and great.

Boaters do see weather from a different perspective, or with a different awareness, than land people. On shore, you can hide from the weather; on the water, you must deal with it.

WEATHER TRACKS

In the U.S., weather systems move in a general west-to-east pattern, shifted north or south in places by a Canadian polar air mass, the jet stream, or a tropical depression. Weather moves in masses of air that are either cold and dry (polar) or warm and moist (tropical); a front—cold or warm—is an area where these air masses collide.

Between VHF broadcasts and television weather maps, you can see how weather moves through an area. For example, in Florida in winter, when the wind is from the southeast (the prevailing wind), the weather is beautiful. The first sign of an approaching front is a wind switch to the south; next it moves through southwest to west, and by then, the rain is probably starting. When the wind goes through northwest and north, the storm will be in full swing, delivering most of its rain and fury. By the time the wind swings to the northeast, the sun is out and the sky is clear, even though there is still a lot of wind in the high-pressure area. Just before the wind veers to the east, it slows considerably, finally returning to the steady, usually pleasant southeast breeze.

In contrast to this predictability, Puget Sound's weather is a complex interplay of ocean air, mountains, and channels. As Migael Scherer explains in *A Cruising Guide to Puget Sound* (International Marine, 1995), "The prevailing flow of air in the sound is from the west, off the north Pacific Ocean. By the time this air reaches the Washington coast it is laden with moisture. Forced up by the Olympic Range, the saturated air cools and forms clouds. Precipitation results; lots of it. . . . No longer sodden but still moist, the air continues to flow inland over the Olympics, then across more water (where it picks up more moisture), up and against more mountains, down and around numerous channels and headlands.

"These mountains, channels and headlands alter the direction and force of the wind, determining where clouds will gather and where rain is likely to fall. As a result, very different levels of precipitation occur within relatively short distances. . . .

". . . boating can be enjoyed year round in Puget Sound. For most, the cruising season is from May through mid-September, when high pressure is usually dominant and (usually) less than 20 percent of the annual precipitation falls. . . .

"The normal summer pattern is for a spell of warm, sunny weather, with north-northwest winds gradually shifting to west-southwest winds that bring in clouds and rain for a few days."

The normal summer pattern in the Great Lakes and on Chesapeake Bay includes more than a fair share of afternoon thunderstorms. The biggest difference is that in Michigan, the storms bring some cooling relief, whereas in Maryland and Virginia, they just make steam.

All cruisers hear about Maine's famous fog, but it's not an all-summer problem. No matter where you're cruising, be aware of the weather patterns typical for the place, and for the time you're there.

WEATHER MAKERS: WIND AND CLOUDS

Winds are sometimes classified by a number on the Beaufort Wind Scale. Originally conceived in 1805, the scale uses a number to describe wind speed as well as the sea conditions that wind creates. Stated as "Force 1" or "Force 5," the numbers cover each step from calm to hurricane.

Cloud families divide into three main types: *cirrus*, *cumulus*, and *stratus*. Since one type often blends into another, the names also connect, to better describe them—for example, as cirrostratus or cirrocumulus. Two more syllables allow even more accurate description: *alto*, indicating high clouds, and *nimbo*, for low rain clouds.

The illustration on the facing page shows some typical clouds, and the wind and wave conditions you might expect with each.

Cirrus
Cirrus clouds are the wispy, narrow bands of white that look like strands of hair. Always high, cirrus clouds are the first indication of a change to wet weather (probably within two days).

When cirrus clouds first appear, you'll hardly notice waves. Force 0 would be a calm day; Force 1, gentle ripples brought by 1- to 3-knot breeze.

Stratus
Sometimes fragmented but usually connected, stratus clouds are the layered look in a fairly uniform gray cloud cover.

If you don't yet have the rain, expect it in the form of an all-day or two-day drizzle.

cirrus

stratus

cumulus

cumulonimbus

You might have a light breeze (Force 2, or 4 to 6 knots) or a gentle breeze (Force 3, or 7 to 10 knots) with a few scattered whitecaps.

Cumulus

The separate, puffy white cotton or popcorn or cauliflower clouds are cumulus. When they're high, it usually means fair weather for the day. When they start to connect to each other and develop dirty bottoms, watch for the possible addition of a thunderhead; afternoon storms could develop. (Ordinary rain showers may come from cumulus clouds; a thunderstorm will come from the cloud combination of cumulonimbus.)

You'll probably see some whitecaps when the wind gets to about 15 knots, or Force 4.

Cumulonimbus

A dense, heavy-looking cloud mass with a tall formation in its midst, this is the classic cloud for thunderstorm development. By the time you recognize the anvil shape, the rains have probably come, but at least they are usually brief.

With the wind at 17 to 21 knots (Force 5), you'll see a lot of whitecaps, and some spray. Winds and waves frequently increase during storms.

- "Mare's tails" are another name for the high, wispy cirrus clouds. Change is on the way, in a couple of days.

- A "mackerel sky" has cirrocumulus clouds that look like sand ripples. Wet weather is coming, perhaps as soon as 24 hours.

- When you see a separation in an all-over cloud cover (a white border overlapping a dark gray background), it is very probably an approaching squall line. Get ready, just in case.

- When you hear a report describing a stationary front, you can't be sure what the weather will do. The front may decide to move, in which case it will affect your weather, but you won't know when. Or, it may simply dissipate.

Lightning

Anybody who is not wary of lightning must be in denial. When you are the lone protrusion on a vast expanse of sea, you understand the meaning of vulnerable. Safety recommendations tell you to protect your boat with a grounding system, and so many boaters do. But even that cannot dispel the mixed feeling of fear and awe that comes with every storm.

Each time, you go through the motions: unplug the electronics (we're told this wouldn't help them if the boat were struck, but we do it anyway); stay away from large metal objects; stay low.

You can estimate the distance between you and a thunderstorm. Sound travels roughly 1 statute (land) mile in 5 seconds. When the lightning strikes, count off the number of seconds between the lightning flash and the thunder roar. You probably won't have your stopwatch handy at this exact moment, so do the slow counting (one thousand and one, one thousand and two . . .). If you get to 10 seconds before you hear thunder, the storm is 2 miles away.

WEATHER PREDICTORS

Weather information comes from many sources: television and radio reports, newspapers, broadcasts on VHF radio, all combined with your own observations of sky and water.

Big Picture

Most cruising boats have a television tucked away in a corner (even though the crew *never* watches it). Other boaters insist on a daily shore trip for a newspaper. Either way, or both, you have access to weather information.

Any weather map that gives you an overview of the whole country is helpful for your do-it-yourself forecasting. Look for the weather-makers: fronts, air masses, storms. Find them again the next day to see where they went, and how fast they traveled. Move them along in the same direction and at the same speed, and you can guess where they'll be tomorrow. Even by that oversimplified process, there is some real, applicable information.

VHF

Boaters get continuous weather reports on the WX channels of VHF radio (Channels 1, 2, and 3). Issued by NOAA, the messages repeat and are revised as needed. Similar broadcasts are heard in Canada on VHF Channels 21 and 83. You'll learn wind speed and direction, humidity and temperature, barometric pressure, and details of cloud cover, fog, or rain. In some locations, river levels and tides are included; broadcasts are prepared to provide information pertinent to a specific area.

Special warnings are broadcast for severe weather conditions. Some newer VHF radios will automatically switch to the weather channel to alert boaters of an approaching weather system.

• Keep a road atlas on board. Weather reports (TV and NOAA) often give weather warnings directed to specific counties; you'd like to know the location of those counties to determine if the weather is moving your way.

• If you're really ambitious, you can pay close attention to the location of those systems, and plot them on your chart (or on a weather tracking chart).

• NOAA reports on the VHF are so thorough these days, you'd be wise to keep a note pad handy and jot down

reports about your general area. Later, you can decide which one's closest to your particular location. After a few days, you'll know the order of the reports: inland, coastal, offshore, farm report, etc. Develop your own shorthand, or you'll miss it the first time.

Barometers

Barometers are reliable predictors. Once you get into a habit of watching your onboard barometer, you won't be surprised by a weather system. When you see a change in pressure, you'll expect the corresponding change in the weather. You can guess how extreme the change might be by how abruptly the barometer rose or fell.

The most familiar onboard type is the *aneroid barometer* (the one that matches the ship's clock). The pointer moves as air pressure changes.

• A steady barometer indicates stable weather; clear skies, light wind.

• A rising barometer means good weather is coming; clouds will decrease, the front is leaving.

• If the barometer falls slowly, expect unsettled weather; clouds, rain, an approaching front.

• When the barometer falls quickly (more than a millibar in an hour), a bad storm is on the way.

- Adjust a new barometer by listening to a nearby VHF weather station on a clear, calm day with a steady weather pattern. Set your barometer to match.

EXTRAORDINARY WEATHER

It's been suggested that if it weren't for the bad weather, we would not appreciate the good. There is probably some truth to that, but it would be nice to exclude certain extremes from that comparison. Still, it's better to know they exist, just so you can make every effort to avoid them.

Disturbed Air

Thunderstorms and squall lines are frightening in themselves, but as bad as the lightning show is the sight of a dark, swirling tail reaching down from a cloud and growing and growing till it touches the horizon as a tornado (on land) or a water spout (over water).

Water spouts often appear in multiples—we once saw seven at one time, in Florida's Keys. You can watch their course, and you can try to evade them. Mostly, you can hope they will simply fizzle out before they get anywhere near you. (Generally, the wind speed in a water spout is much less than that of a tornado.)

Disturbed Waters

Even when local weather is great, disturbed weather far away can send surprisingly high waves into your area. Waves spawned by hurricanes off the Florida coast devastated New York and New Jersey beaches. Storms in the Gulf of Alaska influence weather as far south as northern California. Waves from an "ordinary" norther can create boat-swamping conditions off certain cuts in the Bahamas, even though the weather seems calm on the inside.

Tidal Wave. A *tsunami*, or "tidal wave," does not come from tidal forces. It is a seismic sea wave—the result of a submarine earthquake. Such a wave can travel far from its place of origin, and cause a lot of damage when it finds shore, landing in a series of high, destructive waves.

Storm Surge. Also wrongly called a "tidal wave," a *storm surge* comes ashore with a hurricane, or with any combination of strong wind and an abrupt change in

Wind speed in a water spout is less than that of a tornado. Try to avoid them anyway.

barometric pressure. When a storm surge happens to coincide with high tide, damage to low-lying areas is increased. Most death and destruction from hurricanes are the result of storm surges, not high winds.

Seiche. A *seiche* is described as a "stationary, vertical wave oscillation." That may be hard to picture, but we remember the effects of one in Lake Erie. The water level rose about 2 feet in a very short time. As we watched, the dock to which we were tied submerged; then the water flooded the backyard of the house to which the dock was connected. Finally, the water crept into the house itself, forcing a temporary lifting of all movable furniture and rugs. The homeowners did not find this odd; this was a familiar routine for them.

Disturbed Everything

When severe weather threatens, smart boaters do all they can to protect boat and crew. When winds are expected to be 50 and over, or when tornadoes, hail, and frequent lightning strikes are all mentioned in the same forecast, it's time for all the preparation you can think of.

A severe storm often brings severe coastal flooding, so a marina dock may not be the best place to ride out a storm. The water may come up over the docks, carrying all the boats with it. When they come back down, they probably won't be in the same places. Your boat could land on the dock, or on another boat, or 2 miles inland.

- Travel as far inland as you can, and do it as early as you can. Later, bridges may be closed to boat traffic, if land traffic fills evacuation routes.

- Look for protection in an anchoring spot. Follow local fishing boats' lead: major rivers in any state lead to smaller side creeks.

- Even where fetch is not a problem, flooding may be; the farther inland you are, the less the surge will affect you.

- This is the time to drag out the storm anchor—and whatever others you have on board.

- Don't leave the anchor rode on bow rollers; most are not made for storm conditions.

- Even better than a bunch of anchors, tie to a bunch of trees. Don't stop with two or three; run as many lines as you have.

- If flooding is *not* a concern and you're staying at a dock, add extra lines, especially on the "weather" side, if that's possible. A slip-tie gives you a better chance to keep the boat off posts or pier. If you're stuck with a side tie-up, use all the fenders you have and *add extra spring lines*.

- Add heavy chafing gear to anchor or mooring lines. Try to tie it on securely, or it will slide away. Cover a long area of line with the chafing gear, because the line will stretch and shift position in the chocks.

- Take off everything that's removable. If you don't, the wind may. Canvas and lines are the first to go flying.

- Sailors should secure all sails or remove them. A furled jib increases windage initially, and if it gets loose all those square feet of sail could pull anchors out before the wind would tear it to shreds.

- A line wrapped around the boom many times can keep a sail cover from ripping.

Hurricane Warnings

A hurricane is a tropical cyclone; winds spiral counterclockwise around a calm, center eye. It starts as a *tropical depression* (wind less than 38 mph), grows into a *tropical storm* (39- to 73-mph wind), and becomes a *hurricane* when the wind climbs over 74 mph. The official season is June 1 through November 30; most storms occur in August and September.

Hurricanes start with a 74-mph wind, but the wind can gust to over 200 mph even 30 miles from the eye. Think about those numbers if you're ever tempted to stay on board your boat during a hurricane. Squalls can spread out over a 500-mile diameter.

A record downpour from one hurricane brought 23 inches of rain in a 24-hour period. Storm surge is the biggest problem for coastal lowlands. Water can be 10 feet over the normal high tide.

- The "weak" side of a hurricane is the semicircle to the left of the hurricane's eye and track; there, wind is moving in the opposite direction from the way the storm is moving. On the right side of the eye and track, the hurricane's wind and the storm's forward motion are both going the same direction.

- Most tropical storms follow a storm track that hooks north before reaching the southeast coast of the U.S.; they then dissipate at sea.

- Hurricane classifications:
  Category I—74 to 95 mph winds
  Category II—96 to 110 mph
  Category III—111 to 130 mph
  Category IV—131 to 155 mph
  Category V—156+ mph

Insurance companies, the Coast Guard, and all other boating safety people say don't stay on the boat in a hurricane. But some owners think they cannot leave. In the height of a hurricane, you could not do anything to change whatever the situation might be, so why risk harm to yourself?

WEATHER MAYBES

- *Red sky at night, sailor's delight;*
  Red sky in the morning, sailor take warning.

Dry air holds more dust, which makes the sky appear red. If it's red when the sun sets in the west, then dry weather is coming. If it's red in the east as sun rises, the dry air is past; in a normal cycle, rain may be coming.

- *Mackerel sky and mare's tails*
  Make lofty ships carry low sails.

Mare's tails are high cirrus clouds, the first sign of a change in the weather. In mackerel skies, cirrus clouds combine with cumulus, and rain is usually on the way.

- *Circle 'round the moon*
  T'will rain soon.

The moon is surrounded by cirrostratus clouds; moisture in the clouds refract the light so the moon seems to have a halo. These clouds precede a cold front.

- *At sea with a low and falling glass*
  The greenhorn sleeps like a careless ass.
  But when the glass is high and rising
  May soundly sleep the careful wise one.

(It seems easier to remember "Rising, fair; falling, foul.")

- *Wind before rain, soon set sail again.*
  Rain before wind, your tops'ls mind.

- *Long foretold, long last*
  Short warning, soon past.

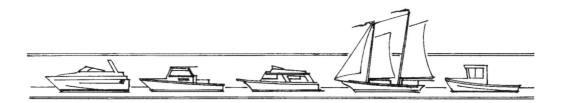

19

Filling Loopholes

Some people like to think of boating as a kind of last frontier: on the water, at least, they're "free to *be*," they "have their space," or whatever other description fits the mood. Unfortunately, it's not quite true. Fifty miles out, perhaps: get naked, get noisy, speed, make a big wake, do what you please. But not when it intrudes on other people, whose ideas of freedom and space could not coincide with yours because you would be in *their* space and disrupting *their* freedom.

This chapter is not meant to spoil anybody's fun, but rather to let you know that even on the water, certain restrictions apply. Better to be aware of them than be surprised (shocked) by a fine you consider disproportionate to an infraction of which you were unaware.

Along with knowledge of rules and laws, you should check a few sections of your boat insurance policy, to avoid misunderstandings that could lead to legal hassles.

LEGAL MATTERS

Navigation directions are not the only rules boaters must follow. Many aspects of boating are regulated, and violations can carry hefty fines.

No-Wakes

Even brand-new boaters would have a hard time pleading ignorance regarding the regulation that holds you responsible for damage caused by the boat's wake. As more boaters share the waterways, and more homeowners build along the waterfront, more no-wake zones will be established, and boaters must be more aware of the extended effects of their movement through the water.

Besides obeying specific signs, you're expected to slow down when overtaking other boats, when going through a fleet of fishing boats, and when passing house docks, especially those with small boats tied parallel to the channel. Then there are bridges, eroding shorelines, workboats, and wildlife to slow down for. But at least you have many opportunities to see the scenery.

• If you speed through a posted no-wake zone, you may be dealing with a Coast Guard regulation, which makes it a federal offense. A Coast Guard "ticket" may be considerably more expensive than the everyday traffic fine you may be expecting.

• In Florida, the Manatee Sanctuary Act created many idle-speed zones where speed is to be "reasonable and prudent" . . . to avoid harming the slow-moving manatees. In Puget Sound, federal law protects whales.

Running Rules

Here are more reasons to learn navigation rules:

• Any person who operates a vessel in violation of the Navigation Rules Act of 1980 may be liable for a civil penalty of not more than $5,000 for each violation.

• If you operate a vessel in a negligent manner—and if your negligence endangers life, limb, or property—you may be liable for a civil penalty of not more than $1,000 ($5,000 for *gross* negligence). And you will not be the one to define negligent, or gross.

• Examples of negligent operation:

Speeding in a congested area

Speeding when fog or rain makes visibility bad

Boating too close to a swimming area

Obstructing a navigation channel

Boating while under the influence of alcohol or drugs

Redundant reminder: designated drivers should drive boats, too.

Clean Rules

• You're asked to report any polluting discharges you see. (Call the nearest Coast Guard.)

Sewage Pumpout

• Your boat should have an approved operational marine sanitation device (MSD).

Some boating areas are designated "no-discharge," so your boat must have a holding tank if you plan to cruise in these areas. In coastal areas, you can pump properly treated waste overboard, except in specific harbors or basins that are designated no-discharge. The only place you can pump untreated waste overboard is outside coastal limits.

Type I MSDs macerate and treat sewage before pumping it into the water. Type II MSDs do the same, to a higher standard of treatment. Type III MSDs use a holding tank, and waste is pumped out at a shore facility.

• Federal law prohibits the discharge of raw sewage in U.S. waters within 3 miles of shore.

• Fines for overboard discharge of waste in coastal waters, lakes, and rivers may be $500 to $1,000.

Garbage Dumpout

• MARPOL is an international agreement to regulate marine pollution. All boats must post a sign listing these garbage dumping rules, preferably close to the main garbage-producing area, for easy reference. For recreational boats: Don't dump anything into inland waters, or within 3 miles of the coast. From 3 to 12 miles out, dump garbage (except for plastic items) *only* if it's ground to less than an inch. Do not dump any plastic, anywhere on Earth, ever.

• If cruising beyond the 3-mile limit, boats 40 feet and over must have a Waste Management Plan. This is a written account of how you plan to collect, process, store, and dump garbage; you must also have a designated garbage collector, processor, storer, and dumper.

Oil Discharge

• Boats over 26 feet must have an oil-discharge placard posted in the engine-room, or close to the bilge-pumping area. This reminds you not to discharge oily waste, and it informs you that the penalty for so doing can be $5,000.

Radio Rules

• You're not required to have a copy of the FCC Rules on board, but you must comply with them. Do not transmit:

A false emergency message

Obscene, indecent, profane words or meaning

General calls, except in an emergency

When boat is on land

• The penalty for sending a false distress call includes prison and fines. The caller is also responsible for the costs of search-and-rescue efforts prompted by the hoax call.

• Bad language will get you a bad fine, and it could get you locked up, too. Think before you key that mike in anger.

Customs Customs

If you plan to travel to a foreign country, call a local Customs office or write to the U.S. Customs Service, Washington, DC 20229. Ask for the publications *Pleasure Boats* and *Know Before You Go*. These booklets explain entry requirements and tell how to report dutiable merchandise purchased outside the country. You'll also find a list of items you should not bring into the U.S.

• Before you leave, get a Customs User Fee Decal so you can return without hassle. Call your nearest U.S. Customs Service office and ask for Form 339. There will be a fee ($25, unless it has increased recently).

• U.S. boats don't have to report to customs when they *leave* the U.S., only when they return.

• Most pleasure boats returning to the U.S. will not be boarded by a customs inspector, but you must call U.S. Customs as soon as you arrive. (Local marinas can provide the phone number.) Once you anchor or tie up, you have entered; only one person can get off the boat to make the call. In most cases, you'll be given a clearance number by phone, at which time everyone else is free to leave the boat.

• To indicate you require customs clearance, fly the yellow quarantine flag until you are officially cleared.

Zero Tolerance

Early heavy-handed enforcement of the Zero Tolerance policy outraged many boatowners: If any amount of illegal drugs was found on a boat, the boat could be seized and placed into indefinite storage at the owner's expense—even when the owner was not responsible for, or aware of, the drugs being on the boat, as when boats were in a charter business and/or hired crewmembers were on board.

Drug possession is still illegal, but now the boatowner usually retains possession until the matter is settled in court.

• If you allow illegal drugs on your boat, you're liable for heavy penalties.

Accident Reports

As with automobile accidents, people are sometimes hesitant to report an accident because they're afraid it will affect their insurance rates. The reasoning—or the reason for the fear—is a whole debate in itself, but report is what you should do, according to the law.

File an accident report when any of the following apply:

Loss of life

A person disappears

Injury requiring more than first aid

Loss of the vessel

Damage to the vessel or other property, when the amount exceeds $500. (Some states may set a lesser amount for the reporting limit; call the Coast Guard Boating Safety Hotline, 1-800-368-5647.)

• File the report with local authorities in the state where the accident occurred. If there was death or injury, file within 48 hours. For other circumstances, file within 10 days.

• Get a copy of the Coast Guard Boating Accident Report by calling the Coast Guard Safety Hotline: 1-800-368-5647.

Good Samaritan Provision

While helping another should be a "your choice" situation, where boating mishaps are concerned you have a legal obligation to help. You must provide assistance to any individual found at sea, or in danger of be-

File an accident report with local authorities.

ing lost, as long as you can do so without danger to your vessel or those aboard.

In this day of million-dollar awards granted in seemingly frivolous lawsuits, fear of a liability backlash is a real concern, even for people who are willing to help another boater in distress. The "Good Samaritan" provision addresses that concern.

According to the Federal Boating Safety Act of 1971, if you offer assistance "in good faith at the scene of an accident or other boating casualty without objection of any person being assisted, you cannot be held liable for any civil damages as a result of offering (rendering) assistance, or of any act or omission in providing or arranging salvage, towage, medical treatment, or other assistance where you act as an ordinary, reasonable, prudent person (would under similar circumstances)."

• Failure to provide assistance can result in a fine of not more than $1,000 or two years in jail, or both.

• On land, "Good Samaritan" help *could* put you at risk of a liability suit.

Boarding

If you're not familiar with Coast Guard boarding/safety inspection policy, here's what to expect. You may be called by radio, or you may suddenly see an inflatable alongside, with three or more Coast Guardsmen inside, one of whom will be holding a notebook or clipboard, and one of whom may be in full dive suit. They'll ask when you were last inspected, which may—or may not—influence their decision to board.

Members of the boarding team will probably be wearing sidearms, but we are told not to be alarmed; that's just part of the uniform. (You'll probably be asked if you have any weapons.)

Once the team is on board, you'll be asked to provide basic information about the boat and the crew; you'll produce boat papers and your papers. Next comes the list of required safety equipment; all will be checked, and if you pass inspection, you get a copy of the boarding report.

Depending on your frame of mind, ask them to sign your guest log. (It's not their fault they must enforce a regulation you don't like.)

• If you were negligent about checking the dates on your flares, or if your PFDs were wrapped up in a seat locker instead of being immediately accessible, you'll be cautioned to "fix" the oversights. But if the boarding officer thinks these items go beyond forgetfulness, you'll be given a Notice of Violation, for which you may be fined.

• As with auto tickets, you can either pay the penalty, or contest it through the Coast Guard's complaint channels.

• If you have a question about a violation, call the Coast Guard where the boarding occurred (name and number will be on your boarding report). You can also call the Coast Guard Boating Safety Hotline for a referral to a legal office: 1-800-368-5647.

• The Coast Guard has the authority to board U.S. vessels anywhere (and they can board foreign vessels in or near U.S. waters).

• The Coast Guard finds some noncompliance in almost half their boardings. Word to the wise: Be prepared. The requirements are, after all, minimal.

• Boaters have heard many bad reports about boardings, some by Coast Guard, some by other agencies, but these are mostly history. Our experience (and we have more than we'd like for an old, slow boat) has been that all boarding crew were polite and professional, and, by the time they left, smiling.

• While the purpose of these boardings is a safety inspection, the Coast Guard can conduct an extensive search of the boat if

Filling Loopholes

they determine it is warranted. No search will be done unless there is "cause for suspicion" that is "developed at the scene based on the facts at hand." Some of those facts might be: what people have said, prior intelligence, the smell of drugs, other law violations.

• If you're really upset about the boarding policy, call the Coast Guard Safety Hotline and register your complaint. And the next time someone tries to tell you drug use doesn't bother anybody else, explain to them this major aspect of "bother."

• If you cooperate—whether you agree with the policy or not—the boarding will go faster.

• Your chances of being boarded are about one in a hundred in coastal areas, except in Florida, the Gulf of Mexico, or Caribbean passages, where the odds are better.

INSURANCE

This is not a complete discussion of the terms of your boat insurance policy, but a few topics concern the boatowner who leaves home waters for an extended time.

Towing or Salvage?
Hopefully, you will never need to call for salvage help, but you should know the difference between ordinary towing and a salvage operation.

Ordinary, non-emergency towing assistance is for a no-damage grounding, a no-start engine, a no-fuel tank. Such towing *may* be covered by a boat insurance policy, but more likely, by separate towing insurance.

When a vessel is in immediate danger—imminent peril—big trouble—that's when salvage help is required. (You've grounded on a submerged jetty and the waves are pushing the boat farther onto the rockpile,

or water is filling the boat faster than you can pump it out.) Fees for salvage would *not* be covered under towing insurance, but by the regular boat insurance policy.

Because a salvor "saves" the boat in disastrous circumstances, salvage fees are usually substantial, much higher than a simple towing fee. (Don't use a salvage contract for an ordinary towing assist.)

Towing
Towing companies usually charge by the hour, starting from the time they get underway to come to you. If you accept their offer to assist, even if the acceptance is by radio and through the Coast Guard, the towing company may bill you even if they do not ultimately tow you (assuming someone else comes along in the meantime and takes you to a dock).

Be clear about the kind of help you need, so the towing company sends only the kind of boat and equipment to do the job. Talk directly to the towing company, if possible, rather than go through a third party. (See Chapter 13 for more on towing.)

Salvage
When your boat is "in peril," you're in a bad position to negotiate, but you should be careful what kind of contract you sign. Because salvage contract forms were originally written for commercial boats, they were not appropriate for recreational boats. BOAT/U.S. cautions boaters not to sign a contract called Lloyd's Open Form (or Lloyd's anything); this was written for commercial shipping interests.

BOAT/U.S. researched the problems of salvage, and prepared a contract designed specifically for a recreational boat salvage job. Their contract can be used by any boater, insurance company, or salvor. It does not insist on a pre-established fee; the salvor bills on his choice of a flat fee, time and equipment, or a percentage of the boat's value "as is" after salvage. There's a provision for arbitration in case of disagreement.

If you find yourself in need of professional salvors, here's what BOAT/U.S. suggests you do:

Call the Coast Guard and explain your situation. If they decide it is not life-threatening, they will send a local salvage company.

Ask for a salvor that uses the BOAT/U.S. salvage contract. If you are talking to a salvor on the radio, tell him you want to use the form and have one aboard. To obtain a copy of the BOAT/U.S. salvage contract, call 1-800-937-1937.

If possible, use the VHF to call your insurance agent. If your boat is insured with BOAT/U.S., they will handle negotiations for you.

Have the salvage company sign the contract.

• For future reference in settling a possible dispute, try to take some photos of the boat and the salvage procedure. Make notes: time called, time help arrived, what equipment, how many crew, whatever is pertinent.

• To avoid confusion: Insurance companies use the term "salvage" to describe a different, though related, situation.

When a boat is declared a total loss following an accident, the insuring company pays the claim, and technically, owns the boat. But often, if the boat is repairable (perhaps on a do-it-yourself basis), the original owner will buy the boat back from the company for a negotiated "salvage" price; ownership reverts to the insured person.

Travel Insurance

• If your home port limits boating to a seasonal basis, your "home" policy may be written for a six-month period (assuming the boat's out of the water the other six). It may also limit the geographic area where you're covered. If you plan an extended cruise, be sure your coverage extends to the times and places you will cruise.

• Some policies establish a separate deductible for the dinghy and motor. Some have different deductibles for different cruising areas. Some have a different deductible for "natural catastrophe"; this could be 10 percent of insured value. These are all fine clauses as long as you're aware of and in agreement with them before any claim dispute.

• The boatowner is expected to maintain the boat "in seaworthy condition." If you accidentally put diesel into the gas tank, you're probably covered. But if you don't take care of the boat and it sinks at the dock, you may not be covered.

• When you first insure the boat, you state how the boat will be used. Using it any other way could void the coverage. (The obvious example: If you're insured as a pleasure boat, don't take out passengers for hire without changing the declaration of use to commercial.)

• If you're in an accident, and according to the rules, you were in the wrong, or partly in the wrong, the insurance company could deny a claim.

• Read your policy carefully, and ask for explanations of any terms that are not clear.

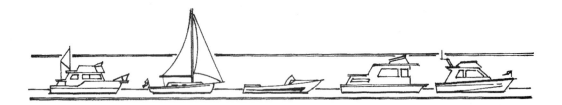

20 Preserving Nature

As a group, boaters feel singled out, put upon, picked on regarding water pollution. A major complaint is the disagreement about discharge from marine heads. When an East Coast city can dump six million gallons of raw sewage into the waterway, and then declare the area beaches safe just a few days later, you can't help but wonder how much effect recreational boats really do have.

Of course, that's salt water, and it's tidal; in freshwater lakes and inland rivers, or the confined waters of sounds and bays, discharge was a different problem, now solved by holding tank requirements.

Perhaps a worse frustration for boaters is the perception that they create all the water's problems, when the facts say most marine pollution does not come from boats at all, but from land "non-point" sources: the non-traceable runoff from cities, farms, and waterfront homes.

Having noted the complaints, boaters as a group are probably already a lot more green-minded than many who would criticize. It is to their own advantage and for their own benefit that boaters will do all they can to minimize boating's effect on the environment that is the basis for boating.

WATER POLLUTION

Boats *do* put unnatural stuff into the water. Boaters *can* prevent much of the most harmful overboard flow.

Fuel

• Keep your engine running well; it will use fuel more efficiently, and less unburned polluting fuel will go into the water.

- Standard two-stroke outboards did not use fuel efficiently. Some better-engineered, minimum-polluting models are already available, with more on the way, designed for improved combustion, so less fuel is sent out with the exhaust.

- Instead of an inflatable-and-outboard combo, get a rowing dinghy; you'll get some exercise as you help keep the water cleaner.

- Instead of an inflatable-and-outboard combo, get a sailing dinghy; you'll have fun, and you'll help keep the water cleaner.

- A 24-foot Zodiac circled the world (40,000 miles) using a 180-hp Merc-Cruiser diesel sterndrive powered by soybean fuel, a renewable, non-polluting energy source. How many soybean plants would it take to power America's marine diesels?

- Don't let diesel fuel or gas spill into the water as you're filling fuel tanks. Catch all the spills and burps with rags.

- One quart of oil spilled into the water could cover an area of almost 2 acres.

Bilge

Bilges still need to be pumped, but with the availability of oil-absorbing pads, cylinders, and pillows, there's no need to pump oily residue out with the bilgewater. Keep the oil-soakers in the bilge at all times, so all you send through the pump is water.

If you see a polluter, call any Coast Guard Group on the VHF to report it.

Head

Rules for responsible use of the head: Beyond 3 miles of the coast, you can pump a marine toilet overboard, whether sewage is treated or not. Other places, pump waste into your holding tank and empty the holding tank at a shore facility, or use an approved treatment device where legal. More

pumpout places become available at marinas each year; those that accept government funding cannot charge exorbitant rates for the pumpout.

Paint

More water-based paints and varnishes are appearing on marine store shelves. (Ten years ago, "they" said it couldn't be done.) Besides being better for the environment, (by eliminating solvents), water-based products work well and are more practical: Boaters who live, and paint, in a climate that is almost always humid could not comply with paint manufacturers' instructions for application to truly dry surfaces; humidity is not such a problem with water-based paints.

Since the banning of tin-based bottom paints, which were shown to harm marine life, most anti-fouling paints use copper. A new paint has been introduced that claims to be more environmentally friendly: No Foul uses hydrogen peroxide to repel growth on the hull—much less harmful than any metal. Another product replaces some of the copper with red pepper. Another adds an antibiotic to the paint to increase anti-fouling properties.

Clean Green

Look for "green" products for cleaning and polishing jobs. Try the natural cleaners first: baking soda, vinegar, borax, lemon juice, salt. Then check Shaklee Products (Cousteau uses them) or Seventh Generation's line of cleaning helps.

- Washing the boat more often with plain water and a scrub brush will bring almost the same results as the occasional scrub with soap.

- Many cleaning products are described as biodegradable, but the process still takes a long time. Look for no-phosphate or low-phosphate, because phosphate is one cause of the algae blooms that result in massive fish kills.

AIR POLLUTION

• Anti-pollution requirements for new outboard motors were established to keep the water cleaner, but the end result is also a first step toward emission controls for cleaner air. (According to the EPA, an older, 50-hp two-stroke outboard motor can emit as much hydrocarbon in 1 hour as a car would in 40 hours.)

• When you run any engine at high RPM, you create more air pollution because the fuel does not burn completely, and goes out with the exhaust. Most engine manuals recommend normal running at two-thirds to three-quarters of an engine's top speed.

• Solar panels are splendid, non-polluting ways to generate power, and can be used on all kinds of boats. They are nearly no-maintenance; they're not inexpensive, but nowhere near the cost of a separate generator motor, which *does* pollute.

• Wind generators are another alternative to fuel-powered generators.

• Electric propulsion power is a reality for small boats that do not travel long or far; someday, it might be feasible for larger boats traveling longer distances—one company has produced a 40-foot electric cruiser.

• Some states now regulate another form of air pollution: noise. In New York, officers take noise meters on marine patrol. A noisy boater faces a fine up to $250 for generating more than 90 decibels.

SHORE POLLUTION

Smart people never did need an international agreement to tell them not to dump trash—plastic or other—in places other than trash dumpsters. Recreational boaters are blamed for a lot of mess they do not create, but guilty or not, it benefits us all to help in the cleanup effort. Besides being ugly, floating plastic junk can mess up your boat's cooling system or propeller.

• Many boaters have probably seen the sad photos of pelicans trapped by fishing line, or fish, turtles, seals, and otters strangling in a six-pack ring. To foil the chance of a plastic ring escaping its garbage bag, cut it so no loops remain. The rings are made of photodegradable material now, but the degrading takes a longer time than a fish or otter might be able to wait.

• Don't let fishing line and hooks go overboard unless attached to your pole.

Pelicans are often caught in fishing line.

• Filters from cigarettes are a small item that can cause big problems for the sea creatures that try to eat them. These don't biodegrade at all.

• The Center for Marine Conservation (CMC) has organized hundreds of volunteers to do beach cleanups each year, and literally tons of trash are picked up and carted off to "proper" disposal sites.

• You don't need to wait for an organized cleanup; adopt your own section of beach and just clean it. (Wear gloves, and don't try to move any large, 5-gallon drums you may find.)

Beaches need regular cleanups to get rid of debris deposited by tide or waves.

• Some marinas now participate in recycling efforts. It is not difficult to keep boat trash separated by type; just allot enough small spaces in boat lockers for aluminum, other cans, glass bottles, plastic bottles, cardboard/paper, and stinky garbage. The last one is the only category you'll need to worry about. Add a new outer bag as needed for smell confinement.

• Turn in your old 12-volt batteries when buying new ones. You won't get a big dollar credit, but the battery will be recycled and *not* at your expense.

• Sails can be made from recycled plastic soda bottles.

• Boatyards, too, are changing for the environmental good. Dropcloths catch scrapings. Sanders collect dust. Boats are "tented" to confine grinding and sanding mess. Paint leftovers are collected for hazardous waste disposal.

SHORE DESTRUCTION

• Because of sometimes narrow channels, wakes can cause serious shore erosion, so watch your wake more carefully in shallow, confined waterways.

• Shore erosion can destroy beach or bank; and it affects wetland "nurseries," the

Wakes can cause shore erosion.

breeding grounds for so much marine life.

• Wakes also stir up bottom sediments, clouding the water so life-sustaining light cannot get to the submerged sea grasses.

• Underwater plants are the start of the marine food chain, the base of that natural food pyramid.

• Stay away from seagrass beds; underwater grasses stabilize bottom sediments, creating the habitat for small fish and shellfish.

• Beach grasses help to keep the beaches in place. In many coastal areas, a barrier beach protects the mainland; if the beaches go, so goes the first defense against an angry ocean. When you walk a beach, walk *around* the grass.

• Some marine parks in Puget Sound discourage anchoring in order to prevent damage to underwater plants and marine life.

• One anchor and its chain can destroy a lot of coral; the anchor may stay in one spot, but the chain can drag a long distance repeatedly as the boat shifts back and forth with wind or current shifts. After too many breaks, the coral will not regenerate. Coral is terrible holding ground anyway; find some sand.

• If possible, avoid taking the big boat *over* coral formations; anchor away from the reef and come in by dinghy.

• In the Florida Keys, use a mooring when you visit the underwater parks of Pennekamp or Looe Key. Only look—never touch—living coral. Take only pictures.

WILDLIFE PROTECTION

For many cruising boaters, wildlife sightings are one of the best things about boat travel. It is so exciting to see creatures living where they belong. Try not to frighten any wild creatures in your enthusiasm to take a better close-up picture. In some places, you might be required to stay 200 yards away from a National Wildlife Refuge, charted as "NWR."

• Without a lot of extra effort on your part, you will see a lot of wildlife on any waterway trip. Dolphins, manatees, sea turtles, and rays; blue crabs, horseshoe crabs, fiddler crabs, and hermit crabs; jellyfish and flying fish; sea lions, otters, and seals; maybe sharks and whales: orca, gray, or humpback; too many birds to list.

• Shore scenes are equally varied: mangroves in Florida, cypress swamps in the Carolinas, rocky cliffs and pine forests in Maine and the Great Lakes.

• If you're a birder, watch from the boat; don't disturb nesting colonies.

• Turtles nest on certain Florida beaches. Because light influences the directional instinct of turtle hatchlings, property owners in nearby residences have established lights-out times. Join the effort, and don't disrupt mama turtles when they're nesting; sea turtles are on the endangered list.
(If you ever see a granddaddy loggerhead drifting along in the ocean, you will forever be more careful of turtle-nesting beaches.)

• Sportfishermen are holding more and more catch-and-release tournaments, doing their part in the effort to help fish regain safe population levels.

• Manatees are associated mainly with Florida, but they do migrate seasonally. In summer, they may go west to Alabama and north to the Carolinas or Virginia (one solo wanderer decided to check out New England in the summer of '95). In winter, they follow snowbirds' lead and go south again, heading inland where waters are warmer.

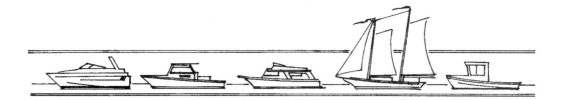

21 Minding Manners

Even when actions are not specifically illegal, they can be inconsiderate and, as more boaters use the waterways, intolerable. There will always be a few people with an I-don't-care attitude, and it's doubtful they'll ever change. It is unfortunate that the rest of the boating community must suffer because of the actions of those few. When municipalities or neighborhoods start looking for legislation to keep boats out, boaters must look for ways to alter the guilt-by-association perception.

Boating organizations have proved influential in some government decisions, but as a group, boaters are loosely connected, usually by choice. Without getting involved in any organized effort, individual boaters can at least call attention to activities that could be viewed as inconsiderate, and hope the unsolicited advice is considered.

When a boater drags the dinghy onto a state park beach and starts scraping barnacles, it might be that the scraper just didn't think about how that activity would affect other people trying to enjoy the park. If another boater helps the dinghy owner to think, that's better than the park's prohibiting all future dinghy landings.

Relationships between boaters is another story. People who cruise for any length of time realize the silliness of the separation of sail and power. Whatever your propulsion preference, it's a lot more pleasant to smile and give a friendly wave to a passing boater than to shout and give another kind of wave. Why waste your time being angry?

This chapter shows a few of the more common situations that antagonize shore people or other boaters. Don't put yourself in any of the pictures.

APPEARANCES

Admittedly, it's hard to carry all the cruising necessities on a small boat without leaving something out on deck. But "something" easily gets out of control. Items are added one at a time; you get accustomed to seeing a space occupied, so the item is no longer noticeable—to you.

Organization

Try to look at your boat as a non-boating shore person might see it. Will they be glad you are part of the waterfront scene? If the answer is at all questionable, do some serious eliminating or stowing, but get the excess out of sight so you can see the boat again.

Flag Waving

A pet peeve, perhaps, but if you're going to fly your country's flag, fly one that is still in one piece and still showing its real colors. A shredded, faded flag is depressing.

• Americans cruising in U.S. waters can fly either the U.S. ensign (the 50-star flag) or the yacht ensign (the 13-star with anchor flag).

• If an American boat goes to a foreign country, it's proper to show the U.S. ensign (*not* the yacht ensign).

• In addition to the U.S. flag, when you visit a foreign country, it's a courtesy to fly the flag of that country while you're there. Be sure to fly the courtesy flag from the appropriate place: on a powerboat, from the bow staff; on a sailboat, from the starboard spreader.

• You're *not* supposed to leave the foreign flag on the boat once you return to the U.S., though many boaters seem to forget to remove courtesy flags.

• Put the flag out in the morning (tradition says 0800) and take it in at sunset.

ACTIVITIES

Shore people are usually friendly and sometimes exceptionally accommodating to cruising boaters, but don't be surprised by an occasional attitude that seems less than cordial. While you have done nothing to warrant a negative response, you are a boat person, and in some ways will be stereotyped according to each shore person's previous experience with other boaters. The following lists should explain why boaters may be regarded with suspicion.

Boaters and Homeowners

• Don't leave garbage where it doesn't belong (most specifically, on private docks or property).

• Don't make noise where it doesn't belong.

• Don't sneak into marinas under cover of darkness and after closing hours to take water, leave trash, take showers, and do laundry.

• Avoid demonstrations of chutzpah, like the captain who complained to a town's chamber of commerce because the electric power (free) at the town dock (free) was not adequate for his air conditioning needs. Or another who chained his bicycle to a property owner's fence, then crossed (trespassed) private property to go grocery shopping.

• Don't settle long-term into a busy, residential community where you stick out like the proverbial thumb; and, most especially, don't park a car in such a neighborhood so you can get around more conveniently.

• Leave your clothes *on*, where they do belong.

*Don't have noisy
parties when you're
anchored close to a
private dock in
a residential
community.*

• Respect private property. Not all beaches in the U.S. are public. Find out the rules of the area you're cruising.

• Put yourself in the waterfront home-owner's place, and think of a modified, marine version of the Golden Rule.

Boaters and Boaters

• Don't monopolize an anchorage by using excessive scope on a single anchor, or by using multiple anchors if they're not needed.

• Don't be a top-anchorer. Try not to anchor in front of or too close to a boat already in the anchorage. If you misjudged the positioning, pick up your anchor and move to a better spot. It's polite, it's safer, and the first boat to be anchored has the "right-of-anchorage"; if you're interfering with its swinging circle, you are obligated to move.

• Sailors should learn how to tie off halyards so they do not clank all night. Those who find the sound appealing should find a solitary anchorage.

• Anyone who plans to use a generator should try to choose a spot downwind where noise (and exhaust) will be carried away from other boats. Better yet, don't run a generator at all from sundown to sunup.

• Try to confine your musical prefer-ence to your own space. If you like coun-try, like it quiet, or you'll have to listen to the competition's arias in the background. Quadraphonic anything doesn't fit the tranquility picture; use headphones, where necessary.

• Similarly, try to limit the frivolity of your party to your group. The neighbors have their own exploits to brag about.

• Sound carries loudly and clearly across water. Before you express a difference of opinion to your crew, realize everyone in the anchorage will follow every word.

• Try not to perpetuate antagonism between sailors and powerboaters. What can you say about the subject that hasn't been said already, too often by misdirected writers who think they are teaching a course in abrasive writing? Put name calling out of mind, like nice folks usually do when they pass puberty; then surprise somebody. Be friendly to—better yet, offer some help to—a member of the opposite persuasion. For starters, it's fun to see the expression on the other person's face. First surprise, followed by suspicion, and finally, the simple question, "Why are you doing this?" Because, often, a friendly encounter ensues.

ATTITUDE

Despite any sometime downsides, the rewards of cruising far outweigh the hassles. New friends, new places, new experiences—and possibly, a whole new way of life.

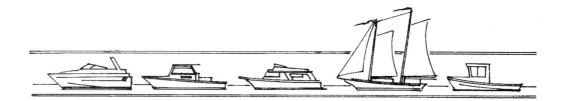

Appendix:
Checklists

PAPERS

Boat documentation or registration (and
   title in some states)

Radio license
   (if voyaging outside the U.S.,
   or using SSB)

Radio operator's license
   (if voyaging outside the U.S.
   or using SSB)

Oil placard

Garbage placard

ENGINE MAINTENANCE
AND REPAIRS

Engine oil

   Oil-changing kit

   Oil filters

Fuel filters

Filters for fuel-water separator

Coolant

Additives:

   Fuel (condensation, anti-bacteria,
   sludge breakup)

   Oil

WD-40, Corrosion X, CRC
   (anti-corrosive spray)

Special tools for engine
   (metric or motorcycle-size)

SPARE PARTS

Zinc(s)

Propeller(s)

Engine parts
  (refer to manual for specifics)

Extra water pump

Water pump impellers, seals, and water
  pump grease

Alternator belt

Flax (stuffing box)

Grease and proper grease gun

Thermostat

Spare fuel cans

BILGE

Extra bilge pump (manual)

Float switch

Bilge pump repair kit

DINGHY AND OUTBOARD

Registration paper

PFDs

Anchor and line

Gas can

Spare hose, squeeze bulb

Paddle

Bailer

Flashlight

Whistle

Propeller

Oil

Shear pin

Spark plugs

Portable tool kit

Lower unit lubricant

Carburetor kit

BATTERIES/SHORE POWER/ LIGHTING

Two-battery system with switch

Hydrometer

Distilled water

Inverter/battery charger with regulator

Portable generator

Shore-power cord with alternate
  end plugs

Polarity tester

Spare wiring

End fittings and wire connectors
  (and proper installation tool)

Circuit breakers/fuses

Bulbs: 12-volt and 120-volt

Liquid electrical tape

Plastic electrical tape

Lantern wicks

Lamp oil

SAFETY EQUIPMENT

Personal Flotation Devices, each with
  whistle and strobe light

Safety harnesses

Throwable life ring

Visual distress signals (flares, flag)

Emergency boarding ladder

Crew-overboard retrieval system

Horn/bell

Spotlight

Fire extinguishers

Fume detectors

Backfire flame control

Proper ventilation
    (bilge blower with gas engines)

Radar reflector

Lightning protection

Wood plugs
    (for broken through-hull fitting)

EPIRB

Survival kit

Sea anchor/drogue

First aid kit and references

NAVIGATION TOOLS AND RULES

Charts

Coast Pilots

Tide tables

Light Lists

Cruising guides

Parallel rules/course plotters

Dividers

Pencils

Erasers

Note pad/Post-It Notes

Flashlight(s)

    Spare batteries and bulbs

Red lens for flashlight

Red lens for chart-reading light

Compass

Binoculars

Hand-bearing compass

Rangefinder

Night scope

Navigation rules reference book

Day shape (ball and/or cone)

Barometer

Weather radio or VHF radio

Leadline

WATER

Water hose (white, for filling tanks)

Spray nozzle

Fill cap opener

Water bottles

Sink and drain hoses

HEAD

Holding tank treatment

Extra discharge hose

Head repair kit

ELECTRONICS

VHF radio

Hand-held VHF

Ham or SSB radio

Electronic chart plotter

Depthsounder

GPS/loran receiver

Autopilot

    Spare belt(s)

ANCHORING GEAR

Two or three "regular" anchors

One storm anchor

Line and chain

Chain hook

Chainstopper

Windlass

Chafing gear: hose, leather, small line to tie on

Bucket with line, or wash-down system

MOORING LINES

Lines

Chafing gear

Boathook

Fenders

Fenderboard

TOOLS

Good assortment for:

Engine

Plumbing

Electrical wiring

Miscellaneous repair projects

Carryable box, or tray

Magnet

C-clamps

Prybar

Prop puller

Plumber's "Snake"
(to clean out hoses)

Snorkel/scuba gear, for underwater maintenance

Suction handle, for underwater maintenance

REPAIR MATERIALS

Underwater epoxy putty

Liquid steel/aluminum

Marine-Tex or other epoxy putty

Five-minute epoxy glue

Small fiberglass repair kit:

Cloth

Polyester or epoxy resin

Acetone

Cabosil/microballoons

Gelcoat touchup

Caulking (in closable tubes)

Teflon tape

Hose patching tape

Wire

Liquid gasket

Duct tape

Reinforced strapping tape

Stainless steel fasteners

Stainless steel hose clamps

Spare through-hull fitting

FABRIC/SCREEN REPAIR

Patches of acrylic fabric

Patches of screening material

Heavyweight Dacron thread

Large needle

Self-adhesive nylon tape

Grommet kit

Vinyl glue
(VLP: to seal small cuts in
vinyl cushions)

CLEANERS/WAXES

Hull cleaner, wax

Bilge cleaner, biodegradeable

Oil-absorbing pads, pillows

Spray cleaner, for interior surfaces

Cleaner/polish, for soft plastic ports

Rain X or similar product, for clear wind-
shields

Long-handled scrub brush

Long-handled mop

Hand scrub brush

Whisk broom/dustpan set, or 12-volt
or battery-operated vacuum cleaner

Moisture-displacing spray

Metal cleaner/polish

COATINGS

Paint or varnish

Appropriate thinners

Scrapers

Sandpapers

Masking tape

Brushes

Small amount of bottom paint,
to touch up waterline area

FOR SAILORS

Sail slides

Shock cord with hooks
(for quick mainsail furl)

Sail repair kit:

Sailcloth patches

Dacron thread, needle

Sailor's palm

Ripstop tape

Spare battens

Inverted cone day shape
(when motorsailing)

Stainless steel cable and end
fittings for a stay

Turnbuckle

Cotter pins

BOATING COURSES

For a list of boating courses in your area,
call BOAT/U.S., 1-800-336-2628. Courses
are taught by U.S. Power Squadrons, the
U.S. Coast Guard Auxiliary, or the American Red Cross.

Index

gas pump: fast-fill, 104
gauges. *See* engine gauges
generator: etiquette, 196
gill nets, 89
Global Positioning System. *See* DGPS (Differential Global Positioning System); GPS (Global Positioning System)
"Good Samaritan": liability/definition, 124, 127, 186–187
GPS (Global Positioning System) units, 35, 44–47; crew-overboard, 152; Mayday Mike distress call, 151. *See also* DGPS (Differential Global Positioning System)
Great Lakes: bridges, 74–75; radiobeacons, 46; VHF channels, 60; waves/weather, 158, 159, 176
grounded boat: sound signals, 33, 100
grounding, 28, 95–101; bottoming out in inlets, 161; dredges/clear channel aids, 28; hull damage/repairs, 101, 202; towing assistance, 101, 127–128; towing insurance, 127–128, 188
grounding, refloating techniques, 95–101; with engine, 95–96; falling tide, 100–101; kedging off, 96–97, 98, 101; heeling boat, 97; rising tide, 98, 101; towing/pulling, 99–100, 125–126; wake, 100
guidebooks. *See* cruising guides
Gulf Stream: waves/current, 159

ham (amateur) radio, 64–65; Morse code/SuperMorse, 65; Technician license, 65
hand signals: nighttime alternatives to, 141; for towing, 126
harness, safety. *See* safety harness
head, 155, 201. *See also* holding tank; marine sanitation device; sewage pumpout
heaving-to: in storm, 163
heavy weather. *See* weather; storms; thunderstorms
heeling. *See* sailboats
High Seas Operator, 64
hoisting tackle: for overboard recovery, 154
holding tanks, 184, 190, 191
hose clamp: substitute for, 113
hoses, fuel. *See* fuel lines
hull: checking bottom growth, 108–109
hull, damaged/holed, 101, 155; repairs, 101, 202
hurricanes, 180–182; classifications, 181–182
hypothermia, 156–157

injury: accident report, 186
inland waters: charts, 15; demarcation line, 23
inlets, 160–162; entering, 160–161; exiting, 161–162
Inside Passage: lighted aids to navigation, 23
insurance, boat, 183, 188–189; accidents, 189; claims/deductibles, 189
insurance, towing. *See* towing insurance
International Association of Lighthouse Authorities (IALA): IALA-A/IALA-B buoyage systems, 10
international waters: demarcation line, 23
Intracoastal Waterway (ICW): bridges, 68, 70; charts, 1, 4, 15, 41; locks, 76; navigation aids, 4, 8; nighttime navigation, 23

jetty: marker, 21; submerged, 160
jibe: avoiding in storm, 165

kedging off: to refloat grounded boat, 96–97, 98, 101
kilometer, 15, 41
knot, 41

ladder, boarding. *See* boarding ladder
latitude: degrees of, 14; loran position, 44; minutes of, 14; parallels of, 14
leadline, 42, 133

leaks: stopping, 100, 150, 155. *See also* gas leaks
leeway, 46
lifelines: care/condition, 155; netting, 155
liferaft, 150–151, 156
life ring, 153, 155
Lifesling, 150, 154–155
life vest/jacket. *See* PFDs (Personal Flotation Devices)
lighted aids to navigation, 20–23; channel markers, 21, 84; chart description, 4, 5, 10; flash sequence/characteristics, 4, 5, 10, 20, 21–22; foghorn/sound characteristics, 29–30; leading lights, 10; major harbor entrance, 20, 21; Morse Code "A," 21, 22; outer sea buoy, 21; powering of, 23; range lights, 21; in rivers, 167. *See also* lighthouses; Light List
lighthouses, 20, 21–22, 29–30; chart description, 4, 5, 10; flash sequence/characteristics, 4, 5, 10, 20, 21–22; foghorn, 29–30; leading lights, 10; red sector, 20. *See also* Light List
lighting, cabin: checklist, 200
Light List, 16–17, 20, 21–22; foghorn/sound characteristics, 29–30; light/flash characteristics, 4, 5, 10, 20, 21–22; RACON identification, 46
lightning, 178
lights, navigation. *See* navigation (running) lights
lightships: buoys (ELBs), 7
light signals, 141
line of position (LOP), 46, 48–49
lines. *See* anchor lines; dock-lines; rope; snubbing line; tie-ups; tow lines; tripline
Lloyd's: salvage contract (Open Form), 188–189
lobster pots: avoiding fouled prop, 87–88
locks, 76–82; calling (VHF), 77; entry, 77–78; etiquette/cautions, 78; lines/tie-ups, 78, 79–82;